The Christ Worker:

Devotions for Career and Workplace

Kevin J. Cooney

William (Bill) Dudley

Jonathan Lantz

Christopher Sean Meconnahey

Tammy L. Peavy

Stephen Pincus

James D. Slack

Editors

Foreword by Gary E. Roberts

EMETH PRESS
www.emethpress.com

The Christ Worker: Devotions for Career and Workplace

Copyright © 2017 James Slack

Printed in the United States of America on acid-free paper. All rights reserved. No part of this book may be reproduced, or stored in a retrieval system or transmitted in any form or by any means, electronic, mechanical, photocopying, recording, scanning or otherwise, except as permitted by the 1976 United States Copyright Act, or with the prior written permission of Emeth Press. Requests for permission should be addressed to: Emeth Press, P. O. Box 23961, Lexington, KY 40523-3961.
http://www.emethpress.com.

ISBN 978-1-60947-107-1

Library of Congress Control Number: 2016958419

Dedication

This book is dedicated to the glory of God. Without our Lord, this project could not have been accomplished. All praise goes to Him.

His mercies begin afresh each morning.

- *Lamentations* 3:23(b) [NLT]

Contents

Foreword / vii

Preface / ix

Acknowledgements / xi

Daily Devotionals (Week 1, Day 1 through Week 52, Day 5) / 1

About the Editors / 379

Foreword

The great mission field of the 21st century is the workplace. As society transitions towards a post-Christian world, men and women of faith will be under increasing pressure to demonstrate authentic religious commitment to a cynical world. *The Christ Worker* is an invaluable ministry tool to encourage and equip the saints for the marketplace mission field. As formal religious affiliation dwindles, the only Christian that many coworkers will know are the readers of *The Christ Worker*. Hence, this is a powerful Great Commandment and Great Commission tool to take the love, grace, mercy, and salvation of Christ to the lost.

The Christ Worker is a powerful means for encouraging and equipping the reader to be "light and salt" to a dark and dying world and to reject the pernicious temptation of compartmentalizing our faith – church on Sunday then embracing the self-interest and moral relativism of the world on Monday. *The Christ Worker* reinforces the basic theological and Christian character attributes for a vital relationship with God in a practical and humble fashion. The collective wisdom represented in these daily devotionals are "cool drinks of water" in the workplace desert of conflict, narcissism, stress, and work overload. They are pearls of wisdom on how to work out our salvation with fear and trembling. The devotionals provide hope, encouragement, and laughter to the readers enabling them to begin each workday with a word from the Lord.

One of the great strengths of this book is that each entry is self-contained and provides a coherent message independent of the others; hence, the reader can select those devotionals germane to their needs and life circumstances. In an aggregate sense, the "whole is greater than the sum of its parts," and clear themes emerge that will speak to the needs of the reader as directed by the Holy Spirit.

I want to thank the founder of the original *Christian Public Servant*, Dr. James (Jim) D. Slack, for his Godly heart, courage, commitment, perseverance, and love for marketplace ministry. I had the honor and pleasure of working alongside Jim for three years at Regent University and observed how the *Christian Public Servant* provided a conduit for God's living waters to bless readers with teaching, ministry, and prayer. (The *Christian Public Servant* continues to bless readers via a daily blog and Facebook postings.) The Lord used Jim and the entire editorial team including several of my excellent students – William (Bill) Dudley, Jonathan Lantz, Christopher Meconnahey, and Stephen Pincus – to fill a void in the support of workplace believers. Jim and the team (also including Kevin J. Cooney and Tammy

L. Peavy) "counted the cost" devoting many hours of editing (sometimes re-writing), as well as early morning risings to provide the devotional with that cup of coffee at the start of each day.

This volume is a reflection of the body of Christ in all its glory – a grand symphony of different personalities, skill sets, and experiences that combine to produce a Romans 8:28 anointing of blessing from workplace situations of all types: the good, the bad, and the mundane. It is my pleasure and honor to reflect upon this collection of gems and to provide the great compliment of the Lord to the faithful editors and authors of *The Christ Worker*, "well done good and faithful servants."

Gary E. Roberts, Ph.D.
Professor of Government
Regent University
Virginia Beach, Virginia USA

Preface

A *Christ Worker* is someone who works for Christ. It is the person who surrenders life to Christ – and thereby surrenders work to Christ, as part of that life. This is not a radical definition of Christianity. Quite to the contrary. It is what Christ means when He reminds us in Luke (14:26-27, 33) just what it takes to be His disciple. It takes a lot, and there is no time-out at the workplace.

So a *Christ Worker* does earthly things in the public, nonprofit, and private sectors. However, he or she does those earthly things for His glory – each minute of the workday. The *Christ Worker* acknowledges earthly bosses but kneels and serves only the One True Boss.

This devotional began in 2012 with the introduction of an electronic workplace ministry called *The Christian Public Servant*. Through this ministry, people continue to receive work- and career-devotionals five mornings a week. Eventually growing to nearly 20,000 readers on six continents, *The Christian Public Servant* is found on our blog and on our Facebook page. If you would like to receive the electronic weekday devotional, find and "follow" us at: https://christianpublicservant.com.

The electronic devotionals are written by volunteers from across the globe – men and women at all levels of employment and all types of organizations. The authors are no different than you – facing the same workplace and career challenges as you and struggling to keep Christ centered in their workplace- and career-lives. While the majority of authors hail from the public and nonprofit sectors, the lessons are equally applicable to employees and leaders in the private sector. *Christ Workers*, after all, are needed and found in all types of work settings and career-paths.

This volume of workplace devotionals is a collection of the best from the electronic version – ones that have never been published in print. Each devotional, by design, is intimate – written informally as if you are talking with a close friend over a cup of coffee or tea. Each follows a simple and short format that allows ample fit in your busy workday.

Just like the electronic ministry, each week's readings in this book conclude with a devotional by a special *Christ Worker* – a convicted murderer who lives on death row in an American prison. (Yes, this man works for Christ and calls his workplace "Life Row.") His observations bless thousands of readers on six continents, and we believe his offerings will be a blessing to you.

Preface

Pax Christi,

Kevin J. Cooney
William (Bill) Dudley
Jonathan Lantz
Christopher Sean Meconnahey
Tammy L. Peavy
Stephen Pincus
James D. Slack

Acknowledgments

We are blessed with loving families who inspire us each day: The Cooney family – wife Atsuko, children Aiyana and Kian; the Dudley family – wife Annette, children Stephen, David, Tiffany, and Faith; the Lantz family – father Ivan, mother Loie, sisters Mikaela and Elizabeth, brother Daniel; the Meconnahey family – wife Samantha, daughter Madelyn; the Peavy family - parents Grady and Kathren Robbins; the Pincus family – wife Amy, sons Stephen, Jr. and Mark; the Slack family – wife Janis, children Sarah, Samuel, and Brandon.

This book of the law shall not depart out of thy mouth; but thou shalt meditate therein day and night, that thou mayest observe to do according to all that is written therein: for then thou shalt make thy way prosperous, and then thou shalt have good success.

Have not I commanded thee? Be strong and of a good courage; be not afraid, neither be thou dismayed: for the LORD thy God is with thee whithersoever thou goest.
    - Joshua 1:8-9 [KJV]

Week 1, Day 1

make sure your heart is engaged

Reading

Proverbs 11:12(a); 16:24 [ERV] Stupid people say bad things about their neighbors... Kind words are like honey; they are easy to accept and good for your health.

1 Peter 3:9(b) [ERV] don't insult anyone to pay them back for insulting you. But ask God to bless them. Do this because you yourselves were chosen to receive a blessing.

Reflection

My dad was a carpenter. He carved wood, but he also carved words. When I was upset about something said, he'd warn: "Be careful what you say - don't speak until your brain is engaged." He normally added, "And **make sure your heart is engaged**, too!"

The spoken word can change your day. It can brighten it and give hope, or it can cause trouble and dismay. Words can give you confidence, or they can take away your strength.

The workplace is not always known for kind words. As a nurse, I am fully aware of the egos that come into play. Quiet but deliberate bullying also takes place. And, of course, there is the traditional backstabbing that goes on with words you never hear.

Today at work, be sensitive to what you say. Forgive those who speak ill toward you. Remember *you are the healthy one*. As a *Christ Worker*, you are blessed as one of His followers. So, as my dad would remind you, **make sure your heart is engaged**!

Prayer

Dear Jesus, help me to be more careful and thoughtful about my words and actions toward coworkers, clients, and citizens – especially that one person who gets on my nerves. Before I speak, reconstruct my heart so that my words reflect Your will. In Your name, I pray. Amen.

Patricia Baum

Week 1, Day 2

more powerful than any earthly temptation

Reading

1 Timothy 1:12 [NLT] I thank Christ Jesus our Lord, who has given me strength to do his work. He considered me trustworthy and appointed me to serve him, even though I used to blaspheme the name of Christ. In my insolence, I persecuted his people. But God had mercy on me because I did it in ignorance and unbelief.

1 Timothy 3:2(b) [NLT] exercise self-control, live wisely, and have a good reputation

Reflection

A secular rap song asks "Turn down for what?" The meaning refers to any act of rebellion against rules, values, or protocols that regulate excessive behavior. As public servants, we see people like this each day – clients and citizens who suffer the consequences of their excessive behavior. Sometimes we see excessive behavior in colleagues and coworkers, don't we? In fact, none of us is free from such sin.

As a middle-aged man, it's easy for me to review my deliberate sinful past and revel in the fact that Christ saved me from these indiscretions before something overly tragic happened. It's an honor and blessing to now serve God as a *Christ Worker*. But while many of my worldly ways are behind me, I would be lying if I said I never refer to some of my history as the "good times."

At work today, join me in remembering this simple message: God's love is **more powerful than any earthly temptation**. Remember it for your own sake, and find ways to forward this message to coworkers, clients, and citizens. Greater prosperity and happiness will come to those who understand that excessive behavior gives no glory to God.

Turn down for what? Your day will be a better one – a blessed one – if you only remember that God's love is **more powerful than any earthly temptation!**

Prayer

Dear Lord, please continue to guide my heart with actions that demonstrate Your love for all humanity. While I am fallible and susceptible to the temptations of the world, please repel my worldly selfishness in order that I may be a credible public servant and a vessel of Your divine word. In Your name, I eternally pray. Amen.

Steve Butler

Week 1, Day 3

high time to awake

Reading

Romans 13:11(B)-12 [NIV] The hour has already come for you to wake up from your slumber, because our salvation is nearer now than when we first believed. The night is nearly over; the day is almost here. So let us put aside the deeds of darkness and put on the armor of light.

Reflection

I recently buried a loved one. As I gazed down into the cold, wet grave, once again I was reminded that it is **high time to awake** from my sleep. My salvation – and that of my family, coworkers, and the clients and citizens I serve – is nearer than when I first believed.

As a Christian, you know *the time is at hand* because scripture tells you so. But how do you operationalize this concept? Have you cast off the works of darkness in your own life and put on the armor of light?

And what about the darkness in our workplaces? As *Christ Workers*, surely you and I cannot be good stewards of the public trust if we don't have our own lives in order.

So think not that today is just another day at the office. No, sir! No, ma'am! It isn't. Stop and realize that today may be your last day at the office. Today at work, know it is **high time to awake**; for the night is far spent, and the day of your eternal reckoning is at hand.

In ways that only God can lead you, with whom will you share the Good News of salvation today? Will it be with the one at work who is begging to hear it most? Will it be with the one at work who thinks she needs to hear it least?

In ways that only God can lead you, it is **high time to awake**.

Prayer

Father, thank You for Your Divine Word that tells me emphatically that it is **high time to awake**, for my salvation is nearer than when I believed. Use me today, Lord, in a purposeful way to put on the armor of Your light to my family members, clients, citizens, and coworkers. In the mighty name of your Son, my Lord and Savior, Jesus Christ, I pray today. Amen.

David Boisselle

Week 1, Day 4

what can mere people do to you

Reading

Psalm 118:6 [NLT] The Lord is for me, so I will have no fear. **What can mere people do to me?**

Isaiah 43:2 [NLT] When you go through deep waters, I will be with you. When you go through rivers of difficulty, you will not drown. When you walk through the fire of oppression, you will not be burned up; the flames will not consume you.

Hebrews 13:6 [NLT] So we can say with confidence, "The LORD is my helper, so I will have no fear. **What can mere people do to me?**"

Reflection

The *fire of oppression*. I think we all feel it at times – especially at work. It may seem like you are the only Christian around. Where is the Body of Christ? Enemies are fighting you for being a public servant who believes in God. Coworkers, who show white teeth in your presence, speak curses and deceitful words behind your back. They stab you in the back to hurt you – not because you are a poor employee, but because you try to work as a Christian – as a *Christ Worker*. And you think you are all alone.

It seems particularly challenging to follow Him in law enforcement. It must be true throughout the world. You are expected to be tough, ever-watchful for those breaking the law. You always see first-hand the very worst of what humanity can do to itself. It is easy to become suspicious. It is easy to think that showing the love of Christ might be viewed as a weakness.

Yet surely in law enforcement, as in all public service, there must be room for Christ. Surely there is need for Christ. And thank God there are many *Christ Workers*, including law enforcement, but so many more are desperately needed – around the world.

At work today, trust God to show His power. The *fire of oppression* will not consume you if you rely on God's protection. He will be with you through the high waters of the workday. He gives you the Holy Spirit and the Body of Christ. Both are somewhere in your workplace. Both are in your prayer kingdom. You are not alone. Now **what can mere people do to you?**

Prayer

Thank You, God, for all the *Christ Workers* around the world who are my personal prayer warriors today. Let them stand with me, as I stand with them – in the Body of Christ. The *fire of oppression* will not end, but the Body of Christ will not be consumed. I trust in You, God, to show Your power. It is in Your Son's name that I pray. Amen.

Amelia Monaheng

Week 1, Day 5

tempted by powerful sin

Reading

Genesis 39:9 [NIV] No one here has more authority than I do. He has held back nothing from me except you, because you are his wife. How could I do such a wicked thing? It would be a great sin against God.

Reflection

I am in a place where sin is powerful. To some brothers, *powerful sin* is very enjoyable. It is hard not to be **tempted by powerful sin** when it seems to be all around you. But rest assured, God's presence is here with me and others, and His presence flows mightily!

My place is not so different from Joseph's because he also was **tempted by powerful sin**. Joseph was not worried about sinning against man. He did not say that, by touching Potiphar's wife, he was sinning against him or her. No, he said it would be *a great sin against God.*

Do you work in a place like Joseph's and mine? Is your place really so different? Each day you leave home to go to work, and out there are many opportunities to be **tempted by powerful sin**. I remember. The temptation of not liking others. The temptation of stealing something that does not belong to you. Like Joseph, the temptation of adultery.

At work today, you will be **tempted by powerful sin**. Do not let it blind you from the fact that God is being very good to you, as He is to me and as He was to Joseph. So make *God-choices*, not flesh-choices. If you have the heart and spirit not to *sin against God*, you truly will be a *Christ Worker*. You will change people's lives.

It happens in prisons every day – it can also happen in your workplace!

Prayer

Father, in the name of Jesus, I pray. Thank You for all that You bless me with, but I especially thank You for supplying me with my daily bread. It is all I need. I have no need to sin against You. Amen.

Jimmy Davis, Jr.

Week 2, Day 1

the Hope of all nations

Reading

1 Peter 3:15(b) [NIV] Always be prepared to give an answer to everyone who asks you to give the reason for the hope that you have.

Romans 1:16(a) [NIV] For I am not ashamed of the gospel

Reflection

A young African, living in the United States, was invited to speak at a local public school. But the school principal warned, "Sir, make sure you don't talk about God because that could get us into trouble with the parents or even the court if we were to get sued." To this, the young African replied, *"Madam, I appreciate your concern, but for your information, I am not planning to talk about Jesus. I intend to share my life story of having been a street child and becoming who I am today because of Jesus and what He has done. Jesus is everything I am today and everything about my life story – so much so that I can't tell it without referring to Him."*

The young African's story was one of redemption, transformation, and hope <u>by</u> Jesus and <u>for</u> Jesus. Jesus is the hope of mankind, and therefore, He is **the Hope of all nations**. Reflecting on our past as lost souls and where we are with Jesus today, there is a much bigger story of redemption, transformation, and hope.

Yet are we willing to share that story to bless and encourage those in need?

Jesus, **the Hope of all nations**, is the hope of every *Christ Worker*. As you look into your neighborhood, town, and nation, there certainly are many souls out there longing for that hope. So don't be ashamed to genuinely live Jesus out in your actions. Share Him through your words.

Through your work, may **the Hope of all nations** reach out and bless for eternity the people of your neighborhood, your town, and your nation!

Prayer

Dear Father in heaven and on earth, I pray for a special level of Your strength, grace, and anointing upon Your people whom You have redeemed, transformed, and blessed with hope. May Your Spirit help me to freely, willingly, and obediently share that story of hope with my neighbors today and tomorrow – until

Jesus' reign and hope become complete over all the nations. I pray in Jesus' name. Amen!

Sosthene Maletoungou

Week 2, Day 2

the seed or the nourishment to the seed

Reading

John 4:34, 36-38 [NLT] Then Jesus explained: "My nourishment comes from doing the will of God, who sent me, and from finishing his work. The harvesters are paid good wages, and the fruit they harvest is people brought to eternal life. What joy awaits both the planter and the harvester alike! You know the saying, 'One plants and another harvests.' And it's true. I sent you to harvest where you didn't plant; others had already done the work, and now you will get to gather the harvest."

Reflection

A dear friend kept asking, "Why am I a part of the discussion? They don't really care nor understand the issues our constituents face." She felt like her voice was not being heard, and her attendance, research, and communications in each of the meetings were a complete waste of time. Might it be that her role was only to plant the seed and that the harvest would come later? Could it be her voice was heard and she was watering the seed planted before her? Perhaps her passion and the spirit of God were shining brightly, and God's Will was being done.

It's easy to miss the opportunity to serve and not meet the purpose that God has designed for you in each season. Before you dismiss the value you add, remember that those things added unto the glory of God will manifest later into a plentiful harvest.

So today – as you make decisions, evaluate programs, and provide input to a decision you think is already made – give it your all, and recognize that your voice may be **the seed or the nourishment to the seed** that was planted before you.

Prayer

God, I thank You for creating seed planters, nourishers, and harvesters. I thank You for allowing me to act in any capacity that brings You glory. Lord, I pray whatever role You have for me throughout this day I will serve in that role with great honor, humility, and respect. In Jesus' name, I pray. Amen.

LaShonda Garnes

Week 2, Day 3

love all others – period

Reading

John 13:34(b) [NIV] By this everyone will know that you are my disciples, if you love another.

Reflection

As public servants, you and I come under close scrutiny of those we serve and those with whom we work. Because of that scrutiny, there's pressure to keep our faith under wraps. If you display a cross in your workspace, you may need to keep it low-key. A bible should not readily be seen. If you wear a crucifix or cross, it's better to have it tucked under your shirt or small enough not to attract much notice.

It seems you are expected to hide your *Christianity*.

But what makes you a Christian? Is it a cross on your wall? A bible on your desk? That pendant around your neck? No. Of course not.

Jesus tells what makes you a Christian. He states succinctly what you need to do: **love all others – period**. As a Christian, it couldn't be simpler. So as a *Christ Worker*, you must find ways to love supervisors, coworkers, and the citizens you serve.

And you can do this without displaying anything.

So at work today, *do what it really takes* to be His disciple. All you need do is the simplest thing. All you need to follow is the simplest truth.

Yes today at work, **love all others – period**.

Prayer

Lord, help me focus on the simple truth of Your word. I need Your help to put others first. May my actions toward everyone at work be true to Your teachings. You showed me the way; I want to follow in Your footsteps. In Your name, I pray. Amen.

Larry Ketcham

Week 2, Day 4

that business of making all things new

Reading

Revelation 21:5a [NKJV] Then He who sat on the throne said, "Behold, I make all things new."

Reflection

Remember when you were made new in Christ? Born again to the New and Living Hope. You could feel and sense it. That newness was quite noticeable to you. I bet your newness was noticeable to others, too. Right?

But things get routine when you come down off that mountaintop. Sure, you still get excited at times, probably in church, but that feeling can get lost in the shuffle of life. It can especially get lost at work, and that is where you spend the vast majority of waking hours.

You know, Jesus is still in **that business of making all things new** – in my life and in your life. We must never forget that! As a matter of fact, you and I should anticipate every day what Jesus would like to make new. With a strong sense of spiritual vigilance, we need to anticipate what Jesus needs to make new in your life and mine.

Today at work, partner with Him in **that business of making all things new**. Go back to that mountaintop. It's just around the corner, maybe next to the Xerox machine.

Yes, today, partner with Him in **that business of making all things new**.

Prayer

Lord, You are the New and Living Hope! Renew me today at each corner of my worklife. Let my newness be humbly noticeable to those who need Your same renewal. In Your name, I pray. Amen.

Chris Summers

Week 2, Day 5

no longer fishing for catfish

Reading

Luke 5:10(b)-11 [NLT] Jesus replied to Simon, "Don't be afraid! From now on you'll be fishing for people!" And as soon as they landed, they left everything and followed Jesus.

Reflection

I love fishing. I used to fish in streams around my home. With a bamboo pole, I sat there and waited for the catfish – my favorite fish to eat! Sometimes they came my way, but many times they did not. I just sat there all day, and that was fine with me!

But I am **no longer fishing for catfish**.

Last week, I came across a situation where two brothers wanted to fight. As I stepped between them, they yelled, "Stay out." I told them I would not – that I wanted to cover each of them with the Lord's love, mercy, grace, and favor. In return, they would be changed for life.

Risky? Well, what would happen if I said nothing? You know, I wasn't just fishing for those two brothers. I was fishing for all the brothers who did not speak up and were content to watch a fight until a correctional officer broke it up.

As I said, I am **no longer fishing for catfish** – and not just because I'm on Life Row. No, it is because of my Lord's command to fish for men who need Him. My "stream" is actually larger now and not without nibbles, bites, and some catches. And my day is more exciting – more important now – than when I sat along my old stream. I am truly fishing on His behalf!

At your place of work, what are you fishing for? A nice time along some make-believe stream? Or are you **no longer fishing for catfish**? People may not break into physical fights, but I bet there are fights of a different kind. Fights that His love, mercy, grace, and favor can only resolve. And are you not placed in a position to speak up in fights over injustice? Hatred? Abuse? Fights within the heart of a coworker? Fights within the heart of a citizen you serve?

As a *Christ Worker*, today put down your nets. Leave everything and follow Jesus. That's His commandment. Like me, you are **no longer fishing for catfish**.

Prayer

Father in the name of Jesus, I pray. Continue to equip and prepare me to go fishing to bring glory to Your Son, Jesus Christ. Amen.

Jimmy Davis, Jr.

Week 3, Day 1

have to believe

Reading

Romans 14:8 [NIV] If we live, we live for the Lord; and if we die, we die for the Lord. So, whether we live or die, we belong to the Lord.

John 3:16 [NIV] For God so loved the world that he gave his one and only Son, that whoever believes in him shall not perish but have eternal life.

John 11: 25(b)-26 [NIV] I am the resurrection and the life. The one who believes in me will live, even though they die; and whoever lives by believing in me will never die. Do you believe this?

Reflection

A coworker lost his son to a tragic accident. It immediately took me back to the day my daughter was murdered. I see the pain in my friend's face that I still feel to this day about my daughter. No parent should have to lose a child. The hurt is indescribable.

But God knows that pain. He watched His son die – a horrible death on a cross. He let it happen so you and I could belong to Him. However, it isn't an automatic free "get out of death" card. You **have to believe** God sacrificed His only son for you – for you – because He loves you that much! Yes, you **have to believe**.

Well, my coworker believes and so did his son. I believe and so did my daughter. And we will all be together in the Lord some day because of that belief. Yes, this time is hard and life on earth will never be the same for my coworker – or me, but we will be with our children again, just as God is with His child.

So realize you, too, **have to believe**. In living and dying – and all the details in between – you **have to believe** you belong to the Lord.

So do you? What about your children? What about the coworker you see every day?

As a *Christ Worker*, this is the most important fact you can pass along. And you do so by word and deed. And if you do, people will begin to ask why you act the way you do. In the face of death. In the face of daily responsibilities and deadlines. In the face of challenges to hopes and dreams, jobs and careers. People will begin to ask.

Today at work, show and tell how you **have to believe**. How this gives you strength to take the next step. Let all know your secret about living and dying: you **have to believe**.

<u>Prayer</u>

God, I thank You for Your willingness to sacrifice Your son for <u>me</u>. Jesus, I thank You for Your willingness to do Your Father's will on <u>my</u> behalf. I am blessed with the privilege to believe and show others Your love. In Jesus' name, I pray. Amen.

Greg Smith

Week 3, Day 2

to die with loose ends

Reading

James 4:14 (MSG) You don't know the first thing about tomorrow. You're nothing but a wisp of fog, catching a brief bit of sun before disappearing.

Hebrews 13:16(b) (MSG) don't take things for granted and go slack in working for the common good; share what you have with others. God takes particular pleasure in acts of worship—a different kind of "sacrifice"—that take place in kitchen and workplace and on the streets.

Reflection

A local council member lost his wife due to a massive heart attack. It happened so quickly. At first, I thought that's a good way to die – *quickly* so the pain would be limited. But thinking more, I'm not so sure. What if it were me, and I had a bad day? What if I yelled at my kids before work and died before I could get home to hug them? What if I had an argument with my husband over the phone at work and died before we could make up? What if I left a work meeting, having been accusative toward someone? What if I said some really ugly things to a coworker? And what if I didn't compliment, encourage, or embrace someone who really needed it in their job or career? Good Lord, what if I died before I could take back all the stuff I said or did that day?

Well, it dawned on me that I do not want **to die with loose ends**.

You ever say or do something you wish you could take back? Do you try to do so immediately, or do you wait thinking you will have time to make amends tomorrow?

Today at work and at home, remember to never take life for granted. Be sure about this: one day *there will be no tomorrow*. So think before you speak, reflect before you act, and rejoice in the common good you may do today – before you disappear.

Yes, today make a different kind of sacrifice. You do not want **to die with loose ends**.

Prayer

God, thank You for allowing me to have this day – and maybe no other – with my coworkers, friends, and family. Give me strength to think before I speak and do and to love with all of my heart. Give me wisdom to apologize, to compliment, and to embrace – *immediately*. I do not want **to die with loose ends**. In Your Son's name, I pray. Amen.

Maureen Bereznak

Week 3, Day 3

God's handiwork of change

Reading

Isaiah 40:8 [NIV] The grass withers and the flowers fall, but the word of our God endures forever.

Psalm 105:5 [NIV] Remember the wonders that he has done, his miracles, and the judgments he pronounced.

Reflection

I always enjoy the changing seasons because everything looks so different in the various times of the year. It reminds me to slow down a bit and look at the miracles both small and large – as one season emerges and then dies into another season.

As a *Christ Worker*, perhaps you need to slow down and examine your own seasons and surroundings. What miracles are happening in your life and workplace? What things are now changing, and what will be changing in the near future? In each season of change, how can you best serve citizens and coworkers? Are you wholly committed to living for Christ in each season of your career and life?

Taking a step back and admiring **God's handiwork of change** can be refreshing and insightful – regardless of what season of life you're in. Seeing the miracles removes all fear and anxiety.

Today, you have an opportunity to observe **God's handiwork of change** in your workplace. Don't be afraid, for each season of your life shines with His miracles. Today at work, let God show You the amazing things He is doing to you and your workplace in this particular season.

Take time to observe **God's handiwork of change** – and be blessed!

Prayer

Lord, You are working out a plan that is more wonderful than anything I can imagine. Today, help me take time to marvel at Your handiwork in my workplace and my career. Help me mirror Your majesty to those whom I serve. It is in Your name that I pray. Amen.

Jonathan Lantz

Week 3, Day 4

God at the office door

Reading

Isaiah 63:9(b) [NIV] He lifted them and carried them...

Psalm 5:11(a) [NIV] Let all who take refuge in you be glad.

Reflection

Disturbance. Yes, we are all familiar with that workplace stress-maker.

When things get busy, the last thing we have time for is disturbance. If you're like me, you burrow your head in the task-at-hand and leave the rest of the world to fend for itself. You may even put a *do not disturb* sign on your door to keep everyone out.

But do you also keep God out? Do you keep **God at the office door**?

Too often in times of challenge, we show God the *do not disturb* sign – when we think we're only showing it to coworkers.

Today at work, remember you are the centre of God's attention. Are you sure He is the centre of yours? This shift in perspective is all God needs to show you His miraculous work!

So especially when challenges stack up today, you may decide to minimize disturbances by tacking up a *do not disturb* sign. You may need to keep others out to get the work down. But don't keep God out. No, take refuge in Him and be glad He wants to carry you in times of stress.

Yes, at work today, do not keep **God at the office door**. Let Him in!

Prayer

Lord, help me be disciplined in my faith. Thank You for always treating me as Your priority. Help me leave this world full of disturbances at the office door. But let me never forget You. Let me always keep my door wide open for You. In Your name, I pray. Amen.

Stephanie Van Straten

Week 3, Day 5

eyes to see Jesus

Reading

Job 42:5 [NLT] I had only heard about you before, but now I have seen you with my own eyes.

Reflection

When I was young, my mom told me all about Jesus. My grandma also told me all about Jesus. Even an older couple, who took me to church each Sunday, told me all about Jesus. I don't blame these people, but as they told me all about Jesus, I had no **eyes to see Jesus**.

It is a shame to be told about someone so wonderful and not to know Him well enough to see Him. For us to let others see Jesus, we can't just talk about Him. We have to release His love, peace, joy, mercy, and grace. We have to release Him to others by our words and behavior – each day. We have to stop judging and disqualifying others as we keep talking about Jesus. We have to stop telling them about Jesus and start opening their **eyes to see Jesus**.

It is easy to open eyes at church but much harder at work. Yet your true ministry, like mine, starts outside the church. It starts right in your workplace as it does on my row. For both of us, it starts right now.

Today at work, show someone His love, peace, joy, mercy, and grace. Keep releasing Him through your words and actions. Yes, today, open someone's **eyes to see Jesus**.

Prayer

Father, in the name of Jesus, I pray. Give me Your wisdom and strength so I can open the eyes of all who have just heard about Your Son – so that, through me, they can experience His love, peace, joy, mercy, and grace. Amen.

Jimmy Davis, Jr.

Week 4, Day 1

wake up and shake off the dust

Reading

Matthew 10:14 [NIV] If anyone will not welcome you or listen to your words, leave that home or town and shake the dust off your feet.

Ephesians 5: 7-8(a), 14,17 [NIV] Therefore do not be partners with them. For you were once darkness, but now you are light in the Lord… This is why it is said: "Wake up, sleeper, rise from the dead, and Christ will shine on you."… Therefore do not be foolish, but understand what the Lord's will is.

Reflection

A friend in prison is breaking up with his girlfriend. After years of prayers for a sound relationship, she doesn't value him. God calls him to **wake up and shake off the dust**. Another friend has prayed long and hard for a renewed relationship with her brother, but she still bears the brunt of his animosity. God also calls her to **wake up and shake off the dust**. A colleague is leaving a position at a large Christian NPO. Despite years of prayerful petitioning, he claims the culture there is killing Christ. He believes God calls him to **wake up and shake off the dust**.

Personal relationships, family problems, institutional dysfunction – all can adversely impact your ability to survive and perform in the workplace. So you pray about many things. You pray long and hard for remedy. And you don't want to give up because God answers all prayers. But *sometimes God's answer is "no."* For His reasons yet unveiled, He commands you to let go. It may be for your good or the good of someone else or even the good of the agency. But the fact is He sometimes wants you to rise from the dead and get out of the darkness.

At work today, continue to pray mightily about that which is broken – those sharp pieces that cut into your life, including the workplace. Pray long and hard to understand His will. If the answer is "no," get out of that darkness! Find peace and closure elsewhere in His light. Oh sure, you may mourn – but you'll know it's His will to **wake up and shake off the dust**. Follow Him.

Prayer

Father God, give me eyes and ears to see and hear Your will. You may need me where it is dark and broken. But if You have reason to wake me from my sleep – raise me from the dead – I know You will shine on me wherever You take me. It is in Your Son's name that I pray. Amen.

James D. Slack
Week 4, Day 2

what lies ahead

Reading

Philippians 3:13(b) [NIV] I focus on this one thing: Forgetting the past and looking forward to **what lies ahead**.

Reflection

As I look down at the letter in front of me, I suddenly get a flashback to June 1975. Then, I was signing my acceptance letter in the Canadian Federal Public Service. I remember the excitement in my heart – I just knew this was a new season and the start of a great journey. But today, I find myself signing my retirement letter.

To be honest, I felt anxious about retirement. I asked the Lord to help me understand why I'm afraid to let go. I heard the Lord ask back, "Why are you afraid?" So I reflected on what I love about being a *Christ Worker*: learning, training, traveling, contributing to my country, and making a difference. But most of all, I love serving Him through my work.

Then I realised that was my uneasiness. Would I remain a *Christ Worker*? And the answer is "yes"! He will use me after my career just as He has used me during my career. He will continue to make my path straight.

While I don't want to forget the past, my focus is now on **what lies ahead**. I will remain a *Christ Worker*. When you retire, you will too.

Is today your day to sign those retirement papers? Or is it tomorrow? Do not worry about **what lies ahead**!2 He will keep your path straight!

Prayer

Lord, give me the wisdom and strength to move forward and not stay stuck in the old. You are a God of new beginnings, and Your mercies are new every morning. Give me the power to move forward even if I don't know **what lies ahead**. In Your name, I pray. Amen.

Anne-Marie Couturier

Week 4, Day 3

one of the least

Reading

Mark 8:36 [NIV] What good is it for someone to gain the whole world, yet forfeit their soul?

Matthew 25:40(b) [NIV] whatever you did for one of the least of these brothers and sisters of mine, you did for me.

Reflection

I am self-employed – for the most part, a stay-at-home pawnbroker without cash lending. I sit on the internet and refresh classified pages waiting for underpriced items. I then purchase the items – sometimes low-balling and sometimes offering more than a seller's asking price to cut out other buyers. I will lie to make a deal. Even worse, I "side hustle" people to take their business.

I feel I am forfeiting my soul for worldly gain. Also, I have not opened the Bible in 14 years. I do not know what it means to be a Christian. Truly, I feel like I am **one of the least** in this world.

But something's happening. I don't know exactly what it means, but I yearn to become a *Christ Worker*. And I am looking for others to help.

When you go to work today, look around. There is someone just like me – someone who is hungry to know Christ but has a history. This person is a coworker or a citizen you serve. You don't have to pull out your Bible and preach, but neither should you judge, mock, or ignore him. I am told we are all **one of the least** of His, and this is why Christians help everyone.

Today at work, help that person who needs Him most – help **one of the least** because you, too, are **one of the least**. Don't let you and that person forfeit anything with Christ.

Prayer

Dear Lord, give me the knowledge and ability to open my eyes to You. Surround me with Your people to help me become strong in following You. Let me help others stay strong in You. We are all the least of Yours, especially me. In Your name, I pray. Amen.

Michael Barnes

Week 4, Day 4

enter His gates with thanksgiving

Reading

Psalm 100:1,4(a) [NLT] Shout with joy to the LORD, all the earth!... **Enter his gates with thanksgiving**

Reflection

For a long time, I only had a *weekend God*. I attended church every Sunday, but I prayed just when I needed something from Him. While petitions are good unto our Lord, I was not praying how grateful I was for everything He did for me.

But my profession opened my eyes to the violence, despair, and depravity that go hand-in-hand with living in a sinful world. Watching (and being able to help) other people survive life's crises – *only by the hand of God* – became a turning point for me. The focus of my prayers changed. A weekend God was not enough as He was at work 24/7 – in my life but also in the lives of all whom I serve.

You know, public servants in law enforcement talk about not going into a dangerous situation without "backup." Every day and every workplace is dangerous in one way or another. When I decided to let God be my 24/7 backup, I truly became a *Christ Worker*. I started to give God all credit and thanked Him for all things. I became grateful. In fact, the healthiest emotion I now have is gratitude. Grateful prayer makes me more resistant to stress and less susceptible to negativity. I am happiest when I am grateful, and so I shout with joy as I **enter His gates with thanksgiving.**

At work today, you **enter His gates with thanksgiving**. Engage in prayerful gratitude that will strengthen your personal relationship with Him and help you be a better public servant – a *Christ Worker* who acknowledges that everything you have, and everything you do, comes about only because you have decided to make Him your backup.

So today at work – be grateful, shout with joy to your Lord, and **enter His gates with thanksgiving!**

Prayer

Father, thank You for the blessings You bring each day. I am grateful for Your consistent faithfulness in my workday despite my sins. All good that I experience comes from You and only You. I pray this in Your Son's name. Amen.

Richard J. Conroy

Week 4, Day 5

a different way of life

Reading

Proverbs 10:17(a) [AMP] He who heeds instruction *and* correction is [not only himself] in the way of life [but also] is a way of life to others.

Reflection

One day last week, chaos and confusion struck my tier. It was very cold, and there was no heat. When this happens, you sleep with your coat, hat, and gloves on. The concrete floor in your cell chills every joint of your lower body – up to your hips. Brothers on Life Row become irritable when it's either very cold or very hot. (Do you?) Well, it was easy to get angry on that day.

So a brother falsely accused five Christian brothers and me of violating a rule. We did nothing wrong, but that did not matter. The accusation was made. The five Christian brothers became angry. They started to shout and cuss him out. I also felt like shouting and cussing him, but the Holy Spirit instructed me to remain silent and pray. The five Christian brothers saw what I was doing and stopped cussing. Their anger went away, and they no longer wanted to fight. They joined silently in prayer. The brother making all the trouble now had no one to agitate.

All it takes is one person to heed the instructions of the Holy Spirit and correction can follow. You become corrected in the way of your own life, but you also help others become corrected in the way of their lives. Instruction and correction can come regardless of how much chaos and confusion strikes you. Where I live, it can come in the middle of winter or the hottest part of summer. I bet it's the same with you. It can come on my tier and in your workplace. If instruction and correction can come in my life, surely it can come in your life.

Chaos and confusion will strike you today – in all parts of your life, including at work. Do not join in. Instead, listen to the Holy Spirit. Heed His instruction and correction. Even when you are wronged, *heed* and show someone else **a different way of life** – His way of life.

Prayer

Father, in the name of Jesus, I pray. Thank You for mercy You give me each day, but also thanks for Your wisdom in Your instructions and corrections. Keep me in Your way of life, and help me show others Your way of life. Amen.

Jimmy Davis, Jr.

Week 5, Day 1

give and receive unwarranted forgiveness

Reading

Ephesians 4:32 [NLT] Instead be kind to one another, tender-hearted, forgiving each other, just as God in Christ also has forgiven you.

Reflection

I was in a meeting last week. There was a heated discussion over an important issue, and two coworkers took the debate personally – exchanging very harsh words. This went on for about a minute, and I began to pray under my breath. As I prayed, anger began to be replaced by expressions of hurt and sorrow. The exchange ended with an outpouring of tears from both coworkers. One asked for forgiveness.

Regrettably, the request was not well received. The other coworker did not turn to tender-heartedness. Instead, she let the wound fester during the rest of the meeting.

Afterwards, I talked with the coworker who asked for forgiveness. I wanted to support her. I let her know that I admired how she had handled the situation once she realized her own rage. I told her I was inspired seeing her tender-heartedness sprout up in spite of how the exchange started.

Unfortunately, the *attitude of unforgiveness* seems predominant in too many workplaces. It is in mine. Is it in yours? Unforgiveness contaminates relationships and undermines productivity. As *Christ Workers*, you and I must be lights to our peers in the workplace. You and I must demonstrate tender-heartedness – just as Christ has done for both of us. Yes, you and I must show others how to **give and receive unwarranted forgiveness.**

So today at work, offer and accept forgiveness. Do so freely. Encourage other coworkers to do the same. As a *Christ Worker*, turn to tender-heartedness when tensions boil – especially if yours has already boiled. Show what a difference it can make to **give and receive unwarranted forgiveness!**

Prayer

Heavenly Father, help me throughout this workday not to take offense easily and forgive others freely – just as You forgive me. In Your Son's name, I pray. Amen.

Suzanne Denis

Week 5, Day 2

that Hand will move

Reading

Isaiah 41:10 [KJV] Fear thou not; for I *am* with thee: be not dismayed; for I *am* thy God: I will strengthen thee; yea, I will help thee; yea, I will uphold thee with the right hand of my righteousness.

2 Corinthians 12:9 [KJV] And he said unto me, My grace is sufficient for thee: for my strength is made perfect in weakness. Most gladly therefore will I rather glory in my infirmities, that the power of Christ may rest upon me.

Reflection

My dear father-in-law, who is now with the Lord, would always remind me in times of stress, "Prayer moves the Hand that holds the world." Yet here I sit – overly anxious about the pressures of the day.

Do you feel those pressures? Worrying about possible work outcomes. Agonizing about performing well on an important examination or job interview. And will there be enough cash to see out the month and pay all the bills?

My friend, be more like my dear father-in-law. Pray and **that Hand will move**. Trust in the promises of God. Be dependent upon Him. After all, He is God!

So as you set out on today's journey, *learn not to fear* what the day may hold. In your weakness, there is strength – His perfect strength. He is giving you strength to cope with whatever trial or anxiety you are passing through. His strength will be perfect and His grace sufficient.

Yes, regardless of trouble, be not dismayed. Pray. Have faith. And **that Hand will move**.

Prayer

Most gracious God, I give thanks unto Thee that Thou art so mindful of me in all my times of pressure and stress. Thy compassion is such that Thou art willing to lift me up when I am down. Even amidst all my fears and anxieties, Thou wilt never leave me or forsake me. Give me that needful strength when I feel so weak and fearful, and help me to know and follow the way that Thou, in Thy infinite wisdom, have planned for me. My prayer, I lift up to Thee, in the precious and worthy name of our Lord and Saviour, Jesus Christ. Amen.

Alan S. Flint

Week 5, Day 3

the Ultimate Fixer

Reading

Matthew 6: 25(b)-27 [NIV] do not worry about your life, what you will eat or drink; or about your body, what you will wear. Is not life more than food, and the body more than clothes? Look at the birds of the air; they do not sow or reap or store away in barns, and yet your heavenly Father feeds them. Are you not much more valuable than they? Can any one of you by worrying add a single hour to your life?

Philippians 4:6-7 [NIV] Do not be anxious about anything, but in every situation, by prayer and petition, with thanksgiving, present your requests to God. And the peace of God, which transcends all understanding, will guard your hearts and your minds in Christ Jesus.

Reflection

I come across many challenges throughout each workday – whether with my students, coworkers, or even a parent. I tend to get consumed with finding a solution and making the situation "all better" because I consider myself a fixer. But I often find myself overcome with worry and fear that I may not be the fixer I think I am.

Are you this way at work?

You know, scripture says worrying serves no purpose at all. The Word says I have a savior who has it under control – that He is **the Ultimate Fixer**. So I must not forget He has already solved the ultimate problem of my humanity and sinful nature by sacrificing Himself for me.

Today at work, this is what I will dwell on: I may be a fixer, but He is **the Ultimate Fixer**. And there are some challenges I simply cannot fix – by myself. And many only He can fix – by Himself.

At work today, why don't you put all worries into His hands? In the end, He is the one who will ease them anyway, with or without your help.

So let Him guard your heart and your mind. He is **the Ultimate Fixer!**

Prayer

Dear Heavenly Father, please forgive me for trying to solve problems without first going to You in prayer. Grant me strength and patience to trust that all challenges are in Your capable, loving hands. In Your Son's name, I pray. Amen.

Laura Ashley Missildine

Week 5, Day 4

put all the chaos aside

Reading

Colossians 3:15(a) [ESV] And let the peace of Christ rule in your hearts, to which indeed you were called in one body.

Reflection

Last minute to-dos, parents to be contacted, grades to be entered, lessons to be written, paperwork to be completed and turned in. These are just a few of the many things that occupy my day. And when things don't go as planned, chaos easily becomes part of the equation.

But I have to **put all the chaos aside** once the students enter the classroom. If they sense anything out of order, it can completely alter their learning. And that defeats the day.

If you're like me, it's hard to stop and find needed peace in the craziness of the workday. Yet scripture directs us to be *peace setters* – even in the workplace. And that peace comes from the One above.

At work today, remember your actions speak louder than words, and your actions may even strike up a conversation. So let the peace of Christ shine through your actions during this busy, hectic workday. And when someone asks how you remain so calm, use it as a great opportunity to talk about where your peace truly comes from.

So today, shine peace and **put all the chaos aside**. Let His peace rule your heart.

Prayer

Lord, as I begin another work day, I thank You for the opportunity to shine Your peace to others. I pray that, as chaos begins seeping into the day, Your peace will fill my heart, and You will redirect my thoughts to Your will. In Your name, I pray. Amen.

Morgan Best

Week 5, Day 5

the biggest word ever

Reading

2 Chronicles 16:9(b) [MSG] GOD is always on the alert, constantly on the lookout for people who are totally committed to him.

Reflection

For me, the word "committed" is a big word. Is it for you? I don't mean grammatically. I don't mean by the number of letters in that word. Lots of words are bigger than "committed."

It is *a big word* because it requires a lot – maybe more than any other word. I mean, it really takes a lot to be committed.

Now, you may be committed to your job. You may be committed to your career. You may be committed to circumstance. You may be committed to lifestyle.

But the word gets bigger when you become committed to our Lord. Yes, it becomes **the biggest word ever** because He is on the lookout for you.

Today at work, use **the biggest word ever**. Be committed to God.

Prayer

Father, in the name of Jesus, I pray. Thank You for not only loving me but being on the outlook for me! I commit my life to You, and I promise to show others how committed I am. Amen.

Jimmy Davis, Jr.

Week 6, Day 1

on knees and not in flesh

Reading

Romans 12:3 [KJV] For I say, through the grace given unto me, to every man that is among you, not to think of himself more highly than he ought to think; but to think soberly, according as God hath dealt to every man the measure of faith.

Reflection

As a public administrator for nearly twenty years, I've learned many lessons. Holding a place of authority, there are occasions when I have to react fast. Such instances don't need my flesh on parade or my chest pushed out saying "I'm the boss." Getting the bighead, as they say, isn't the answer. Being a *servant leader* is the answer!

Being a *servant leader* means holding on to God and truly allowing the Word to lead and guide. There are so many pressures and responsibilities that come with leadership. If I don't humble myself and seek the Father daily, I won't make it. So I have to check myself daily to remain in a place of humility – yet operate through the power of God in the position He has called me.

This journey isn't easy, but God sustains me. It isn't by my power or my might but by His spirit; that places me in a position to lead. I am not called to serve citizens by sitting behind a plush desk in a big office – but by truly being a servant from a place **on knees and not in flesh**. It is never about me, even though it feels like it sometimes. It's always about God.

At work today, will you respond from a place **on knees and not in flesh**? Regardless of where you work and what level of employment, will you be a *servant leader*?

Prayer

Father God, thank You for entrusting me to lead Your people. Thank You for placing me in a position to help others. You are the Master of the universe, the Great I Am, and the Master of all. Thank You, Father, for Your word and Your love to lead and guide me into all truth. I pray I may continue to humble myself under Your mighty hand. In the name of Jesus, I pray. Amen.

Wendy Mahoney

Week 6, Day 2

no bad days at the office

Reading

James 1:2-4 [NIV] Consider it pure joy, my brothers and sisters, whenever you face trials of many kinds, because you know that the testing of your faith produces perseverance. Let perseverance finish its work so that you may be mature and complete, not lacking anything.

Reflection

Many days I leave home, and the closer I get to the office, the more I get overwhelmed with extreme anxiety. And that sets the tone of my day. I then react emotionally with angst, distrust, and, well, type-A activity. Not only does this take a physical toll on me, it negatively impacts workplace relationships. And chaos prevails.

The only way I can end the chaos in my thoughts is to realize God is not going to wipe off from the face of the earth all the difficult people and crazy assignments – just because I get nervous. He's not going to end deadlines in my work – just because I give into anxiety. No! He places trials in front of me to test my faith, and testing my faith produces perseverance.

So I know there are **no bad days at the office**. Really. In fact, happiness is a choice, one that I can make at any moment – if I have faith. And if I have faith, I gain perseverance – and that is how I control my thoughts and emotions. That is how I fight chaos.

How about you? Suffer from workplace anxiety? See only workplace chaos? Difficult to maintain healthy workplace relationships? Always feeling tested?

Before you go to work today, have faith in Him. Let perseverance finish its course. After all, there are **no bad days at the office**. How could there be – with Him in charge?

Prayer

Father God, as my workday begins, let me give my anxiety to You. Help me shift my focus from feeling burdened to feeling like Your good servant. Only through You, I know I am in control of my thoughts and emotions. Through every trial today, my faith will let me persevere. In Your Son's name, I pray. Amen.

Shelia Granger-Malone

Week 6, Day 3

dressed for success in any season

Reading

Ephesians 6:13 [NIV] Therefore put on the full armor of God, so that when the day of evil comes, you may be able to stand your ground, and after you have done everything, to stand.

Reflection

A while back, a new employee joined our staff. From the start, she dressed in a professional manner. Once, she asked me, "How do you dress in the fall and winter for this job?" I was not thinking much when I responded, so I just told her what I normally wore. But when I got home that night, I realized I gave her bad advice. I should have said to wear the full armor of God, and she would be **dressed for success in any season**!

It's easy to go to work with the wrong "clothes" or with no "clothes" at all. All that grumbling about the job – all the stress and all the work – you are simply undressing yourself and going to work *spiritually naked* – vulnerable to attacks from the devil throughout the workday.

So today, before you leave home for work, be sure to dress appropriately – *wear the full armor of God* – and stay that way on the work-battlefield for the Lord.

And I promise you will be **dressed for success in any season**!

Prayer

Dear God, thank You for being the top designer in fashion history and for providing me with the wardrobe I need to make it through work and, more importantly, through life. In Your Son's name, I pray. Amen!

Adrieme Walker

Week 6, Day 4

not my responsibility

Reading

Matthew 5:41[NIV] If anyone forces you to go one mile, go with them two miles.

Reflection

Ever hear a coworker say, "That's **not my responsibility**." Ever hear yourself say it? Or do you limit that phrase to just the thought that drives your "polite" response?

If you're like me, I bet you've thought and said it more than once!

On some workdays, or at certain points in each day, you and I get tired. And I would like nothing better than to think something really is **not my responsibility**. That student or citizen asking the umpteenth question. That client with yet another opinion needing a researched response. That elected official with a smart sound-bite aside that requires a reflective answer from you. And, yes, there is a need for limits and boundaries – some things really are above the pay grade. Some issues can only be addressed and answered by someone who is not you or me.

But like the Pharisees in the time of Jesus, a moment of fatigue or a legalistic approach is used too often as a cover to avoid taking responsibility for solving a problem at its root.

When you think or say a situation is **not my responsibility**, you are really saying the person and the problem are not worthy of your time. And then you find yourself denying Christ's command of going that extra mile.

Today at work, ask yourself: is it really **not my responsibility**? Then go that extra mile!

Prayer

Lord, when lost sheep wander into my path, I promise to take time to lead them to the correct pasture. I promise to go that extra mile so that I can give You the glory. Let me honor You with patience and love. In Your name, I pray. Amen.

Gary E. Roberts

Week 6, Day 5

in a manner worthy

Reading

Philippians 1:27(a) [NLT] Above all, you must live as citizens of heaven, conducting yourselves in a manner worthy of the Good News about Christ.

Reflection

A couple of weeks ago, two brothers on Life Row were planning to do something very evil. Something that could have hurt a lot of people here. I was in a position to stop their plan, and I did – not by force but by other means.

There are brothers like that everywhere. Thinking of various ways to hurt others. While my situation involved physical hurt, your situation may involve hurt of other kinds. And like my "workplace" here on Life Row, your workplace probably has one or two who want to do some kind of damage to someone else.

But when you and I live our lives at work (or anywhere else) **in a manner worthy** of the Good News about Christ, we are able to live as citizens of heaven. And, as citizens of heaven, we have an obligation to stop others from hurting others – not by force, but by showing a better way.

So today at work, take the challenge. Be a citizen of heaven. And conduct yourself **in a manner worthy** of His Good News. Your authority will greatly increase!

Prayer

Father, in the name of Jesus, I pray. Continue to strip me of my reputation so I can allow Your reputation to flow through my life to others. I want to be **in a manner worthy** of You. Amen.

Jimmy Davis, Jr.

Week 7, Day 1

the virtue of spiritual poverty

Reading

Matthew 5:3 [NKJV] Blessed are the poor in spirit, For theirs is the kingdom of heaven.

Reflection

When I served in the military, it was too easy for me to forget my subordinates were fathers and mothers themselves – people who represented the knowledge of the world to their children. I was *humbled* when I realized they were so much more than merely "troops" or "sailors." When I began to check my ego – stopped talking and started listening – my unit became an effective organization.

You know, Jesus teaches us **the virtue of spiritual poverty**. His lesson is this: we don't know everything. Therefore, we should *remain humble* knowing it's God's grace that permits you and me to be what we are. That we <u>all</u> are His children – His sons and His daughters. So humility is perhaps the most important Christian virtue – it is, after all, the first beatitude.

One of the great strengths of public and nonprofit administration may be the high level of technical expertise brought to the table. But being technically right isn't always, well, right. In fact, the technically correct decision often turns out badly – when "people" knowledge is discounted or ignored.

So today at work, really listen to others – staff members and residents living closest to the problem or setting. Practice **the virtue of spiritual poverty**. Remember, everyone is a child of <u>your</u> God. And remember <u>you</u> don't know everything.

Yes, at work today, be humble with your expertise. Practice **the virtue of spiritual poverty**.

Prayer

Lord, I pray that You re-teach me today the value of humility. By Your grace, and only by Your grace, I can be a better servant and disciple. Keep me humble, Lord, so that I might be Your instrument in building the Kingdom of Heaven by listening to and helping others. In Your name, I pray. Amen.

Allen Stout

Week 7, Day 2

when a bully comes your way

Reading

Proverbs 11:12 (NKJV) He who is devoid of wisdom despises his neighbor, But a man of understanding holds his peace.

Reflection

A few months ago, I had to deal with a bully. That person cussed me, accused me, pointed his finger right into my face, and called me a liar. He was out of control, and let me tell you, it was awful. I really wanted to let him have it – lord my authority over him and tell him what's what.

But I didn't. Instead, I tried to keep cool. I kept whispering, "Dear Father, help."

Obviously, the incident was dreadful, and I was bothered all day. And so I went home wondering if I did the right thing in that exchange – keeping my cool and not lording over the person.

A brother heard about my day and, that night, forwarded a devotional from the on-line publication, *The Christian Public Servant*. Now I had never heard of this publication, and the devotional he sent was rather unique. You see, the author was not a government employee. No, it was written by a man in prison – a man on death row. Here was a man with no control over anything in his life, yet his words reinforced in me what Christ wants: I need to stay in control. Even when events get out of control, I need to keep myself under control.

I felt better that evening. Through that author's words, God assured me I did a good job. I did what was right because I came to my Father asking for His help. And He came through.

Today at work, you do the same. When pressed, don't lord it over others. Be like our brother on death row. Be wise and understanding **when a bully comes your way**. Ask for God's help, and He will come through for you, too.

So at work today, need only Him **when a bully comes your way**.

Prayer

Father, I ask for Your help today as I strive to be the public servant You call me to be. Give me wisdom and understanding. I will give You all the glory. In Your Son's name, I pray. Amen.

Ronald Wilson

Week 7, Day 3

like a passing shadow

Reading

Psalm 144:4 [ESV] Man is like a breath; his days are **like a passing shadow**.

Reflection

They call them New-Agers. Millennials. And they're all part of Generation Y, which is just a little younger than Generation X.

Young people – knowing so much, demanding so much, and expecting so much more than you think you did at their age. Truth is, you and I were like them just yesterday – maybe 10 years, maybe 20 years, maybe just a short 30 years ago.

When David was older, he began to see the frailty of humankind. He understood that time passes faster with age. He started to realize his days were numbered – **like a passing shadow**.

And so it is with you and me.

There was a time we'd go to work and our youthful energy and shallow short-sightedness would keep us from seeing life's brevity. But with each added year, we'd start to worry about our frailty – becoming more cautious in our bets and wagers about the future. Oh yes, worry did set in some time ago.

Serving Jesus with all of your heart, mind, soul, and strength is the only consolation for that brief frailty called life.

And so it is also with that millennial you see at work today. No matter your age or station in life, take a moment to pray for grace to see God's wisdom in our collective plight of human brevity and frailty.

And pray especially for that all-knowing New-Ager.

As you are, she too is **like a passing shadow**.

Prayer

Father, You know my time is brief – shorter than what I hope. Use me today like it is my last day on earth. Help me be more than a passing shadow today at work. Let me use each minute to glorify You through my diligence and accomplishments. In Your Son's name, I pray. Amen.

Chris Summers

Week 7, Day 4

not just for rest but for praise

Reading

Genesis 2:3 [NKJV] Then God blessed the seventh day and sanctified it, because in it He rested from all His work which God had created and made.

Revelation 4:11 [NKJV] You are worthy, O Lord, To receive glory and honor and power; For You created all things, And by Your will they exist and were created.

Reflection

I'm just starting out in my career. In fact, I am currently looking for a job. I am not lazy. Far from it. I plan on burning the midnight oil to be successful. Believe me; I will work long and hard.

But I pray I will be able to have one day off – **not just for rest but for praise**. It may not be Sunday, I understand that. But it will be one day a week to worship Him.

God, himself, set the example for you and me. As *Christ Workers*, we need to follow His example. We need to reserve one day – **not just for rest but for praise**. Having fun, sure. But spending time with family and glorifying Him. Spending time in worship with family. Spending time with Him.

This week, reserve one day – Sunday if possible – **not just for rest but for praise**.

And you will be refreshed to burn that midnight oil!

Prayer

Dear Lord, thank You for creating this world and me. Let me reserve one day – **not just for rest but for praise**. All glory goes to you, my Lord, only to You. In Your name, I pray. Amen.

Paul Bayer

Week 7, Day 5

the best training ground

Reading

Luke 22:3 [NLT] Then Satan entered into Judas Iscariot, who was one of the twelve disciples,

John 13:12 [NLT] After washing their feet, he put on his robe again and sat down and asked, "Do you understand what I was doing?"

Reflection

This may sound strange, but I thank God I did not get saved while I was out in the free-world. And for about 10 years here I was still not saved. But then our Lord touched my heart, He changed my life, and death row became Life Row.

You may ask: why wouldn't I have wanted to be saved on the outside? Well, prison is **the best training ground** for me because there are a lot of demonized people who believe in their own abilities, their own will, and their own desires. And, until Jesus flooded my life with His blood and I surrendered to the Great Authority, I was just like those demonized fools.

That's how I got here.

So when I see someone who has not found Christ, I think of how Jesus treated that one demonized fool called Judas. He loved him. He served him. Jesus washed Judas' feet, just like He washed the feet of the other disciples.

When I realize that people who don't know Jesus are being driven by Satan, I know I must show them the love of Jesus – especially them – just like Jesus showed Judas. Like He showed me.

My setting is no different than that of the disciples – for they also had **the best training ground** for learning to follow Jesus.

Where you live and work, is it any different? Look around at all the people who do not know Jesus. Look closely.

Today at work, understand you also have **the best training ground** to learn and do His work.

Prayer

Father, in the Name of Jesus, I pray. Thank You for helping me see You in everyone – especially those guided by Satan. No matter how bad they act, let me love and show Your example. Thank You for placing me in this training ground. Amen.

Jimmy Davis, Jr.

Week 8, Day 1

lead by the heart, not by the world

Reading

1 Samuel 16:7 [ESV] But the LORD said to Samuel, "Do not look on his appearance or on the height of his stature, because I have rejected him. For the LORD sees not as man sees: man looks on the outward appearance, but the LORD looks on the heart."

Reflection

A long time ago, a coworker and I became really good friends. The best of friends. We had lunch all the time, went shopping together, and knew each other's family. Then she got a big pay raise and a promotion, and her attitude changed. She acted better than me, and she no longer had time for me. No more shopping and no more invitations to her home. It was clear she couldn't afford to be friends with me anymore. She wasn't my supervisor, but it was still rough since we remained working in the same department and saw each other every day.

Something like this ever happen to you?

Losing a friend is difficult, but the hardest thing is working near that person. When that former friend ignores you, it's like you're no longer good enough. You get angry and hurt, and you want to get even somehow because others see your worldly emotions.

Yes, you want to do or say something to get even – but don't.

God doesn't want you that way. He rejects those who act and react on the basis of the height of someone's stature. God wants you to lead by His example – **lead by the heart, not by the world**.

So at work today, don't fret about how others treat you based on the height of stature. After all, God is rejecting that person. Instead, be His example. Take a deep breath and **lead by the heart, not by the world**.

For it is the heart that God sees.

Prayer

Thank You, God, for giving me the guidance I need to get through difficult times in the workplace. Remind me constantly that you are looking at my heart.

Let me carry my heart throughout the workday, and let me show others the result in my reactions. In Your Son's name, I pray. Amen.

Maureen Bereznak

Week 8, Day 2

letting the evil one get to you

Reading

Psalm 18:1 [NIV] I love you Lord, my strength.

Exodus 15:2(a) [NIV] The Lord is my strength and my defense

Reflection

Ever have a workday when you're completely overwhelmed because of so many demands? You begin to think you can't possibly get it all done by the deadlines imposed. And then there is the work at home and perhaps in school. It all adds up. You feel like screaming, "I can't do it!"

Doubting yourself. Doubting your ability. Doubting your strength.

You know what you're doing, don't you? You're **letting the evil one get to you**. You're letting Satan have his hand at convincing you that maybe – just maybe – you're unable to cut it. He's whispering to you, in the most vulnerable moments, that you're not qualified to do the work – let alone give sound advice to an employee or supervisor.

Friend, I'm here to tell you that God is your strength, and He will get you through these overwhelming times of stress and doubt. When feeling dazed, I have learned to look at what I've accomplished over the years – and I bet you have many victories, too! Then I realize God has brought me this far and He surely is not going to abandon me. I begin to relax with the certainty that He will protect and defend me when the evil one tries to sneak doubt into my mind about myself and the day's tasks.

So at work today, stop **letting the evil one get to you**. Your strength comes from God. And so must your confidence!

Prayer

Dear Heavenly Father, thank You for all that You have allowed me to accomplish in my life. I praise You for getting me through the difficult tasks, and I ask You to continue to be my strength. I know You are God, and there is nothing I can't do because You have equipped me to do Your work right here and now. And when there is doubt, remind me of my past victories! Remind me of You!! In Jesus' name, I pray. Amen.

Wendy Standorf

Week 8, Day 3

desires of your heart

Reading

Psalm 37:3-4 [ISV] Dwell in the land and feed on faithfulness. Delight yourself in the LORD, and he will give you the desires of your heart.

Reflection

I don't like dealing with "bad news" on the days I teach because it distracts my focus. Recently, I received an email bearing disappointing employment-related news. It put me in a kind of funk right before a class. On my knees, I prayed that God would cover my disappointment with His grace and allow me to "do good" for my students. God was faithful to me when I really needed to draw on Him.

It's during times of disappointment that "faithfulness" and "delight" and "doing good" (regardless) – all can be difficult. You can become oblivious to His faithfulness because you can't see beyond the setback.

As a *Christ Worker*, you need to trust in Him, continue doing good for those whom you serve, and recognize His faithfulness during your ups and downs.

Today at work, resolve to always delight in Him believing in faith that He will ultimately give you the **desires of your heart**.

Prayer

Father, thank You for the opportunity to serve Your purpose for my life. Thank You for covering me with Your grace when I need it most and even when I cannot seem to get past my fleeting disappointment. Help me walk this journey in complete faith in Your promise to fulfill my heart's desires. In the mighty name of your Son, my Lord and Savior, Jesus Christ, I pray today. Amen.

David Boisselle

Week 8, Day 4

His gift of diversity

Reading

1 Corinthians 1:12 (NLT) The human body has many parts, but the many parts make up one whole body. So it is with the body of Christ.

Revelation 7:9(a) (NLT) After this I saw a vast crowd, too great to count, from every nation and tribe and people and language, standing in front of the throne and before the Lamb.

Reflection

My husband and I awoke in the middle of the night and found ourselves talking about the differences between our respective sisters. Believe me, there is much to contrast! Then we chuckled about the differences between his family and mine. We come from such diverse backgrounds; how did we ever find each other?

Our Lord proclaims diversity as bountiful and good – within families, churches, and communities. Yet many struggle with **His gift of diversity** and do so in peculiar ways. Some are suspicious – fearing the gift rather than praising God for sending it. Others celebrate the gift but forget Who sends it – claiming it to be a secular right rather than a right founded on scripture.

And so often these struggles accompany us everywhere – including the workplace.

Do you come to work suspicious of **His gift of diversity**? Do you celebrate it for the wrong reasons? Or do you come to work fearlessly celebrating the miracle of differences among coworkers – every nation and tribe and people and language – all made in His Image and all giving strength to the One Body?

At work today, look around and look within. Celebrate **His gift of diversity**. Take that celebration with you at the close of the workday. Carry it always in your heart.

Celebrate **His gift of diversity** – for soon, we will stand together in front of the Lamb.

Prayer

Lord, at work today, teach me to celebrate the uniqueness and strength of Your gift of diversity. Then let Your teachings accompany me after work. Let me carry always these teachings and share them freely wherever I go. In Your name, I pray. Amen.

Patricia Baum

Week 8, Day 5

not to your cave

Reading

1 Kings 19:9 [MSG] Then the word of GOD came to him: "So Elijah, what are you doing here?"

Reflection

Like Elijah, I cannot count the number of times I run to my cave – not to Jesus – when I am in trouble. The tendency is always there. And once in that cave, it is easy for me to pretend I am still loving Him, caring for His flock, and doing what He needs of me. Worse, it is easy for me to pretend that I – alone – can either solve my problems or hide from my troubles.

But how can I really love Him, really care for His flock, and really do what He needs – when His voice asks, "What are you doing here?" And why do I think I am not hiding when He has to repeat, "What are you doing here?"

We all find caves, and when we enter them, they become prisons. We think we are safe, but we're not. And the walls limit our responses to Him.

Today, at work and in your life, don't wait for God to ask, "What are you doing here?" You know what you are doing for you, and more importantly, you know what you're not doing for *Him*.

When things get tough at work today, run to Jesus, **not to your cave**. You will hear Him better, and you will know where He is!

Don't wait for Him to ask even once. Today run to Jesus, **not to your cave**.

Prayer

Father, in the name of Jesus, I pray. Thank You for being my refuge in troubled times. Keep reminding me that my cave denies me Your presence and power. I promise You will not have to ask me again – what am I doing? I am out in the open. I am with You, Lord. Only You. Amen.

Jimmy Davis, Jr.

Week 9, Day 1

His power rests on you

Reading

2 Timothy 1:7 (KJV) For God hath not given us the spirit of fear; but of power, and of love, and of a sound mind.

1 Corinthians 14:20 (NIV) Brothers and sisters, stop thinking like children. In regard to evil be infants, but in your thinking be adults.

Reflection

There are moments at work when I need to remember God's command *not to fear*! It may not be what most people call "evil," but stuff happens that runs counter to scripture in and around any workplace. Not that Christianity deserves special rights or privileges, but it just seems Christians are usually fair game to attacks and ridicule.

Does it happen in your workplace, too? Using the Lord's name in vain when something doesn't go right. A condescending comment "here" and an inappropriate observation "there." An unsolicited remark by a coworker in the parking lot or the elevator or the break room. Sometimes it comes out in conversations with supervisors. All this can truly generate fear in the heart and soul of the practicing Christian – the Christian who is mindful of our Lord.

Yes, we must be infants when it comes to knowing evil. But should we remain silent when our faith and fellow Christians are questioned and mocked? I mean, it's nice to stay cradled in the arms of our Savior, but aren't we expected to think as adult Christians and go out into this evil world with a spirit of power, love, and intellect to fight His good fight?

The spirit of **His power rests on you** every moment of the workday! His words are meant to wake you up so the words you speak will be His words. Your actions will be His actions.

Today at work, arise from your slumber and enter the spiritual battle that surrounds you – with coworkers, supervisors, and the citizens you serve. As a *Christ Worker*, use the spirit of love and a sound mind. And remember: **His power rests on you.**

Prayer

Oh, Lord God, You are the strength in my weakness. You promise wisdom if only I ask. Your repeated words command me to stand up and not to fear. The

Holy Spirit is my divine Helper. I have all I need. Thank You. In Jesus' mighty and powerful name, I pray. Amen!

Ellen C. Stamm

Week 9, Day 2

more like God

Reading

Psalm 78:36-39 (NKJV) Nevertheless they flattered Him with their mouth, And they lied to Him with their tongue; or their heart was not steadfast with Him, Nor were they faithful in His covenant. But He, being full of compassion, forgave their iniquity, And did not destroy them. Yes, many a time He turned His anger away, And did not stir up all His wrath; For He remembered that they were but flesh, A breath that passes away and does not come again.

Reflection

A friend was on the verge of losing his job. He had to complete an important report and everything had to be perfect. He asked for my help, and I coached him through it – crosschecking every last word and number in the report. His final product was truly excellent, and I was proud of him. But after he turned in the report, his supervisor altered it with bad data and edited it to include grammatical errors. My friend lost his job.

As hard as it may sound, my friend forgave his supervisor. He didn't grieve, and I was furious. I offered to testify in a lawsuit as to the integrity of his work, but my friend said he had done his best, and it was clear his supervisor didn't want him around. So he chose to forgive and move on. He decided to be **more like God**.

Today's scripture deals with a similar situation except it is God who is being lied to by His chosen people. And yet He forgave them. God remembered they were human – just like my friend remembered about his boss – and He forgave them – just like my friend did.

We all deserve God's wrath, but God chooses to forgive our human weaknesses. This is why my friend chose to do what he did.

Today at work, take time to ask God to help you to forgive like He forgives. It can be quite liberating. And you will be **more like God**.

Prayer

Lord, help me forgive as you forgive. I am very deserving of Your just punishments, but I know You came to earth so that I might receive Your forgiveness.

Help me show that same forgiveness to others who do wrong to me. Help me see everyone I meet through Your eyes. In Jesus' name, I pray. Amen.

Kevin J. Cooney

Week 9, Day 3

gentle words and patient persuasion

Reading

Proverbs 25:15 [NIV] Through patience a ruler can be persuaded, and a gentle tongue can break a bone.

Reflection

Do you ever get an assignment and complete it only to have your work questioned?

How do you respond? Get red-faced? Fist clenched? Storm out of the office?

All of these reactions are not doing you or the situation any good. Your response should be just as the verse says – using **gentle words and patient persuasion**.
If your work is questioned today, talk to your supervisor. Patiently ask what is wrong and how it can be improved. Then patiently listen. Sometimes a conversation can help explain much better than a directive and a reaction.

So today at work, use gentle words and patient persuasion. You may win or you may lose the conversation. Regardless, you will be following His word.

And that will make everything – even the redo – pleasing to God.

Prayer

Father, give me the patience of a farmer – let me be slow to judge and slow to anger when my work is not accepted. Give me a gentle tongue to talk to my supervisor so that I may be a light to the situation and remedy. In Jesus' name, I pray. Amen.

John F. Long, Jr.

Week 9, Day 4

the first step in healing

Reading

James 5:16 [MSG] Make this your common practice: Confess your sins to each other and pray for each other so that you can live together whole and healed.

Reflection

Got one of those phone calls last night. You know the type. A good friend in a distant place with a workplace problem. In a nutshell: her supervisor shouted an obscenity at her and kicked her out of his office. She was trying to get a much-needed answer to complete a project, but he was stressed-out over his own deadlines. In the resulting grievance, she discovered her supervisor did not have the capacity to apologize. After all, he viewed the problem as her fault – he was forced to be abusive because she couldn't understand how much work he had to do.

Well, the grievance went in her favor, but her phone call centered on concerns about working with someone who is unable to say "I'm sorry." You see, she learned something about her supervisor's character.

I told her that apologies are essential in two situations: (1) when you're truly wrong and (2) when you truly hurt someone's feelings – regardless of whether you did right or wrong. I reminded her of how everyone has an unlimited supply of apologies – even in the workplace – if your apologies are authentic. And just one heartfelt "I'm sorry" is **the first step in healing**.

As a *Christ Worker*, make this your workplace practice. Confess when you make a mistake. Confess when you hurt someone. Confess to encourage the other person to confess. Confess because it shows your character – that you are a child of God.

So today at work, use as many "I'm sorry's" as needed. (There's a bowlful in the break room.) If you run out, use your unlimited supply of "I was wrong's." (Those are in your pockets.)

An apology does not remove a problem, like my friend's supervisor blaming others for his outbursts. But an apology shows character.

And it is **the first step in healing**.

Prayer

Father God, humble me so that I may apologize for wrongdoings or hurt feelings I might cause during this workday. Help me make the workplace whole and healed. In Your Son's name, I pray. Amen.

James D. Slack

Week 9, Day 5

even in a land of affliction

Reading

Genesis 41:52(b) [KJV] For God hath caused me to be fruitful in the land of my affliction.

Reflection

It's not easy living in a land of affliction. In my case, a land separated from family and loved-ones. Living and sleeping in a 5' by 8' space 23 hours each weekday and 24 hours each weekend day. Waking up and going to sleep knowing I am convicted of killing a man who did not deserve to die. Knowing that man's loved-ones wake up and go to sleep not deserving to suffer. Oh, yes, I feel all this – I feel the illness every day of my life. Truly this is a land of affliction.

And you, too, may also live in a land of affliction. Things that happen at your home. Things that you bring to the workplace. Things that you take home with you. Loneliness. Worriedness. Anxiety. Anger. Hurt. The pain of hating others. The pain of hating yourself. Yes, yours is truly a land of affliction.

You and I may not be able to leave our land, but we both have our Lord. His power can cause us to be fruitful – **even in a land of affliction**.

So today at work, be filled with hope. He can bear fruit – if you let Him. Yes, He can bring good things to you – **even in a land of affliction**.

Prayer

Father, in the name of Jesus, I pray. Thank You for Your power to cause me to be fruitful regardless of where I am – **even in a land of affliction**. All the glory goes to You. Amen.

Jimmy Davis, Jr.

Week 10, Day 1

it's faith that gets you places

Reading

Mark 11:23 [NIV] Truly I tell you, if anyone says to this mountain, 'Go, throw yourself into the sea,' and does not doubt in their heart but believes that what they say will happen, it will be done for them.

Ephesians 2:8-9 [NIV] For it is by grace you have been saved, through faith – and this is not from yourselves, it is a gift of God – not by works, so that no one can boast.

Reflection

Ever have a coworker who just happens to be so good at everything and receives all the praise and support from upper management? That person never has to try, nor does he fail a couple times before he gets something right. It's frustrating, right?

Cheer up. When it comes to careers, remember it's *not just by works*. Actually, **it's faith that gets you places**. Now I'm not saying you can be successful without knowing the job – but faith is the key to doing better. It will give you strength to try harder and to learn more. It will allow you to find the place where He needs you most.

So when you're back at work with that one person who gets all the praise for his work, don't fret. Just remember **it's faith that gets you places**. Have steadfast faith. Show how your faith can move a mountain when it comes to improving your skills.

Yes, **it's faith that gets you places** – and many great things will come to you!

Prayer

Lord, You bless me in so many ways. Continue to see favor in my efforts and deeds for You. Help me move a mountain in my workplace. My faith in You will get me where You need me. In Jesus' name, I pray. Amen.

Sara Garth

Week 10, Day 2

check your heart

Reading

Romans 12:2 [KJV] And be not conformed to this world: but be ye transformed by the renewing of your mind, that ye may prove what is that good, and acceptable, and perfect, will of God.

Reflection

When I stopped by the corner store, a man begged money for food. As I handed him some loose change, he smiled and said, "God bless you!" As I entered the store, a lady told me the man was always outside begging for change. She said he probably had more money than me and it was all probably a scam. She went on to say that's why she doesn't give to beggars because they are just trying to game people.

The lady's harsh words made me pause. I never want to harden my heart toward the work of the Kingdom of God.

How about you?

Will you **check your heart** about someone today? The man you see in the vacant lot on the way to work? The woman you see sitting on the curb on the way home? How about the coworker next to you who has troubles? How about the citizen you serve who is so desperate?

Today at work, take a moment and **check your heart**. Your kindness is needed in the Kingdom

Prayer

Heavenly Father, help me remember how merciful and patient you are to me. Let me be the same to all I see and hear today at work. In Jesus' name, I pray. Amen.

Crystal Featherston

Week 10, Day 3

cross that road

Reading

Luke 10: 31-34 [NIV] A priest happened to be going down the same road, and when he saw the man, he passed by on the other side. So too, a Levite, when he came to the place and saw him, passed by on the other side. But a Samaritan, as he traveled, came where the man was; and when he saw him, he took pity on him. He went to him and bandaged his wounds, pouring on oil and wine. Then he put the man on his own donkey, brought him to an inn and took care of him.

Reflection

Last week, I took some time off to assist my brother with a construction project. We had gone to the store and obtained lumber and other necessary supplies. After loading and strapping down the lumber in the rear of my pick-up truck, we began to proceed to the work site. But in our haste, it became obvious we didn't tighten the straps sufficiently. Hitting a bump, the entire load fell off into the middle of the road. From out of nowhere, two gentlemen **crossed that road** and helped us lift the load back into the truck bed. My brother and I had never met these men before, but we were truly grateful for their help.

Many public servants have jobs that demand they **cross that road** to help those in need. In fact, it's often a matter of law for public safety personnel to be the *Good Samaritan*. They may even face the danger of going into a crime scene or a burning building to render assistance.

Now your position as a teacher, accountant, office manager, or city manager may not require you to go into areas of danger. But as a *Christ Worker,* your Lord wants you to go out of our way and **cross that road** for others.

At work today, share the love for Jesus by acts of kindness and service. Search for opportunities to **cross that road**.

Prayer

Father God, You want me to assist Your children in trouble. Let me never be blind to their needs or be too pre-occupied with my own duties. Use me to share Your Good News through my actions of assisting others. I thank You for all of the good Samaritans who have rendered assistance to me, and I ask for Your continued blessings for them. In Your Son's holy name, I pray. Amen!

Stephen Pincus

Week 10, Day 4

use your inner lens

Reading

Romans 1:20 [*ESV*] For his invisible attributes, namely, his eternal power and divine nature, have been clearly perceived, ever since the creation of the world, in the things that have been made. So they are without excuse.

Reflection

When was the last time you took a stroll around your community with a camera? Even if it is just with your smartphone, I bet you have the ability to pick out unique items that most people without a camera just walk past. I bet, if you try hard enough, your smartphone lens can pick up God's creation, in any part of town, a little differently than the person with no camera.

As a *Christ Worker*, **use your inner lens** to find the uniqueness of Christ anywhere in your community – including in your workplace. After all, God makes things that radiate his "eternal power and divine nature" – especially in the people you meet each day.

So when you go to work today, "see" what God might see. "Capture" those who need God – His grace, His love, and His hope. And **use your inner lens** to picture the Christ shining in everyone you meet!

Prayer

Lord, let me see You and Your workings in my community today. Bless all those near and far. In Your name, I pray. Amen.

Joseph N. Harrell III

Week 10, Day 5

the right formula

Reading

Psalm 23:5 [KJV] Thou preparest a table before me in the presence of mine enemies: thou anointest my head with oil; my cup runneth over.

Reflection

The other day I awoke in my usual state. Not very refreshed and so uncertain. But once I sat down at the feet of Jesus and read this scripture, my spirit came alive. All day I could not sit still. Anyone walking by my cell, I just had to tell about my cup running over. But it didn't stop there. All day and night, wherever and whenever I could, I showed my brothers and the correctional officers just how much my cup was running over.

You see, David found **the right formula** to have his cup running over. First, he allowed the Lord to prepare his table – right in front of all those who deemed him an enemy. My, what a statement made by God! The battle was not David's but the Lord's – and everyone knew it!

But then David allowed the Lord to anoint his head with oil. That made him refreshed and certain – giving him the courage to show how his cup was running over.

Before you go to work today, choose to allow our Lord to use **the right formula** so that your cup will run over. Have patience, and let Him prepare your table – it will not be done in secret. No, it will be done so that your enemies can see. Then take time to let God anoint you – to refresh you and give you confidence for the day.

Let God let your cup run over today. Let it run over in your workplace. Let it run over in your life.

Prayer

Father, in the name of Jesus, I pray. Thank You for protecting me from my enemies. Thank You for refreshing me. Thank You for having my cup run over to show others Your love and grace. Amen.

Jimmy Davis, Jr.

Week 11, Day 1

the condition of the heart

Reading

1 Samuel 2:3 [HCSB]. Do not boast so proudly, or let arrogant words come out of your mouth, for the LORD is a God of knowledge, and actions are weighed by Him.

Reflection

We've all heard the saying "actions speak louder than words." And in the workplace, it's easy to get caught up in responding to credit given for a job well done. A simple "thank you" for compliments and commendations somehow turns into "did you hear what was said about me?"

In scripture, Hannah knew this. But she also knew that **the condition of the heart** would generate her actions and guide her reactions. With a devoted heart, she gave all the Lord had given her, and God was faithful to give her the desire of her heart. She had no reason to be arrogant or boastful.

Today at work, may your actions match your devotion to Jesus. The Lord is a God of knowledge, and your actions, not words, are weighed by Him.

So at work today, check **the condition of the heart**.

Prayer

Father, fill my heart with Your intent. Let me not be boastful of doing my best nor be arrogant in accepting credit. In Your Son's name, I pray. Amen.

Chris Summers

Week 11, Day 2

when the work is burned

Reading

I Corinthians 3:13(b)-15 [NKJV] and the fire will test each one's work, of what sort it is. If anyone's work which he has built on it endures, he will receive a reward. If anyone's work is burned, he will suffer loss; but he himself will be saved, yet so as through fire.

Reflection

A few years ago, a former student wrote to me. This student never earned a grade better than "C" from me, yet he wrote to thank me for never giving up on him and encouraging him through every failed test. But there was something more. In his email, he expressed a desire to earn a graduate degree and needed a letter of recommendation. He knew I could not give him a strong letter, based on his performance in my classes, but he asked if I could help him nonetheless. He closed his note by saying he is also asking God for help. "If You give me a chance, Lord, I will make both You and Professor Cooney proud."

Well, he was right. I couldn't write a superlative letter, but I wrote the best one I could. And I'm sure God was doing much of the heavy lifting because this former student was admitted into a good graduate program. He eventually graduated with honors! Throughout the graduate experience, he glorified God and made me very proud.

I could've refused his request, and maybe he still might have been admitted. But I realized the grades he earned from me were consumed by fire – they were short-term at best. And he had a chance, through the experience of that same fire, to be more successful and receive a reward.

Whether you are a manager or a professor, you appraise others. Some will be rewarded while others will suffer a loss. That's only fair. But remember you are more than a teacher or a professor. You are more than a manager-assessor. Recognize that the fire of assessment is meaningful but short-term. The person is not condemned but has another shot – if not in your shop or classroom, certainly somewhere else.

Today at work, be honest about the rewards you can offer. But also be understanding so *the fire does not consume the individual.* You are a *Christ Worker* so, even **when the work is burned**, be encouraging while you are being honest. There is always something to salvage. There is always something to save – the coworker, his future, and his salvation.

Today, make a difference in the lives of others – be encouraging even **when the work is burned**.

<u>Prayer</u>

Lord, let my work survive the fires of this life and not be consumed so that I may glorify You. Yet let me also have confidence that my work does not equal the entire being of Your creation. Help me remember that the work of others also does not constitute their whole being as Your creation. In Your name, I pray. Amen.

Kevin J. Cooney

Week 11, Day 3

cling onto His promise

Reading

Isaiah 43:2 [NIRV] You will pass through deep waters. But I will be with you. You will pass through the rivers. But their waters will not sweep over you. You will walk through fire. But you will not be burned. The flames will not harm you.

Reflection

The world admires perfection, but worldly people just aren't perfect. Things might not always go as desired or planned. Some may not always see eye to eye with their boss or coworkers. Others may be overworked and underpaid. All of us may be denied that promotion or unable to get the new job we want. Fact is we live in a fallen world, and that means we, too, are fallen. Fact is God promises no one an easy road, a straight path, a perfect life.

Yet God promises to pass through the waters with us. He promises the flames won't overcome us. The reality is you and I can be used by God when we are broken, worn-down, and just plain tired because that's when we come to the end of our rope. That's when you and I usually start relying on God's strength and not our own.

So today at work, you may be treated unfairly. But your hope lies in Jesus. You may be broken and scared. But God is there.

Yes, today at work, **cling onto His promise**: whatever river you are passing through, whatever fire is in front of you, lean on God's strength and not your own. Be courageous in knowing that He is guarding and guiding you. All you need do is to **cling onto His promise**!

Prayer

Father, I bow before You as a broken and worn-down believer. I am on a different path than I intended, but I know You are with me. I cling onto the promises You give me personally. I am <u>not</u> defeated because You bless me with a dependent heart and an encouraged soul. Thank You for using me right where You put me – guarded and guided by You. In Jesus' name, I pray. Amen.

Kathryn Saunders

Week 11, Day 4

cease striving and just be

Reading

Psalm 46:10(a) [NIV] Be still and know that I am God

Psalm 46:10(a) [NASB] Cease *striving* and know that I am God;

Reflection

This may sound weird, but I think God wants us <u>to just be</u>. A simple command, but most of the time we are busy *doing* rather than being. In fact, we practice the doing so much that we forget what it means <u>to just be</u>. When you are just being, you are fully listening to someone speaking rather than planning how you will respond. When you are just being, your response is genuine, transparent, and God-felt. When you are just being, you shake hands and mean it rather than viewing the ritual as a process leading to the next step. When you are just being, you hug someone longer than they hug you. When you are just being, you are more compassionate because you want to imitate Christ, and you know that He is God.

It's not easy, but I believe God is calling His workplace servants to <u>*be*</u> *more than* <u>*do*</u>*.* So at work today – listen, respond, greet, hug, and touch the hearts and minds of those around you with the being of Christ. You will accomplish much more work when you **cease striving and just be**.

Prayer

Father, today I pray that You will teach me to just be. Show me how to imitate Jesus in being fully there for the people You love. Help me not to be busy doing without being there, too. I am Your vessel through which all of Heaven flows. In His name, I pray. Hallelujah! Amen.

Ellen C. Stamm

Week 11, Day 5

exceptional for His sake

Reading

2 *Corinthians* 5:20 [NLT] So we are Christ's ambassadors; God is making his appeal through us. We speak for Christ when we plead, "Come back to God!"

Reflection

Do you know how exceptional we can be? I am not bragging. By "exceptional," God means rare. There are too few people willing to be Christ's ambassadors, and He needs all of us.

One day I was writing a letter in my cell and had my headphones on. A correctional officer shouted down my tier wanting to know what I was up to. Half-listening, I shouted back that I was writing a letter. I would have kept writing, but a brother down the row said the officer needed a Bible verse. That is why he asked what I was up to. So I stopped writing, took off my headphones, and wrote down a scripture. I sent it up the row, and he thanked me.

You see, God was appealing through me, and He needed me to plead to that officer. He was showing how exceptional I am for His sake – how rare I am to be His ambassador.

Today at work, God will need you to be His ambassador. He will need you to make His appeal to someone. Someone will ask for help, or someone will need help but will not ask. Today, God will need you to be **exceptional for His sake**. He will need you to be that rare person who will stand up and plead "Come Back to God!"

Can you be **exceptional for His sake**? Can you be rare for His sake? Can you be Christ's ambassador? Can He appeal through you?

Today, will you speak for Christ? Will you be **exceptional for His sake**?

Prayer

Father, in the name of Jesus, I pray. I come to You as a little child, thanking You for continuing to mold and shape me to be exceptional – so You can appeal through me. So I can plead for You. Amen.

Jimmy Davis, Jr.

Week 12, Day 1

kneel before others

Reading

1 Peter 5:6 [NLT] So humble yourselves under the mighty power of God, and at the right time he will lift you up in honor.

Romans 8:17(b) [NLT] But if we are to share his glory, we must also share his suffering.

John 13:5(b) [NLT] Then he began to wash the disciples' feet

Reflection

To humble yourself. Just what does that mean? When I was a child, I thought I knew. Then, it only meant to get on my knees and pray – with my family every night before bed and in my church every Sunday. But as an adult, I grew to know it had to mean more than kneeling in prayer at home and at church. I learned that it meant serving others as Christ serves me.

To humble yourself – to **kneel before others** in only His glory as He once did for His disciples. Now that's a tough thing to do, especially in the workplace. There are so many conflicts on any given day: among units for more resources and power, within units over how resources will be used, between coworkers who yearn for power and promotion. Too often, we forget on Mondays what we learned on Sundays. Too many times, we forget in the morning what we learned on bended knee the night before. Too frequently, we forget what Jesus did to humble Himself – and we forget why He did so.

And so He calls us to humble ourselves – to **kneel before others** in His name only – not just in comfortable environments like home and church. He wants us to serve others in the least comfortable and most dangerous places – like our own workplace.

Today at work, follow the footsteps of Christ and suffer as He once did. Suffer as He still does for you and me. Forget misguided ambition that does not glorify Him. Serve others to meet their needs – in this world and in the next. He will reward you in His right time.

Yes, today **kneel before others** as Christ still does. Do so in His name and for His glory.

Prayer

Father, I confess I am far too preoccupied with me. Forgive me and give me a servant's heart to **kneel before others** like Jesus once did. Give me courage to do so as He <u>still</u> does on this very workday. Let me find Your ways to humble myself so that others will see You in me and, in that way, You are glorified! In Your Son's name, I pray. Amen.

Wilisha G. Scaife

Week 12, Day 2

pray and seek His face

Reading

2 Chronicles 7:14 [NKJV] if My people who are called by My name will humble themselves, and pray and seek My face, and turn from their wicked ways, then I will hear from heaven, and will forgive their sin and heal their land.

Matthew 6:33 [NKJV] But seek first the kingdom of God and His righteousness, and all these things shall be added to you.

Matthew 5:10 [NKJV] Your kingdom come. Your will be done. On earth as *it is* in heaven.

Reflection

As a public servant, my job is to find solutions to the problems facing my city. In my area, the economy is still not the greatest. There is a shrinking job market, and there is an aging population. Frankly, it's not easy being a public servant – especially an elected one at that. I mean, most elected officials could find simpler challenges to master in the private sector. You and I both know it's just very difficult to heal our communities.

As a *Christ Worker*, I know I do not have all the answers. In fact, by myself, I actually have very few answers – if any. But I do know that to **pray and seek His face** is my most powerful weapon in healing my community. And when I seek Him first, the healing is always a little nearer than what I thought. So it is only when I **pray and seek His face** that I can be His tool in doing His will on earth – especially in my city.

Yet so often, I default back to leaning on my own will and pride. Why is that? Why is it so hard for me to **pray and seek His face** on every issue facing my constituents? I guess it's because I'm still a work-in-progress and I just need to trust Him more.

As you approach the problems facing the citizens you serve, remember to seek Him first. As a *Christ Worker*, know you can be His tool in doing His will in your workplace and community. But like me, you are still a work-in-progress. So trust Him much more than before.

Today at work, we both have to **pray and seek His face** if we truly want our lands healed.

<u>Prayer</u>

Dear Lord, help me to trust You more, focus on You always, give thanks to You each day, and worship You every workday. In Jesus' name, I pray. Amen.

Matt Whitman

Week 12, Day 3

fight through the waves

Reading

1 Peter 1:6-7 [KJV] Wherein ye greatly rejoice, though now for a season, if need be, ye are in heaviness through manifold temptations: That the trial of your faith, being much more precious than of gold that perisheth, though it be tried with fire, might be found unto praise and honor at the appearing of Jesus Christ.

Reflection

An old cliché says "Problems come in 3's." That may be true for some, but in my life, they don't always come in 3's; they come in *wave after wave*.

Now a surfer has to fight *wave after wave* to get out to the point where he can position his board for a smooth and enjoyable ride. I believe that's what happens in our trials. God is allowing us to **fight through the waves** of pain, sorrow, failure, and confusion to position us spiritually to begin to ride the waves and see the beauty around us.

At work, you may be fighting waves of confusion due to policy changes. They might be followed with waves of stress because of the tasking of a superior. That may be coupled with a wave of family illness or sorrow. Then waves of financial hardship hit. Finally, waves of pressure arise to provide a good testimony in the midst of the pounding rocks of all the situations.

Brothers and sisters, keep pushing and a'paddling! He is positioning you in that *special place* where you will get to ride the wave of praise. He will place you atop that wave, and oh, the glory that will be revealed!

So today at work, have His courage and strength to **fight through the waves**!

Prayer

Father, give me strength this day to face my struggles at work, to face my fears and failures. Lift me beyond the circumstance of my job to see Your marvelous hand at work and experience the beauty of Your love. In Jesus, name, I pray. Amen!

Bill Dudley

Week 12, Day 4

don't become weary

Reading

Galatians 6:9 [NIV] Let us not become weary in doing good, for at the proper time we will reap a harvest if we do not give up.

Reflection

For years, it seemed my friend was the only one at his agency who treated others with respect, followed the rules of the office, and was always honest. He watched others do whatever it took to impress managers – while they were in the room. But when his supervisor retired, my friend was selected as the new supervisor.

A bit shocked, he asked why he was chosen. "You never grow weary of doing good," the former boss responded, "even when you think no one is watching."

Like my friend, you may be ridiculed or ignored at work. Still, **don't become weary** of doing good. Do whatever is required, and do it with excellence. You never know what impact you'll have on others – your coworkers or managers.

And true, no one may ever acknowledge your good work. That's still OK. One day you <u>will</u> reap a harvest more plentiful than you can imagine! The Lord always blesses those who continually do His work.

So don't give up today, my friend! No, **don't become weary**. Keep doing what is right in the Lord's sight in all situations. Ultimately, you <u>will</u> reap a harvest!

Prayer

Lord, today at work, help me not to grow weary of doing good at whatever I am assigned. Please bless my hard work at Your appropriate time. But may it bless others right now, and may it glorify You always. In Your name, I pray. Amen.

Reagan Hinton

Week 12, Day 5

put on Jesus

Reading

Colossians 3:10 [NLT] Put on your new nature and be renewed as you learn to know your Creator and become like him.

Reflection

It is so easy to get too busy in this world. This is true even on Life Row. I read my devotions early each morning, and I attend a bible study group when we're permitted. But I get too busy with a lot of other things. I write letters each day, and I deal with family concerns. I get into many conversations about a lot of things with other inmates, and I watch TV – sometimes too much TV. Sometimes I get busy watching movies instead of the 700 Club or other Christian programs. I can get so busy that too often I forget to **put on Jesus**.

I am sure it is the same with you. You get busy with your job, and you get busy with family and church. Like me, sometimes when I leave my cell, I bet you can leave your home each morning with too much on your mind.

It is easy to forget to **put on Jesus**, and then we find ourselves in uncomfortable situations. Our old nature starts showing up: selfish, unforgiving, prideful, lacking self-control. We begin to respond to others with our old nature, and that can lead to trouble.

Today, remember to put on your new nature. As you prepare for work, **put on Jesus**! Throughout your busy workday, learn from Him. Change the atmosphere in your workplace, and carry that renewed atmosphere back to your family and your church.

Don't get too busy to **put on Jesus**. You will be renewed, and you will become more like Him.

Prayer

Father, in the name of Jesus, I pray. Slow me down, Father! Please move into my heart so I can dress in Your Son. Help me **put on Jesus** so I can help others take off what has them bound. Amen.

Jimmy Davis, Jr.

Week 13, Day 1

a better formula

Reading

Proverbs 12:1; 19:11 [NIV] Whoever loves discipline loves knowledge, but whoever hates correction is stupid ... A person's wisdom yields patience; it is to one's glory to overlook an offense.

Psalm 138:8 [NIV] The LORD will vindicate me; your love, LORD, endures forever— do not abandon the works of your hands.

Reflection

There is no shortage of arrogance in the workplace. It's great when your unit takes pride in the quality of its work, but there are forms of destructive egotism that suck the life out of coworkers and cause division and conflict.

One of the poisonous states of arrogance is the "know-it-all" boss or coworker. You know, the one who has all the answers. Any time you offer an alternative opinion, the know-it-all's eyes roll, shoulders shrug, and you get that blank stare. On some days, it's like the "drip, drip" of a leaky faucet, and on other days, it's a maddening itch. Your pot of anger begins to boil. The great temptation is either to feed that rage or hide in your work cave.

But scripture has **a better formula** than rage or hiding. Be disciplined and patient. Don't let the know-it-all get under your skin. Just let the Lord vindicate.

Today at work, don't fight those battles with your own strength. You will only engage in another form of destructive arrogance – that of playing the role of God. Instead, take the high ground, be patient, and ask the Lord for the strength to love like Jesus and leave the change process to Him.

Yes, at work today, remember scripture has **a better formula** to handle that know-it-all.

Prayer

Lord, help me to be patient and love those who irritate me at work. In Your name, I pray. Amen.

Gary E. Roberts

Week 13, Day 2

just pushing through the day

Reading

John 8:12(b) [ESV] I am the light of the world. Whoever follows me will never walk in darkness, but will have the light of life.

Reflection

Ever have problems **just pushing through the day**? You know what I'm talking about. Rolling out of bed is a bit harder. And once at work, staying motivated becomes a challenge – especially with umpteen different tasks thrown in your direction.

Everyone has workdays like this – when the struggle seems more than the day is worth.

Is this how your today is going?

If so, remember your strength comes from the Lord. God promises He will provide – if you seek His will and His direction in all situations. He will provide in everything, and this includes this day when you don't think you can push forward.

So if you're having trouble **just pushing through the day** – getting out of bed, tired, dragging at work – then intentionally take time to seek His help in prayer and in devotional.

Seek His light, and He will provide.

And you will be doing much more than **just pushing through the day**!

Prayer

Lord, thank You for another day of opportunities to serve You in my workplace. Thank You for always shining Your light into in my life. As I go throughout my workday, help me try even harder to seek You in all situations. Fill my heart and mind with motivation and positivity. In Your name, I pray. Amen.

Morgan Best

Week 13, Day 3

not Maslow's, but Christ's

Reading

John 4:31-34 [NIV] Meanwhile the disciples were urging him, saying, "Rabbi, eat." But he said to them, "I have food to eat that you do not know about." So the disciples said to one another, "Has anyone brought him something to eat?" Jesus said to them, "My food is to do the will of him who sent me and to accomplish his work."

Reflection

At one point or another, we've all studied Maslow's hierarchy of human needs. Remember the first level of need: food, drink, shelter, clothing? Those come first because they are the most basic. Without this foundation, there is little to be desired and little to be accomplished.

But for a *Christ Worker*, the first level of human need is spiritual. Our foundation is to do the will of God. Now this is not to say we don't eat physical food. But our every breath is dependent on doing the will of God.

At work today, consider Jesus' example. His is a lofty goal. After all, doing the will of the Father is life and worth more than anything else for real living.

So today at work, ask yourself: What would it look like to do the will of God?

Then just do it. Follow **not Maslow's, but Christ's** hierarchy of your needs.

Prayer

Father, Your hierarchy of my needs starts with serving Your needs. And at the top is eternal life. Today, let all things I do serve Your needs, for that is the basis of my needs. In Jesus' name, I pray. Amen

Chris Summers

Week 13, Day 4

serve and show love

Reading

John 13:14-15 [NIV] Now that I, your Lord and Teacher, have washed your feet, you also should wash one another's feet. I have set you an example that you should do as I have done for you.

Reflection

After working in public service for thirty-plus years, I have come to realize that the time is <u>now</u> for *Christ Workers* to really step up and demonstrate our love of Christ by the way we treat one another – even those who would betray us.

You know the workplace can be quite cutthroat. And we happen to deal with some citizens who are desperate. And some are criminals. The question is how do you react?

Living in the world and being Christ-like is hard. Christians are called to do things that run counter to human flesh and emotions. We must not be afraid to follow Jesus' example – even if it means we **serve and show love** to all – even to those who do us wrong. After all, even knowing the consequences of Judas' betrayal, Jesus knelt down and washed his feet.

You and I are commanded to do no less. This means we must wash the feet of those who will betray or do evil to us or our community. Yes, we must **serve and show love** to those who crush our spirit and our neighbors' spirits by their action – even in a cutthroat workplace – even among desperate citizens – even with criminal citizens. That's what following Christ means.

Yes, living in the world and being Christ-like is hard. *But Jesus sets the example.*

Now go **serve and show love** – sacrifice as He commands – so you can join Him in His Resurrection!

Prayer

Heavenly Father, I send You all glory, honor, and praise as I remember the greatest sacrifice – Your Son, Jesus, laying down His life for the forgiveness of my sins. Help me always follow Jesus' example by willingly forgiving, loving, and serving everyone – even those who commit wrongs against me – even those who commit wrongs against my community. In Your Son's holy name, I pray. Amen.

Stephen Pincus
Week 13, Day 5

the simple thing

Reading

Luke 5:18-19 [KJV] And, behold, men brought in a bed a man which was taken with a palsy: and they sought means to bring him in, and to lay him before him. And when they could not find by what way they might bring him in because of the multitude, they went upon the housetop, and let him down through the tiling with his couch into the midst before Jesus.

Reflection

How many times do we make excuses for not helping others find Jesus? We get shy, fearful, nervous. We claim it's too complicated. Yet all God requires is **the simple thing**. Like saying *"my Lord* helped me get the job done on time" instead of "boy, was I <u>lucky</u> to get it done today!" Or saying, "I am *praying* for you" instead of "My <u>thoughts</u> are with you."

Doing **the simple thing** is the best way to share the Gospel – just like those brothers brought that man with a palsy to Jesus. The man's illness was something to make them nervous. But they did not worry about catching what he had. The streets were complicated, clogged with so many wanting to see Jesus. But that did not make them shy away. Getting on someone's roof could have made them fearful. But they did not worry about that either. *No excuses!* Those brothers just did **the simple thing** to lay that man before Jesus.

Like me, you live in a world that begs for excuses. Like you, I am a *Christ Worker*. We both work for the Lord in a place where it's easy to put Him off because of situations. But we must not worry about such things. Like those brothers carrying that man, *we have no excuses*.

So today at work, do not let your shyness complicate matters. Do not let your fear of others or your nervousness about things become excuses. No, do **the simple thing** your faith requires.

Yes, today just do **the simple thing** and lay that person before Him.

Prayer

Father, in the name of Jesus, I pray. Thank You for giving me Life so I can help show Life to others. Take away all of my excuses so I may seek the simple ways to do Your will. Amen.

Jimmy Davis, Jr.
Week 14, Day 1

believe and don't be afraid

Reading

Mark 5:36(b) [NIV] Don't be afraid, just believe.

Jeremiah 33:3 [NIV] Call to me and I will answer you and tell you great and unsearchable things you do not know.

Reflection

How many times do you have a grand idea but are afraid to follow through with it? How many times do you think a dream is beyond your capability? I know life can be pretty daunting when you look at things from just your own seemingly tiny perspective.

What do you want to accomplish a year from now? What's your biggest challenge? Whatever it is, don't limit yourself. Remember *God makes the impossible possible.*

Yes, don't succumb to worldly bounds and human perspective. God's calling is so much greater than that. Just **believe and don't be afraid**. Take time to ask God what you do not know, and then give it all you've got!

God will do the rest.

As a *Christ Worker*, you have the opportunity to show others just how spectacular God's work is. You can inspire others by pursuing what God has laid out for you.

Today – this year – at work or in study for work – **believe and don't be afraid**!

He knows the unsearchable and great things about you! He always has.

Prayer

Father God, thank You for allowing me to put all my faith in You. Give me courage to call on you to teach me those unsearchable things about me and my abilities. Remind me how possible the impossible is with You by my side. In Your Son's name, I pray. Amen.

Stephanie Van Straten

Week 14, Day 2

always better than yours

Reading

Isaiah 55:8(a) [NIV] For my thoughts are not your thoughts neither are your ways my ways...

Matthew 7:7 [NIV] Ask and it will be given to you; seek and you will find; knock and the door will be opened to you.

Reflection

Ever been in a rut?

A pastor once told me, "A rut is a grave with no end in sight!" If you've held your current position for any length of time, you know what I'm talking about. You do the same things each day. You perform each task the same way. You no longer think outside the box. You process and suddenly, bam! You're in a rut.

It may be your job that's the problem, or it may be just the tasks you're required to do in your job. Or maybe it's you. But on some days, it really doesn't matter.

Every day can be an adventure. As a *Christ Worker*, I truly like my own profession, and I love my students and my school. So each day I try to find excitement in what I do. But then again, I know it's easy to fall prey to ruts.

And there you sit. Without a clue as to how to get out of your rut. Do you try to change tasks? Do you look for another job? Do you search for another career?

You do everything but take *the surest way* out of that rut. You forget to turn to God. And the thing is He's already telling you that His thoughts and ways are **always better than yours** – in the tasks of the day, in your job, in your career – in what you do.

So why don't you turn to the Creator of the world you call Father? The One who already knows your problem and already knows your solution. Why wouldn't you knock on His door?

Yet you hesitate. Are you so far down in the box you can't see Him?? *Ask, seek, knock!!!!*

Today, if you find yourself in that rut, admit His thoughts and ways are **always better than yours**. Then *ask, seek, knock*! You may not leave your job. You may not change the way you do a task. But you'll be out of that rut because you will listen to His thoughts and ways, not yours.

Trust me, today will be a better day because His is **always better than yours**.

<u>Prayer</u>

Dear God, forgive me for leaving you out of my daily lesson plan. You alone know my future and my past. You alone know each soul that crosses my path today. Please keep me out of that rut so I may see the excitement and adventure of this workday. In the precious name of my Lord, I pray! Amen.

Debra Neal

Week 14, Day 3

His way and choose life

Reading

James 4:1 (NIV) What causes fights and quarrels among you? Don't they come from your desires that battle within you?

Deuteronomy 30:19 (NIV) This day I call the heavens and the earth as witnesses against you that I have set before you life and death, blessings and curses. Now choose life, so that you and your children may live.

Reflection

Last night, I helped my son with a homework assignment based upon scripture. Little did I know, in the process of teaching my son, I would relearn that lesson. I taught that, in the heat of any moment, many do not seek **His way and choose life.** Rather, they try to get their *own selfish way* and thereby choose death. I confess, on many occasions I do, too.

As *Christ Workers*, you and I deal with many coworkers, citizens, vendors, and politicians – all trying to get their own way. Sometimes motives are less than rational – they are downright selfish. And we push back because we also want our own selfish way. Such arrogance leads to quarreling and fighting. In our world, this is how disagreements and arguments turn into battles and battles turn into wars. In our workplace, it leads to disciplinary actions, grievances, and cultures of entitlement and resentment.

Today at work, remember the lesson taught by scripture – the same lesson learned by my son and relearned by me. When things get heated because "he" wants his own way for selfish reasons, seek to find **His way and choose life.** If "she" persists, contain your own selfish motives in the struggle – remembering to humble yourself before the Lord.

Just like children of my son's age, too many workplace quarrels center on not getting your own selfish way. And just like my son, you and I need to remember the lessons taught in scripture.

So today, look to God for the best way to solve quarrels. Don't try to get your own selfish way. Instead, seek **His way and choose life.** And surely *He will lift you and your agency up*!

Prayer

Dear Heavenly Father, thank You for blessing me in places I don't expect, like with my son's homework. Help me see from another person's perspective and not judge because of differences. Help me never to enter an argument or make a decision because I want my own selfish way. Rather, help me see what is Your way for all involved. In Jesus' name, I pray. Amen.

Wendy Standorf

Week 14, Day 4

even Mr. Knight

Reading

John 13:34-35 [MSG] Let me give you a new command: Love one another. In the same way I loved you, you love one another. This is how everyone will recognize that you are my disciples – when they see the love you have for each other.

Reflection

An old friend works for a public agency in his country. Because of the nature of the work, he's in contact with others in similar positions in nations all over the world. The messages are usually official, but bonds are formed and sometimes the postings get a bit informal.

My friend called me last night. Seems there's a "Mr. Knight" who, in those informal times, clogs the inbox with tales of his many battlefield feats decades ago – his job as a wartime interrogator – sometimes attaching pictures (yes, pictures!) of those he had just interrogated.

Mr. Knight's unofficial emails sound annoying and inappropriate, but my friend felt one was particularly troublesome – given it was sent on the Thanksgiving holiday celebrated in Mr. Knight's country. And so my friend responded because he felt the email crossed a line. He asked Mr. Knight – especially on his country's Thanksgiving Day – why not just give thanks to his Lord for how <u>he</u> is made rather than give ridicule for how our Lord might have made someone else? Well, Mr. Knight responded arrogantly – after all, you can't tell <u>him</u> what should or should not be emailed!

My friend was angry at Mr. Knight. And so I reminded my friend that he must love everyone – **even Mr. Knight**. *The Lord's commands are simple, but obedience is difficult.* My friend's only important job is to obey the commands of our Lord. So my friend had to find a way to love **even Mr. Knight**.

We all know people like Mr. Knight in our workplaces or professional associations. They come in all shapes and sizes. But as a *Christ Worker*, your task is not just to work with people like that. No, *you must love people like that* – the irritating coworker, the annoying supervisor, the inappropriate citizen you serve.

Regardless of what they do or say, you must love – **even Mr. Knight**.

Prayer

Father God, You place so many people in my life path, and my work-life is no different. While You teach me many things, You always instruct me to love. Give me strength to be obedient to <u>all</u> of Your words – including Your commandment to love. In Your Son's name, I pray. Amen.

James D. Slack

Week 14, Day 5

awake from a selfish sleep

Reading

Psalm 37:4 [NLT] Take delight in the LORD, and he will give you your heart's desires.

Reflection

For some time, I was praying for things my heart desired. Not big things, like a trip to Disney Land, but a lot of things. I desired more time alone – in quiet, away from the shouting talk that goes on and on between men in cells on my row. I desired working as a "runner" so I could get out of my cell and walk around more. I desired nicer weather so I could go outside. I desired something else to eat other than what was on my tray. Yes, my heart desired a lot of things that were all about me.

It's funny. Many people like *Psalm* 37:4, but they forget the first part of the verse. Delighting in the Lord is key to Him giving you your heart's desires.

So very early one morning last week, God shook me out of bed like an alarm clock you don't want to go off. He left the first part of that verse ringing in my heart. I realized I had been concerned with just my own selfish heart's desires. I was taking delight *in me and not Him*. You know, give me this and give me that because those things make me happy.

And now I am **awake from a selfish sleep**.

When you delight in yourself, all you get are worldly desires. The kind that come and go so quickly and never quench the need in your heart. But when you delight in our Lord, you get *Godly desires*. The kind that last forever and take away all need.

So, as you prepare for work this morning, will you also **awake from a selfish sleep**? Will your hopes, dreams, and even prayers be about Him and not you? Which will it be – Godly desires or worldly desires? Delight in yourself throughout the workday or delight in the Lord?

It's up to you. But the alarm is going off.

Will you **awake from a selfish sleep**?

Prayer

Father, in the name of Jesus, I pray. Change my worldly desires to Your desires. Let me delight only in You. Remind me of the reason You let me wake up this morning. Remind me of what You need of me today. Amen.

Jimmy Davis, Jr.

Week 15, Day 1

like sandpaper on your heart

Scripture

Colossians 3:12 [NKJV] Therefore, as *the* elect of God, holy and beloved, put on tender mercies, kindness, humility, meekness, longsuffering

Reflection

I work with someone who has led a tragic life. Abuse. Dysfunctional family. Divorce. These are just some of my coworker's problems. Patterns of life-destroying habits and decisions abound. And I've tried to advise this individual, but it falls on deaf ears. I'm tempted just to write this person off.

Longsuffering. Ahhhh, now that's what scripture reminds us to be. Into your life and mine come those who seem bent on challenging our well-being or demeanor. That's life, and there's nothing you or I can do about it. And who knows, God may well be choosing that person to take off our own rough edges, kind of **like sandpaper on your heart**.

As *Christ Workers*, you and I are called to walk with hearts of mercy, kindness, humility, meekness, and, yes, even *hearts of longsuffering*. And not just in dealing with the easy ones who come into the workplace. We simply don't get to choose. Even the most troubling person, you cannot write off.

Yes, as a *Christ Worker*, you have to show the attributes Christ places in your heart.

So at work today, welcome that most troublesome person because God sends him to take off your own rough edges – **like sandpaper on your heart**.

Prayer

God, open my eyes to see You among all the people I work with. Today, give me a heart to understand Your need for my compassion and kindness in working with even those "sandpaper people." I desire to be longsuffering in Your eyes. In Your Son's name, I pray. Amen.

Jan Bedogne

Week 15, Day 2

only test you need to pass

Reading

Jeremiah 29:11 [NIV] "For I know the plans I have for you," declares the LORD, "plans to prosper you and not to harm you, plans to give you hope and a future."

Reflection

Some time ago, my husband took a big test that would give him a much-needed pay raise. He studied hard for several months. I took our two kids to different places every weekend just to give him time to learn. Unfortunately, my husband and I are both terrible test takers, and he failed. Now he wants to take it again, and I'm trying to figure how we can pay for the test he failed let alone pay for him to re-take it. Like most people, we live paycheck to paycheck.

Well, I got very mad at God. I screamed, "Why did You do this to us?" I cried, "How could You let him fail when You know he tried his best?" I gave up hope, questioned my faith, and even stopped praying – just to show Him how angry I was. A good friend took me aside to remind me of all my blessings: a beautiful house, a good job, two healthy kids, and a loving husband. Yet none of that mattered because all I wanted was for my husband to pass the test and earn the extra money he deserved.

And then something happened... I read something... A glimmer of hope entered when I finally listened to God. Not job nor house nor even pay-raise – *nothing matters other than following Him and knowing He has a plan for me and my family*. And it's only been a few weeks, and the wound is still raw. I try to hold my head up high, but some days are harder than others because we feel so defeated. And I wonder should my husband take the test again? Or is this God's way of saying there's something else? And waiting on God's plan really doesn't help pay the bills.

But I'm no longer mad at Him. My husband and I will get through this <u>with</u> Him and become stronger <u>because</u> of Him. I don't know when He'll let us in on His plan, but that doesn't matter. All I need to do is *follow Him and have faith* in His plan, not mine.

As you follow your own route to work this morning, make sure you also follow Him and have faith. It may be a rough day – shoot, it may be a rough year. Doesn't matter. The **only test you need to pass** is to follow Him and have faith.

Yes, His is the **only test you need to pass**. Then He surely will get you where you need to go.

Prayer

Dear God, thank You for giving me the strength to go on when all I want to do is quit. I know You have a plan much brighter than I can imagine. Thank You for always standing tall and being there when I feel so alone. In Jesus' name, I pray. Amen.

Maureen Bereznak

Week 15, Day 3

really not that far from paradise

Reading

Isaiah 65:17-18 [NAB] See, I am creating new heavens and a new earth; the former things shall not be remembered nor come to mind. Instead, shout for joy and be glad forever in what I am creating.

Reflection

In class yesterday, a young preschooler told me it was *Paradise Day* and "there was no rain on that day." I have no idea where she came up with this idea, but it made me smile. After all, I tend to think of my workplace as a long way from paradise! It's full of messy, noisy children and tired, overworked adults. But on that day, I felt incredible joy thinking about that one word – *paradise* – and realizing my workplace is **really not that far from paradise**!

Like me, you may work in less than ideal conditions – but it's **really not that far from paradise**. As a *Christ Worker*, look past those dirty floors, that "out of order" sign on the restroom door, and your grumbling coworker.

Each day God is making your workplace part of His new earth. So truly look around. Have *eyes like a child*, and shout for joy in what you see!

Your workplace is **really not that far from paradise**.

Prayer

Lord, I love You so much, and I know You are in my life and thus in my workplace. Teach me how to be open and present with You in all my thoughts and actions. Let me see a paradise for Your glory in my workplace today and every day. Like a small child, I will shout for joy and be glad forever. In Jesus' name, I pray. Amen.

Joanna Knight

Week 15, Day 4

firewall against spiritual hackers

Reading

Ephesians 6:13, 17-18 *[NLT]* Therefore, put on every piece of God's armor so you will be able to resist the enemy in the time of evil. Then after the battle you will still be standing firm…and take the sword of the Spirit, which is the word of God. Pray in the Spirit at all times and on every occasion.

Reflection

Lately, it seems every time I log into my city's bank website I face a new layer of PIN numbers, token codes, and security questions. I'm grateful the bank is protecting the city's dollars, but I fume at the nameless people lurking behind the scenes working to steal, disrupt, and delete. It wasn't always like this! What happened to those simpler days? We are in a very real cyber war that drains time and resources from our workplaces.

Yet there is a much greater conflict in the spiritual realm. And He strategically places you and me as earthly parts of His **firewall against spiritual hackers** and their plans to steal and destroy – delete – the souls of our brothers and sisters. He gives us the weapons we need to *stand firm*! We have defensive armor of faith, salvation, truth, righteousness, and the Good News. Even better, He equips us to take the offensive – we can boldly pray and declare the Word over people and situations.

Well, you know how the story ends. Jesus is greater than any evil you'll ever face; He has already won the victory! So don't pine for more peaceful times. No! As a *Christ Worker*, just remember who you are – an earthly part of His **firewall against spiritual hackers**.

Today at work, know you are His updated layer of PIN numbers. His refreshed code. His renewed security question. You are one of His earthly helpers in keeping evil from deleting someone out.

Yes, go to work today and *stand firm* – because He has work for you to do!!

Prayer

Lord, You have all authority in heaven and on earth. I rejoice that you allow me to partner with You to bring Your Kingdom into my workplace. I face today and all tomorrows with joyful confidence in You. In Your name, I pray. Amen.

Maureen Rogers

Week 15, Day 5

miss the right results

Reading

Luke 5:5(b)-6 (NLT) we worked hard all last night and didn't catch a thing. But if you say so, I'll let the nets down again. And this time their nets were so full of fish they began to tear!

Reflection

Simon, a fisherman, never got his nets as full as when he obeyed Jesus.

As *Christ Workers*, you and I must be very careful not to **miss the right results** intended by Jesus. It's easy to let your job or marriage or friendship or family get in the way of following His commands. Even here on Life Row, it's easy to let things get in the way.

Sure, doing what you think is right might still have good results, but you will **miss the right results** – His results. And those results are advancing His kingdom, not yours.

So today at work, don't get too independent. Don't stray away from Him. Don't let things get in the way. You may work hard but not catch a thing. You may do good but **miss the right results**.

Today, follow Jesus' commands, and don't **miss the right results**.

Prayer

Father, in the name of Jesus, I pray. Continue to speak to my heart, Father, so I can not only get the right results but also get to be used by You! Amen.

Jimmy Davis, Jr.

Week 16, Day 1

be the servant, and you will be the leader

Reading

Matthew 20:26(b) [NIV] **whoever wants to become great among you must be your servant**

Philippians 2:3 (NIV) Do nothing out of selfish ambition or vain conceit. Rather, in humility value others above yourselves

Reflection

I once worked in a place where everyone hated the boss. He focused only on himself. If anyone made a mistake, he'd view it as a personal attack. So we all did as little as possible in fear of making a mistake. And nothing ever got done but the boss's busy work.

Maybe you've experienced a workplace like that – a workplace with management but no leadership. So everyone works hard, but the organization goes nowhere. No one really works at all because nothing will satisfy the boss. No one is willing to work for the good of the whole because fear and frustration cause each to focus on self-interest. *A workplace with management but no leadership.*

Management is an easy commodity, but leadership is not. And leadership is something every work unit requires.

As a *Christ Worker*, look to Christ's example for leadership. He will show you how to gain the enthusiasm of everyone to accomplish tasks with efficiency, effectiveness, dignity, and compassion. Through Christ, **be the servant, and you will be the leader**.

This is what Christ teaches you – *leadership, not just management.* He equips you to lead others for His sake, not yours, to accomplish the job at hand.

So today at work, **be the servant, and you will be the leader.**

This is what Christ teaches you. It's what He expects.

Prayer

Lord, I seek to be Your humble servant in my workplace. I will rely on Your guidance to bring honor to Your name. Help me be the leader You want me to be. In Jesus' name, I pray. Amen.

Stan Best

Week 16, Day 2

when anger wells up

Reading

Galatians 6:9 [NIV] Let us not become weary in doing good, for at the proper time we will reap a harvest if we do not give up.

Colossians 3:23 [NIV] Whatever you do, work at it with all your heart, as working for the Lord, not for human masters.

Reflection

A friend of mine had a job that caused a lot of stress. Oh, he can take hard work and deadlines. But as hard as he tried, his work never stood up to his supervisor's critique. *Working* overtime just to redo projects, anger began to well-up. My friend got to a boiling point where he couldn't take it. He exploded at his boss and was fired.

My friend should never have acted that way, but what could he have done? What do you do **when anger wells up**?

As a *Christ Worker* –give Him the stress, and keep doing your best! I know, I know – it's tough not to receive any acknowledgment for good effort and improvement. You may be unappreciated. You may even be ridiculed. And you may never hear anything nice from a particular supervisor. But just keep in mind; you are working for the Lord and not any human master.

Today at work, will you find yourself in the same predicament as my friend? If so, keep your cool. Do your best for Him, not your supervisor. At the proper time, you will reap a harvest for your good work. That, He promises you!

So **when anger wells up**, it's all the more reason to work for Him – with all your heart!

Prayer

Father God, let me not grow weary at work. I promise to give You all the stress and frustration. And **when anger wells up**, calm me and let me work on the areas I truly need improvement. Throughout the day, remind me I work for You – with all my heart. In Jesus' name, I pray. Amen.

Erica Everette

Week 16, Day 3

be bold and testify

Reading

Acts 20:24(b) [NIV] my only aim is to finish the race and complete the task the Lord Jesus has given me—the task of testifying to the good news of God's grace.

Romans 3:23(b)-24 [NIV] for all have sinned and fall short of the glory of God, and all are justified freely by his grace through the redemption that came by Christ Jesus.

Reflection

Have you ever felt compelled by the Holy Spirit to speak out even though you knew it might cost you? After all, as public servants, we serve the government and the taxpayers, right? But as *Christ Workers,* should we not **be bold and testify** about the Good News?

Recently I had the opportunity to be on a local radio talk show. One of the topics was Edward Cornwallis, the founder of Halifax. You see, history hasn't been kind to Cornwallis. He lived in another age in North American history. During the battle between French and English, Nova Scotia's first people sided with the French, and Cornwallis issued a proclamation for their scalps. Many contemporary citizens call for the removal of his statue, as well as the removal of his name from a park, several streets, and churches, and even a river and a military base. When it comes down to it, Halifax is filled with the name of Cornwallis.

So at the radio station, I thought how everyone has fallen short of the mark by sin. I decided to **be bold and testify** to the Good News. So I said to the voting listeners that, if we dug back into the history of every human who ever lived in Nova Scotia, buried under every tombstone in Halifax, we'd learn all were imperfect. We'd know that all today are equally imperfect. Yet, by grace and grace alone through that ultimate sacrifice of Jesus, we are saved – just as Cornwallis was. I concluded my talk by reminding everyone that this is the reason for Easter!

I want people to know I truly am a *Christ Worker*, and I'm willing to **be bold and testify** publically despite potential political cost.

Today at work, remember the reason for the Lenten season. Sometime today, **be bold and testify** to someone about the Good News.

And fear not – your sacrifice could never match His!

Prayer

Father God, I am but a frail human full of weakness. Yet You sent Your Son to save me from this sinful world. Today at work, let me be bold and find opportunities to share the meaning of Lent. In your Son's name, I pray. Amen!

Matt Whitman

Week 16, Day 4

the bottom of the box

Reading

James 1:2-3 [ESV] Count it all joy, my brothers, when you meet trials of various kinds, for you know that the testing of your faith produces steadfastness.

1 Corinthians 11:1 [ESV] Be imitators of me, as I am of Christ.

Reflection

I love gifts – especially opening them! Maybe it's the fun of wondering what could be inside the box wrapped in all that pretty paper. Maybe it's the joy of knowing who it's from regardless of what's inside the box. But sometimes the real gift can get lost at **the bottom of the box** when you pay too much attention to the shiny bows on top.

I once served in an organization that I felt wasn't run well. When offered the chance to take a leadership role, I felt this was a gift to allow me to make changes. In my mind, I only wanted to do good – but others began to see my views as arrogant. During one meeting, my own words were used against me. Criticism came fast and furious. I'm not sure how I finished that meeting without crying.

Wow! Shiny bows and ribbons of leadership. What a rotten gift, I thought. That gift was supposed to change things, but all it did was make people mad at me. And I felt terrible.

But driving home that day, God taught me a lesson. His gift to me was not the pretty wrapping of leadership. There I found only my own ego, and others found my pretentiousness. The real gift from God, one I neglected to find, was an opportunity to represent Christ in my leadership. I guess, in the excitement of opening the box, I failed to see the valuable gift **at the bottom of the box** – the gift of Christ's example. Rather than letting Christ lead me, I tried to lead all by myself.

You know, God's greatest gift is His son, Jesus Christ. That's the gift He gives you at work today. So unwrap that gift! Just don't get mesmerized by the pretty ribbons and shiny bows. Find the valuable gift **at the bottom of the box** – the example of Christ. Be steadfast in using that gift throughout the day.

Yes, count it all joy! Find the valuable gift **at the bottom of the box**. Imitate Christ, not yourself. Let Him change you. And let Christ, not you, change what needs to be fixed.

Prayer

Father, thank You for the gift of Your Son. Let Christ make changes in me as I imitate Him in my workplace. Let all changes be made through Him, not me. In Jesus' name, I pray. Amen.

Jenny Sue Flannagan

Week 16, Day 5

see another side of them

Reading

John 1:46-47 [NLT] "Nazareth!" exclaimed Nathanael. "Can anything good come from Nazareth?" "Come and see for yourself," Philip replied. As they approached, Jesus said, "Now here is a genuine son of Israel—a man of complete integrity."

Reflection

It seems many nonbelievers hold a lot of resentment toward Christians. Perhaps it's because they were hurt by someone responding in a non-Christian way. Maybe it's because of false information spread about our faith or rumors about what goes on in our churches. Whatever reason, nonbelievers judge us – and some even mock us – our faith, our church, and our Lord.

It is way too easy to respond like they do – judging right back or making fun of them. I know you get angry at them. I do, too. But we know that's <u>not</u> how Jesus wants us to respond.

He wants <u>you</u> to **see another side of them** – see the nonbeliever with love and grace – just like Jesus saw Nathanael differently than Nathanael saw Jesus. He wants you to see each one as a *genuine son or daughter with complete integrity*.

Today, as you head out to work, don't return anger with anger, mocking with mocking, judgment with judgment. No, let Jesus' love and grace be <u>on</u> you and ready to pour <u>from</u> you.

Yes, at work today, **see another side of them**.

And let His grace and love change that coworker forever!

Prayer

Father, in the name of Jesus, I pray. Thank You for freely giving me Your love and grace so I can freely give it to others to change their hearts and their destiny. Amen.

Jimmy Davis, Jr.

Week 17, Day 1

matches to light that candle

Reading

Titus 2:7-8 [KJV] In all things shewing thyself a pattern of good works: in doctrine *shewing* uncorruptness, gravity, sincerity, sound speech, that cannot be condemned; that he that is of the contrary part may be ashamed, having no evil thing to say of you.

John 1:5 [KJV] And the light shineth in darkness; and the darkness comprehended it not.

Reflection

A mentor of mine is polite, courteous, and respected by everyone. He is known for the quality of his work and always giving sound advice. He is seen as an example of a godly person. My mentor's walk with Christ is evident to coworkers throughout our building.

But it is certainly not easy to be a godly person in this postmodern age where civility is reconstructed to match the license of each person. Too often, you hear off-color language, dirty jokes, and lewd comments about the opposite sex. Yet in my workplace, my mentor (and a few other godly men and women) silence such license. He doesn't judge, but when my mentor is present, coworkers apologize if license is used. He is like a candle of the Lord illuminating the darkest parts of the room. Not all may understand that light, but all become ashamed of their own darkness. My mentor truly is a *Christ Worker*.

Every workplace should be blessed with many godly coworkers like my mentor. But I have learned it only takes one godly person to start the fire. And as *Christ Workers*, we are the **matches to light that candle**!

Today at work, be the *Christ Worker* God expects. Don't wait for others to light the flame. Be the <u>first</u> of many **matches to light that candle**. The darkness may not comprehend, but you will change your workplace and glorify your Lord!

Prayer

God, help me use the spirit You give to illuminate the lives of my brothers and sisters in my workplace. In Your Son's name, I pray. Amen.

Samuel Henry

Week 17, Day 2

get up and get back to work

Reading

1 Kings 19:13-14 [NLT] When Elijah heard it, he wrapped his face in his cloak and went out and stood at the entrance of the cave. And a voice said, "What are you doing here, Elijah?" He replied again, "I have zealously served the Lord God Almighty. But the people of Israel have broken their covenant with you, torn down your altars, and killed every one of your prophets. I am the only one left, and now they are trying to kill me, too.

Reflection

It's easy to get discouraged and think you are alone in service to the Lord. This is especially true in the workplace. You probably don't know your coworkers like you do people in your Sunday school class. And what you do see of some coworkers may give you an inaccurate snapshot of their faith walk. So you feel alone in trying to glorify God at work. You start to believe you are the only one who truly understands and cares for Christ. A bit pretentiously, you might ponder: if only other coworkers could see how important it is to glorify God through their work, they too would do all they could to serve Him throughout the day.

Elijah certainly felt this way when talking to God. But the gentle Whisper told Elijah to **get up and get back to work**. He was not the only one serving because God had provided 7000 more for the ministry.

God provides. But as we serve, we need to do what we can with what He provides. At work today, look around. Are you really the only one? If He provides many helpers, then join with them. If He only provides you, then work to build the Body of Christ for Him.

And remember what Elijah learned. As a *Christ Worker*, you have to **get up and get back to work**. He will provide more for His ministry!

Prayer

Lord, please keep me humble and in the moment. I know I am not alone in devotion to You. Others are doing their best to glorify You just as I am doing my best. Help me to remember what Your mission is for me, and then give me the courage to do my best in everything You send me to do. In Your name, I pray. Amen.

Stan Best

Week 17, Day 3

that simple rule

Reading

Matthew 7:12(b) [NIV] do to others what you would have them do to you

Ephesians 4:32 [NIV] Be kind and compassionate to one another, forgiving each other, just as in Christ God forgave you.

Reflection

Ever work with someone you really don't like? You know, one of those real pains! Once I worked with a girl who got ruder by the day. I tried to be pleasant, but it was impossible to build an affable relationship. I admit; sometimes I wanted to treat her the same way she kept treating me!

But even when it got tough, God reminded me of the golden rule – *His rule* – to treat others the way you want to be treated – not the way they treat you. And as Jesus reminds us, **that simple rule** sums up all that is taught by the law and the prophets.

I know following **that simple rule** remains a difficult task To be kind and compassionate to a coworker who truly is a major pain. To forgive her so many times a day. To resist treating him just like he treats you. It would just be so easy to act like that coworker, but we are not like that coworker. Are we?

As a *Christ Worker*, know you are not like that painful coworker. While the pain won't go away, you must still follow **that simple rule**. So today at work, treat that repulsive coworker with kindness and forgiveness because that is how Christ treats you – no matter how repulsive you (and I) may sometimes act toward Him!

Prayer

Dear Lord, help me remember the countless times You show me forgiveness and kindness. Help me extend that same forgiveness and kindness to others at work so I may glorify You in all my encounters. In Your holy name, I pray. Amen.

Samantha Pineiro Graham

Week 17, Day 4

pray as your first resort

Reading

1 Thessalonians 5:17 [KJV] Pray without ceasing.

Matthew 7:11(b) [NIRV] How much more will your Father who is in heaven give good gifts to those who ask him!

Reflection

I lost my wallet just a few hours before a business flight. Believe me; I tore apart my suitcases, apartment, and car. No luck. Frantically I called the airline to see what options I had, and those options were not looking good. I searched my apartment again, this time even checking the refrigerator and freezer – but to no avail. In a *last ditch moment*, I kneeled by the side of my bed and broke into prayer. Almost immediately my heart grew lighter, and my mind became clearer. I remembered where I left the wallet – in the bathroom of a restaurant near my apartment. I rushed over, and the manager had my wallet – including all the money! As I raced to catch my flight, I kept praying, "Thank You, Lord!" And He even helped me board the flight with only a couple minutes to spare.

Collapsing into my assigned seat, I thought about what happened. Why did I wait so long to pray? Instead of praying as a last resort, why didn't I pray first? If I had just prayed first, I could have saved myself a lot of grief and worry.

Is it the same way with you? Does prayer seem to be your last resort instead of your first action? Is this particularly true with work-related matters?

Today at work, **pray as your first resort**. Avoid the panic of addressing crises with only your means. If you ask, He will not let you miss your flight. When you ask, He will not let you miss your big break. Because you ask, He will never let you miss your blessing. But if you don't pray first, He will let you lose your peace of mind!

So today, **pray as your first resort**! In fact, just pray without ceasing!!

Prayer

Father, thank You for my direct line of communication with You! Thank You for being my best line of defense against panic, worry, and worst-case scenarios.

Help me to pray _first_ in all of my tasks today. Then let me pray all day! And always let me pray in Jesus' name. Amen.

Kathryn Saunders

Week 17, Day 5

grow in size when you share

Reading

Philippians 2:25 [MSG] But for right now, I'm dispatching Epaphroditus, my good friend and companion in my work. You sent him to help me out; now I'm sending him to help you out.

Reflection

Not long ago I went in prayer and asked God to provide a *pork chop* for me. Yes, a pork chop! I love them, but you can't get them in here. But last week a prison ministry came to Life Row with home-cooked food. And guess what? They cooked pork chops for our lunch! Wonderful pork chops! Glorious pork chops! Delicious pork chops – the way my mama cooked them! And while I was working in a back room helping that ministry prepare the afternoon session, someone who knew how much I love pork chops brought five more just for me!

My pork chop prayer was more than answered on that day!!

But there were three other brothers working with me in that back room. While each of us got one pork chop for lunch, they now saw five extra pork chops on my plate. And while they said nothing, I saw the looks on their faces. They missed pork chops, too, and they were hoping I would share. So I invited each to take as many of my extra pork chops as they wanted.

Yes, God blessed me by answering my prayer. And He used that prison ministry to deliver my blessing. But I was blessed even more when I shared those pork chops with my brothers and saw the smiles on their faces! Those pork chops were a blessing – I can't deny that – but not nearly as much as sharing them.

Every day God blesses you in countless ways. Some are expected and some are surprises. Some blessings are very large, and some are very small. All of your blessings **grow in size when you share**.

It's no different at your place of work. Today you are going to receive many blessings. A beautiful day. A safe trip to work. A new idea. Remembering how to do something. A friendly hello. A text from someone you love. An assuring smile. Whatever those blessings are – expected or not, large or small – they **grow in size when you share**.

And that includes the blessing of sharing your favorite lunch!

Prayer

Father, in the name of Jesus, I pray. Thank You for answering my prayers and blessing me today in so many ways. Give me a heart to share my blessings. Like Epaphroditus, let me use my blessings to be Your instrument in helping others get through this day. Amen.

Jimmy Davis, Jr.

Week 18, Day 1

Jesus is waiting for you

Reading

Psalm 100:2 [ESV] Serve the Lord with gladness! Come into his presence with singing!

Reflection

Especially on Mondays, it's difficult to have joy and gladness about <u>anything</u>. You left a lot of work on your desk last Friday, and it's still *waiting for you*. You may have spent all weekend completing that work, but today other tasks are *waiting for you*. You greet this morning with numbness, exhaustion, and gloom – feeling like you never left the building over the weekend. It's only Monday, but you wish it were Friday. And so, as this workweek begins, it's real hard serving <u>anything</u> with joy and gladness – including our Lord. You just don't feel like coming into His presence with outbursts of song. There's just too much *waiting for you*.

But **Jesus is waiting for you**, too. He wants you to live a sustained vibrant life <u>in</u> Him, but that takes time <u>with</u> Him – in the Word, meditation, and conversation – especially at work.

Yes, **Jesus is waiting for you**. But He wants you to come into His presence with something a bit more than gloom…exhaustion…numbness. Just when your heart feels like singing the least, **Jesus is waiting for you** to sing the most. So today at work, come into His presence with joy!

Jesus is waiting for you. What will you do?

Prayer

Lord, just the thought of You waiting for someone like me makes me fall to my knees in praise! Forgive me for always being so late in entering Your presence. On this Monday, I come to You with special joy and gladness – joy and gladness that glorify You in ways only You deserve! In Your name, I pray all day with outbursts of song! Amen.

Chris Summers

Week 18, Day 2

prayer, praise, and proclamation

Reading

Luke 2:27(b); 36(a); 37-38 [KJV] ...and when the parents had brought in the child Jesus... And there was one Anna, a prophetess... And she was a widow of about fourscore and four years, which departed not from the temple, but served God with fastings and prayers, night and day. And she coming in that instance gave thanks likewise unto the Lord, and spake of him to all them that looked for redemption in Jerusalem.

Reflection

Anna was a very old prophetess who might have been tempted to retire to some 1st century beachfront property or senior citizens home. But she was not the type. Anna was kind of a spiritual workaholic, never leaving the temple and serving God day and night. Her work and life centered on three things – **prayer, praise, and proclamation.**

This philosophy gave her an opportunity to see the Salvation-of-the-World when His parents brought Him to the temple. Through prayer, Anna listened, and God placed her exactly where she needed to be to see Jesus. Then she praised God for sending His son. Then she proclaimed Him to everyone listening – never discriminating as to whom she would tell the Good News.

Like Anna, I want to be a spiritual workaholic! I pray to see Jesus in my workplace today. I will praise God each time I do! I will proclaim His Good News to everyone.

Like Anna, I will focus on **prayer, praise, and proclamation** – especially in the midst of all my work and all my work hours.

Yes, today at work, I'm focusing on Anna's way – **prayer, praise, and proclamation!**

How about you?

Prayer

Dear God, thank You so very much for placing me where You want me to be at this point in my life. I want to see You, high and lifted up! At work today, please grant me the wisdom to pray to You more often, the insight to give You thanks for everything, and the boldness to speak of Your love to everyone. In the name of Jesus, I pray! Amen.

Debra Neal

Week 18, Day 3

without selfishness or envy

Reading

Mark 9:34; 10:41 [NIV] But they kept quiet because on the way they had argued about who was the greatest... When the ten heard about this, they became indignant with James and John.

James 3:16 [NIV] For where you have envy and selfish ambition, there you find disorder and every evil practice.

Reflection

In my work, I study "bad guys" – spies and scoundrels who sell out coworkers, do damage to the security of their country, and endanger lives. Now there's a ton of reasons why bad guys act the way they do, and many center on feelings of exclusion from inner circles of power, economics, or prestige. Once good guys, bad guys stay bad because of envy and selfishness.

In Jesus' day, Judas was a bad guy. Yet, at times, the other disciples also ventured to the bad side. Yes, they <u>remained</u> good guys – but they coveted being at the center of Christ's inner circle. Captured by envy and selfish ambition, they argued about who was the greatest among them. James and John conspired to sit on either side of Jesus.

And we do the same, don't we? Not that we're permanent bad guys, but we become selfish and envious. It can pop up with a lunch meeting to which you're not invited. Or you might lord it over others who, unlike you, aren't in that inner circle.

For good guys, it's so easy to act badly.

Now I'm not suggesting you'll end up selling secrets to foreign governments. As a *Christ Worker*, you <u>are</u> one of the good guys. But you may be tempted to do something to get even or to take advantage – to get into that inner circle. Be careful, and fight against it! The temptation to feel important is a form of spiritual warfare and runs contrary to scripture. And it makes it impossible to work **without selfishness or envy**.

So today at work, serve our Lord through your hard work. Do so **without selfishness or envy**. Follow Jesus, and <u>remain</u> one of the good guys!

Prayer

Lord, help me keep my eyes on You today. Let me be one of the good guys by working humbly <u>in</u> Your kingdom and <u>for</u> Your kingdom in everything I do. In Your name, I pray. Amen.

Mary Manjikian

Week 18, Day 4

do the hope of Christ

Reading

John 5:19(b) [NKJV] the Son can do nothing of Himself, but what He sees the Father do; for whatever He does, the Son also does in like manner

Romans 15:13 [NKJV] Now may the God of hope fill you with all joy and peace in believing, that you may abound in hope by the power of the Holy Spirit.

Reflection

Last year, I interned in a congressional office. My job was to direct constituent concerns to the correct district caseworker. At times, a problem could be quickly resolved. But there were many instances when the issue was substantially more complex. And a few instances where the circumstances were dire. Intense emotions would be expressed because the caller felt cornered. I had to find ways to encourage the constituent. The preferred solution might not be possible, but the constituent had to hear and know that he was not alone. The conversation had to be transformational. There had to be hope.

But what is *hope*? More importantly, what is hope to a Christian? Even with best intentions, we sometimes place our hope in earthly things rather than Jesus. Those we serve are affected when this happens; conversations are not transformational as life wears away earthly hope.

There is both an African proverb and a Quaker saying: when you pray, move your feet. Our God is *a God of doing*. So we must **do the hope of Christ**. You and I need to show that He, and only He, is the source of true hope. And we must find ways to give True Hope to others.

Today at work, you will serve many who have lost all hope. True, they search for earthly remedies, and helping them makes you a public servant. So use your hands and feet to provide the earthly remedies they seek. But as a *Christ Worker*, go a step further. Glorify God. Find ways to **do the hope of Christ** when providing earthly remedy.

Yes today, do what the Father does – **do the hope of Christ**.

Prayer

Heavenly Father, my hope is attached exclusively to You. Inspire me to proclaim exuberantly Your faithfulness and give me courage to take action. Let all see my hands and feet do Your hope. Let Your hope be the hope of many in my workplace. In Your Son's name, I pray. Amen.

Rachael Monnin

Week 18, Day 5

some kind of peace in the middle of the storm

Reading

Luke 8:16 [NLT] No one lights a lamp and then covers it with a bowl or hides it under a bed. A lamp is placed on a stand, where its light can be seen by all who enter the house.

Reflection

Last month a brother was executed in here. Now you might think that's a good thing – a murderer finally paid the price. And that's true; he did. But I knew this brother for many years. And all the correctional officers knew him well. So the day of taking life is not easy for anyone – inmate or officer. It is always sad – an anxious day – kind of like being in the middle of a storm.

Yet, on this day of execution, I felt the peace of Jesus so powerful on me that I sang from morning til night. I sang so loud that everyone could hear me. Joyful hymns. Praises of hope. Songs of confidence in Him. A brother passed by my cell and said, "You are <u>shining</u> all over – *even though death is all around us!*"

I could have hidden my light from the storm I was in. Kept it just for myself.
    But
I did not do that. Others needed the light from that Lamp – inmate and officer. They needed to see it desperately to find **some kind of peace in the middle of the storm**.

A lot of times, <u>you</u> are planted in storms – storms where you work. Storms in your own home. Storms in your community. Storms of fear. Storms of anxiety. And there is always the storm of death around you. Is this not true?

A strong wind may make you want to hide your light – in fear of it going out forever. But don't do it. If you place it under your bed, who will see it? Others are weaker than you, and they <u>need</u> to see it. When you hide it under a bowl, all you do is keep the power of Jesus from those who need Him most. And you never know who needs Him most.

Today as you prepare for work, go to work, come home from work – keep your light uncovered. You never know when a strong wind will pick up. Keep your light on a stand so someone can find **some kind of peace in the middle of the storm**.

And know the wind can <u>never</u> blow out that Flame!

Prayer

Father, in the name of Jesus, I pray. Keep reminding me that the Light of Your son is not for me only but for all others to see and believe in You. Amen.

Jimmy Davis, Jr.

Week 19, Day 1

wear the proper attitude

Reading

Matthew 22:11-14 [NIV] "But when the king came in to see the guests, he noticed a man there who was not wearing wedding clothes. He asked, 'How did you get in here without wedding clothes, friend?' The man was speechless. Then the king told the attendants, 'Tie him hand and foot, and throw him outside, into the darkness, where there will be weeping and gnashing of teeth.' For many are invited, but few are chosen."

Reflection

Everyone likes office parties. They're fun. Plenty to do, see, eat, and drink. And there's chatting with friends and hobnobbing with supervisors and other bigshots.

Yes, everyone likes the social function, but few want to prepare for it. Fewer still understand what it takes to pull together the office event. We rarely take time to celebrate the party workers – the planners, doers, custodians, security, food service people, and staff who put up the tables and take them down – because we are so busy enjoying ourselves.

As a *Christ Worker*, you may do the behind-the-scene work for that office party. In that case, make it the very best event possible. But, if you are one of the invited, do not forget to recognize those who have labored for you. Celebrations, after all, are ordained by God – even secular workplace celebrations are ordained by Him.

So, at the next office social function, wear the proper clothes, of course. But, much more importantly, **wear the proper attitude**. Show how well you truly understand that others made the celebration possible.

Yes, **wear the proper attitude**, or you just may be thrown outside into darkness!

Prayer

Lord, help me never take anyone's work for granted. At times, it's up to me to work, and at other times, it's up to me to enjoy. Regardless of which, keep me in the moment so I can fully appreciate the gift I am given. In Your name, I pray. Amen.

Stan Best

Week 19, Day 2

carry His word in your toolbox

Reading

Isaiah 40:8 [NKJV] The grass withers, the flower fades, But the word of our God stands forever

Reflection

It's part of each public servant's job: an expectation to "know," to have, or to find the information requested by a supervisor, peer, or citizen. When I was younger, I thought it a failure <u>not</u> to have an answer to every question! But I am older now, and I realize no one has all the answers – *except God*. He gives His servants answers through His word and the prayers, visions, and actions that result from His word.

You know you should **carry His word in your toolbox** – that area of the mind where you store workplace information. Or that drawer in your desk where you keep the technical stuff. And yes, that shelf holding all the manuals. His word should be in that workplace toolbox as much as all the other tools you include. And what power flows when you **carry His word in your toolbox**! His word was at the beginning with Him and will be with you and me forever – long after all the current technical fads in that toolbox wither and fade away.

At work today, you won't have all the answers. You <u>will</u> have trouble understanding some of the questions. You might not know where to start looking for possible solutions. Those technical tools may just prove a little ineffective at times.

Today at work, use all the available tools to find answers to questions and solutions to problems. Don't forget to **carry His word in your toolbox**. And use <u>that</u> tool abundantly!

Prayer

Father, thank You for Your word! I really can't solve anything without it. I will carry Your word in my toolbox and use it abundantly. It is in Jesus' name, I pray! Amen.

Ellen C. Stamm

Week 19, Day 3

what we know

Reading

Romans 8:28(a) [NKJV] And we know that all things work together for good to those who love God

Mark 9:23- 24 [NKJV] Jesus said to him, "If you can believe, all things *are* possible to him who believes." Immediately the father of the child cried out and said with tears, "Lord, I believe; help my unbelief!"

Reflection

A friend works in a municipal office. He's a Christian, but he sees himself as being no different from his non-Christian coworkers. One day I asked, "since you knows God, shouldn't you be different?" "Well," he replied, "the same bad things happen to me as everyone else. So how am I different?" I responded, "a Christian *knows* all things work together for good if you love God."

We *know* all things are possible if we believe. I reminded him that his non-Christian coworkers have no such knowledge, and hence, they have no Hope. So **what we know** makes us different.

That changed my friend's perspective, but it got me thinking about my own. Am I that different from my secularist colleagues? I mean; how do I act differently? Is my attitude different? How much of what I know about God really manifests through me at work?

And how about you?

If you and I know God, then we know He is faithful and true. We must know He keeps His promises. No matter what troubles come our way, you and I know that true Hope rests in our belief and love in God. So what counts is **what we know**!

That's what separates *Christ Workers* from non-Christian coworkers. That's what makes us think and act differently. You and I believe and love God.

Today at work, remember it's **what we know** that counts. We know God, and sadly, others don't. And what they *don't know* must make us different.

Prayer

Lord, like the sick child's father crying out, let me also shout: I believe in You. Help me differentiate myself at work today. And help me in my moments of unbelief. Your love and faithfulness give me unshakeable Hope for today and tomorrow. In Your name, I pray. Amen.

Kevin J. Cooney

Week 19, Day 4

only a coworker

Reading

Romans 12:5 [NIV] so in Christ we, though many, form one body, and each member belongs to all the others

1 John 4:20(b) [NIV] For whoever does not love their brother and sister, whom they have seen, cannot love God, whom they have not seen.

Reflection

Yesterday my co-worker learned his brother passed. In the middle of a staff meeting, he received that dreaded phone call. I wanted to console him, wipe the tears from his eyes, but time did not allow. He ran from the office in a panicked state, and there was nothing physically I could do. And besides, I did not know him well. He was **only a coworker**.

So I prayed for God's will to be done. I asked Him to bless me with words of comfort when the time came at the funeral parlor. I asked for God's grace on his family – grace to respond most sufficiently to their brokenness. And I asked for courage to truly be a sister-in-Christ, not **only a coworker**, when he returned to the office.

Today at work, remember that you must love your coworker as you do our Lord. Remember God loves your coworkers – Christians and non-Christians – *equally* – as much as He loves you.

So today, don't be afraid to act like a *Christ Worker*. Regardless of where one is on their Walk, be a brother- or sister-in-Christ to that person. As hard as it may be in your workplace, find and build the Body of Christ. Give encouragement. Give love. Give prayer. Do these things for your boss, your coworkers, and the people you serve.

Begin today, before that dreaded phone call comes to someone who remains **only a coworker**.

Prayer

Dear God, here I am – humble and thankful for the people you've put in my life. I pray You use me to provide the same support to my coworkers that You give me. Transform us all into the Body of Christ. Help me to understand and love my brothers and sisters – all created in Your image – all loved by You equally. In Jesus' name, I pray. Amen.

Krystiana Carr

Week 19, Day 5

rest in the words

Reading

2 Chronicles 32:8 [KJV] With him is an arm of flesh; but with us is the LORD our God to help us, and to fight our battles. And the people rested themselves upon the words of Hezekiah king of Judah.

Reflection

Every day people full of worry, doubt, and fear surround us. On Life Row, there is only one important thing people worry about: facing death.

Last week, I listened to this brother having doubt and fear about what is to come. The Holy Spirit led me to speak to him one-on-one. I told him I didn't know about his faith in God. But I wanted to pray over him because I knew what the God I serve would do on his behalf. He said, "Jimmy, I have faith in God. But it's those people I worry about." He then told me his fears of when it would be his time. I said I didn't know the who's or what's about the future, and I really didn't care because there was one thing I did know: God will fight my battles. I told him that my God will make everything right because He loves him as much as He loves those people. I tried to assure him that God would fight his battle. He had nothing to worry about.

And so we prayed for a long time with my hands laid upon him. Afterwards, this brother's body language changed. He was more relaxed. He came to **rest in the words** God gave me.

At work and in all corners of your life, there are people worried – having doubts – holding on to fears. Perhaps you are one of them. Remember you have more than an arm of flesh protecting you. You have Him fighting your battles.

And you can change people at work – you can change people in your life – with your faith in Jesus. You can help remove their worries, doubts, and fears. Let Him use you to allow someone to **rest in the words** He gives you.

It all starts in your heart.

Prayer

Father, in the name of Jesus, I pray. I do not want to limit You anymore. Equip and prepare me to use the words You give me so that others can rest in them. I know You are fighting my battles, and I have no worries, doubts, or fears. Amen.

Jimmy Davis, Jr.

Week 20, Day 1

prayers will be my weapons

Reading

Matthew 22:21(b) [NIV] Give to Caesar what is Caesar's, and to God what is God's.

Ephesians 6:12(a) (c) [NIV] For our struggle is not against flesh and blood, but ... against the spiritual forces of evil in the heavenly realms.

2 Corinthians 10:3-4 [NIV] For though we live in the world, we do not wage war as the world does. The weapons we fight with are not the weapons of the world. On the contrary, they have divine power to demolish strongholds.

Reflection

I just realized I have not received lately the electronic version of this workplace devotional. So I looked into the reason why. Turns out, the devotional is blocked from our City email system. I find this disturbing.

Not long ago, our (now deceased) Mayor found comfort in knowing that members of his leadership team (and many other city employees) go beyond just an acceptable level of service to the citizens of our great city. They are reminded daily, in part through this devotional ministry, to excel in serving citizens – just as Christ wants them to excel.

Well, my immediate response to the email block was a worldly one. Yes, I was angry. I wanted to know if the block was legal. I was eager to go into battle. But then I realized the real battle is taking place in heavenly realms – not in my city or your agency. It really isn't a struggle against human decisions but a struggle against spiritual forces.

You know, when Jesus commands us to give to authorities, He means much more than financially. Jesus gives us a spiritual command. God uses you and me as His prayer warriors. We give to God our prayers, but in doing so, our prayers are also gifts to our governments. This permits us to keep focused on the real battle and not be distracted by worldly inclinations.

So I don't know what will happen in the short-term concerning the email block. But at work today, I will not wage war as the world does. My weapons will be quite different, and they will have divine power. Yes, today at work, **prayers will be my weapons**.

How about you?

Prayer

Father, I pray that every day in every matter I may serve Your children in a Christ-focused manner and keep my worldly inclinations behind me. In Your Son's name, I pray. Amen.

Alan Cox

Week 20, Day 2

your turn to be bold

Reading

Acts 9:13-14-[NIV] "But Lord," exclaimed Ananias, "I've heard many people talk about the terrible things this man has done to the believers in Jerusalem! And he is authorized by the leading priests to arrest everyone who calls upon your name."

Reflection

New supervisor. Old supervisor. Reorganization. Re-reorganization. Centralization. De-centralization. Forcing square pegs into round holes, and no one sees the problem.

It's so easy to allow fear to creep into the workplace. It makes us cautious, and we bunker down into our own box. Once in there, we don't look up. We crouch in a corner and hope it all works out the way we planned. In that corner, we lose confidence in knowing the difference between what really can work and what is just fantasy. To admit failure – once again – would force departure from that little box. So we invite God to come into our cramped quarters.

It is our undoing when we *try to shrink God into that little box*. He's too big for that. Even His tiniest toe won't fit inside. And, by the way, He really wants you out of that box – but not into another box. You see, He doesn't want you cowering in any corner or wasting your time trying to affix that square peg. No, He wants you to be bold. He was bold for you, after all, when He took your sins to the cross.

Now, it's **your turn to be bold** for Him.

You know you can't hear Him deep in that corner. And sure, He's going to send you where you fear to trod – where you may not want to hear him at all. But He will be with you always, and besides, His glory is more important than your fears or comfort. Right?

So today at work, don't *try to shrink God into that little box*. Whatever you fear, turn it over to Him. Let Him replace it with His boldness. Then join Him, and move forward on His plans.

Yes, today, get out of that box. It's **your turn to be bold**... *for Him.*

Prayer

Here I am, Lord. I'm scared of everything around me. Help me be courageous. I don't want You to be with <u>me</u> – I want me to be with <u>You</u>. Use me. Forget my plan; I want Your plan. I don't even need to know the details because I know Whose plan it is. In Your name, I pray. Amen.

Stan Best

Week 20, Day 3

commit your work to Him

Reading

Proverbs 16:3 [NLT] Commit your actions to the Lord, and your plans will succeed.

Colossians 3:23 [NLT] Work willingly at whatever you do, as though you were working for the Lord rather than for people.

Reflection

It happens in my line of work, and I know it must happen in yours. There just seems to be a lot of drama taking place nowadays. Perhaps it's because of constant fears about lay-offs. Or maybe it's the unspoken threat of elimination through reorganization. It might be a result of so little opportunity for advancement in any workplace. Whatever the reason, the workplace is not bringing out the best in us. Cooperation sinks into subtle treachery, and competition turns into blatant betrayal. It takes very little to turn the workplace into a battlefield.

And Christians are not immune to such drama. I guess we close scripture and lay down the cross so that we can join others in the desperate drama of trying to keep our jobs.

It's all understandable, but that's not how it should be – especially for Christians. I mean; should we lose focus on what is most important just to get something in return? Now think carefully. Your boss may not mind the workplace drama, but what about your Lord?

Today at work, focus on your Priority. Think about the example you must set as a *Christ Worker*. Then avoid the office drama. That's not your job. Working willingly for the Lord – now that's your job. He promises you will be successful if you **commit your work to Him**.

Yes, **commit your work to Him**, and avoid the drama!

Prayer

Lord, thinking of the blessings You have brought me so far in life brings me to tears of gratitude. It is You who helps me persevere through hardship. It is You who uses those hardships to help me grow stronger as an individual and a public servant. I will serve You, work for You, and spread Your word – all to the best of my ability here on earth. In Your name, I pray. Amen.

Meredith Pulsford

Week 20, Day 4

not just fixing the immediate

Reading

Proverbs 19:14(a)-15 [AKJV] House and riches are the inheritance of fathers… Slothfulness casteth into a deep sleep; and an idle soul shall suffer hunger.

Reflection

Now, there once were two men. The first man inherited a decent size farm but cared not to work it. He chose to spend his money on idle pursuits. Quickly he went broke, grew hungry, and died young – leaving nothing for his children. The second man worked his own farm diligently, and when the first man went broke, he bought that farm, too. When the second man died at a ripe old age, he left his children all of his lands and riches.

This story is not one so odd. Though our own parents might not leave large treasures, we do understand the nature of inheritance. The rewards of hard work are for the generations. But idleness is not only bad for the immediate, it also depraves the future.

As Christians, we are to be diligent to leave an inheritance for loved-ones. But as *Christ Workers,* we must also leave a future for our communities. This requires grace, wisdom, and vision to see that we are **not just fixing the immediate** – the incremental tasks completed today will shape the public's tomorrow and tomorrow's tomorrow.

As you go about the challenges of your workday, think in terms of generations. You are **not just fixing the immediate** – you are shaping tomorrow's tomorrow. Don't deprave the future.

Prayer

Father, grant me Your wisdom and vision to see how the little things I do today affect the generations. And teach me how to be a diligent servant of You and my community so that I may leave a godly heritage to those who follow me in work and life. In the Name of the Father, Son, and Holy Ghost, I pray. Amen.

Noah M. Griffing

Week 20, Day 5

His word, nothing more

Reading

Luke 8:15 [NLT] And the seeds that fell on the good soil represent honest, good-hearted people who hear God's word, cling to it, and patiently produce a huge harvest.

Reflection

What are you clinging to? What is your community clinging to? What is your nation clinging to?

In this day and age, it's hard to cling to anything for a long period of time. I see people on TV clinging to many things that do not last. Fashion, music, sports, even politics – none explain anything, and all are gone in a second. So we get confused – families not understanding values, neighborhoods not getting along, and nations not understanding right from wrong. I bet even your workplace doesn't make sense anymore.

We wake up in the morning, but we are not awake. We cling to things that will not be there in the afternoon. We seek something different, but we are afraid of His lasting miracle.

It took me a long time, but I accepted God's miracle. When I finally clung to God's word, He did more than change me. By clinging to His word, a huge harvest grew that changed my family and my community here on Life Row. He can do that for you, too.

So what are you clinging to? Do you want to produce that huge harvest? Do you want to change and change those around you – even your coworkers – even those you serve?

Today, at work and at home, cling to The Eternal and feast on the huge harvest He produces. Don't cling to anything else for it has no value and will soon be gone. Yes, cling to **His word, nothing more**.

Prayer

Father, in the name of Jesus, I pray. Thank You for revealing Your word to help me see that You love me enough to produce a huge harvest – if only I choose to cling to Your word, nothing more. Amen.

Jimmy Davis, Jr.

Week 21, Day 1

great things without number

Reading

Matthew 19:26 [NIV] Jesus looked at them and said, "With man this is impossible, but with God all things are possible."

Job 5:8-9 [NIV] As for me, I would seek God, and to God I would commit my cause, Who does great things and unsearchable, marvelous things without number.

Reflection

Ever wonder why God allows seemingly bad things to happen to His people? Yet, through challenging times, you and I are humbled, and God's glory is truly highlighted. Out of all the man-made impossibilities, our God comes through to do **great things without number**.

For example, several years ago I lost control of my car on an icy patch on the way home from work. I should have been severely injured, but an angel stopped my car from careening into the forest. The car was totaled, but I only had a few bumps and bruises.

Then last year, I lost my job. After more than 20 years of service, the situation seemed impossible. As time elapsed, the possibility of finding a satisfying position grew dim. But God intervened and made a way where man couldn't!

Yes, God does **great things without number**!

So today, have faith – despite the man-made sea of desperation. Going to, coming from, and while at work, anything might happen – even to a *Christ Worker*. There will be trying times. Challenging times. Perhaps horrible times. Yet your God remains in control. He stays with you at every moment – yes, even in seemingly hopeless moments.

Many things are beyond your reach, but nothing is ever beyond His reach. So seek Him, and commit your cause to Him. And rest assured, my friend, He does **great things without number** – things humans cannot accomplish. He is your awesome God!

Yes, today at work, have faith in **great things without number**. He will do it. Count on it.

Prayer

Father, at work today, may I demonstrate my confidence in You to accomplish the impossible in me and for You. Let Your light of possibilities come to life through me so Your glory is made known. In Your Son's name, I pray. Amen.

Suzanne Denis

Week 21, Day 2

where's your sweet spot

Reading

Matthew 23:11-12 [NIV] The greatest among you shall be your servant. Whoever exalts himself will be humbled, and whoever humbles himself will be exalted.

Reflection

So **where's your sweet spot** – being served or serving?

I once knew a woman who cleaned offices on the swing shift. She loved her job for two reasons: "I can be at home to give my kids hugs when they go to school and when they come back." And: "At work, I get to magically make the garbage of yesterday go away, and when the workers come in the morning, they find a fresh, clean day ahead of them." She smiled, *"The best part is that no one sees me do it."*

This lady lives to serve others.

Many people think humility is being a doormat for others to wipe their feet on, but they are wrong. When we are following Him, we are serving Him. Christian service is a mental, emotional, and spiritual state that centers on God's authority and our love for Him. When we do things in service to God, we can be confident that God is demonstrated in our demeanor and personality – rather than our own pride and self-centeredness.

You get it; don't you? When you have Christian humility, you don't have to demand your way. Instead, you partner with Jesus' way of getting things done and submit to His values.

So at work today, **where's your sweet spot**? Serving or being served? Today, be the greatest among your coworkers by being their servant. Let others exalt you by humbling yourself.

Yes today, **where's your sweet spot**? Serve God first, and then everything else will fall into place. After all, you <u>are</u> a *Christ Worker*.

Prayer

Lord, today at work, please give me strength to humble myself and serve – before my coworkers, before the people, and above all, before You. In Jesus' name, I pray. Amen.

Chris Summers

Week 21, Day 3

this kind of hope

Reading

Luke 24:5(b)-6(a) [NIV] "Why do you look for the living among the dead? He is not here; he has risen!

Romans 8:24(a) [NIV] For in this hope we were saved.

Hebrews 11:1 [NIV] Now faith is confidence in what we hope for and assurance about what we do not see.

Reflection

Isn't it wonderful? I mean, isn't it wonderful to be a Christian? Because of our faith in our risen Lord, you and I have hope. No one else in the whole world has **this kind of hope**.

It's amazing how **this kind of hope** changes everything. We are saved. We have assurances in what we do not see. With **this kind of hope**, we have what other religions only wish for. We have what atheists claim they don't need. But you and I know that, without **this kind of hope**, there is no eternal future worth having.

As a *Christ Worker*, take **this kind of hope** to work. Find His ways to share it with coworkers and the citizens you serve. Show all that it brings a new beginning with every step you take.

During this work week, show at work how transformational life can be with **this kind of hope**!

Prayer

Heavenly Father, thank You for **this kind of hope** in the wonderful gift of Your son! Help me to see and show the new wonder of the risen Lord in each day that I serve You and Your children. In Your Son's name, I pray. Amen.

Lyse-Ann Lacourse

Week 21, Day 4

Jesus is found

Reading

John 4:15(a) [NRSV] The woman said to him, "Sir, give me this water, so that I may never be thirsty"

John 4:50(a) [NRSV] Jesus said to him, "Go; your son will live."

Mark 6:41 [NRSV] Taking the five loaves and the two fish, he looked up to heaven, and blessed and broke the loaves, and gave them to his disciples to set before the people; and he divided the two fish among them all.

Reflection

Where I live, there is currently a TV series titled "Finding Jesus." Watching the first episode, I thought I must really be out of touch because I didn't even know Jesus was lost! After a few episodes, I was struck by the series' effort to find some physical connection to Jesus. I couldn't get past the fact that so many people just seem to be *looking for Jesus in all the wrong places.*

Jesus is found when He talked about Living Waters with the Samaritan woman. He is found when He healed the son of the royal official. **Jesus is found** when He served the multitudes with just five loaves and two fish.

He is found when you and I feed our community's hungry. When we build a Habitat home. When, in our capacity as *Christ Workers*, we serve others in His glory and, in doing so, receive a transformational experience ourselves. **Jesus is found** when our agencies give second chances to those who have been incarcerated. He is found when we open welcoming doors to public facilities. **Jesus is found** when the Golden Rule is applied in our workplace.

Today at work, you will find Jesus – repeatedly – if you serve Him by serving others.

So don't worry about "Finding Jesus." Unlike that TV show and so many people, you're not looking in all the wrong places. You know where He is. **Jesus is found** in the miracles He performed as recorded in scripture. **Jesus is found** in the miracles He performs in your own heart and in your own work. Today, **Jesus is found** wherever He leads you.

Prayer

Gracious God, thank You for the gift of Your Son, Jesus Christ. Let me be a faithful disciple in all I say and all I do. Let Jesus be found in how I serve others and how I serve You. In Your Son's name, I pray. Amen.

Larry Hanson

Week 21, Day 5

His Living Plan

Reading

John 3:16 [NIV] For this is how God loved the world: He gave his one and only Son, so that everyone who believes in him will not perish but have eternal life.

Luke 24:5(b) [NIV] "Why are you looking among the dead for someone who is alive?"

Romans 8:38(b)-39(b) [NLT] ... Neither death nor life ... indeed, nothing in all creation will ever be able to separate us from the love of God that is revealed in Christ Jesus our Lord.

Reflection

I was talking to one of my spiritual mentors, and I told him I don't have a Plan B. Jesus is my only plan. My old Plan B was a dead plan. The plan Jesus has is a living plan. You see, when I gave my life to Jesus, I realized that He gave His life for me! He has no dead plan for me, so why should I have a dead plan for myself?

I want **His Living Plan**: love, forgiveness, mercy, and compassion toward others. I need **His Living Plan**: to be a steward of all He pours into me and to be a steward of all I pour out into others – even the ones who don't like me.

Today – as you go to work – *are you ready*? Are you ready to get rid of your dead plan? Everything you think might work without your resurrected Savior is a dead plan. Do you really want a dead plan?

Today, take **His Living Plan**. It's worth it. **His Living Plan** is not a bad deal – for you and I have been involved in much worse Plan Bs – haven't we? And besides, you have no choice – if you want to live with Christ – today and for eternity – you have to take **His Living Plan** and follow it!

You will never die.

Prayer

Father, in the name of Jesus, I pray. Thank You for blessing my life. Thank You for keeping me humble through Your grace. Thank You for the thirst to stay with Your living plan. Amen.

Jimmy Davis, Jr.

Week 22, Day 1

Well done good and faithful

Reading

Matthew 25:29 [NLT] to those who use well what they are given, even more will be given, and they will have an abundance. However, from those who do nothing, even what little they have will be taken away.

Reflection

My church lost its music minister this week. He was a friend to my autistic son who loved watching the minister play. My son insisted we sit in the front pew so he could observe the minister closely as his hands glided across the keyboard. Their friendship led to the flowering of my son's own gift of music. And such relationships happened with so many in the congregation. It was no surprise that the church overflowed for the funeral. For decades, this music minister touched everyone by sharing his talents.

The Lord gives each of us talents – some we are born with, and some He lets us learn and develop. And just like my music minister, He gives us talents to be used in our own workplace.

So what are you doing with the workplace talents God has given you? As a *Christ Worker*, are you using them to glorify God? As others watch, do your workplace
talents bring them closer to God?

Today at work, be like my beloved music minister. Don't bury your workplace talents. Use them to glorify Him in every way possible. Share your talents with others who want to learn. Apply them to serve coworkers and citizens alike.

Yes, during this holy week, share your workplace talents so that they may multiply. At the end of your life on earth, let Him judge, **"Well done good and faithful** *Christ Worker."*

And at the end of each workday, hear Him whisper, **"Well done good and faithful** *Christ Worker."* Truly, you will have abundance.

Prayer

Father God, You bless me with many talents. Please never let me take them for granted. Let me share my talents with everyone in a manner that You receive the glory. I ask this in the name of Your Son, Jesus. Amen!

Stephen Pincus

Week 22, Day 2

what seems the impossible

Reading

Exodus 3:10(a) [NLT] Now go, for I am sending you…

Exodus 3:11(a) [NLT] But Moses protested to God, "Who am I …?"

Reflection

For several years, I volunteered at a church that ministers to the homeless. Early one morning, a man needed a colostomy bag. For days, he wrapped the abdominal opening with an old towel in an effort to absorb the waste. Not only did this cause unbelievable stench throughout the church, he was growing very sick from the backup in his system. I hoped someone else would step in, but the pastor asked me to *handle it.*

Man, I did not volunteer for this. And the stench really didn't invite a personal relationship with this guy. Yet everyone was busy, so I searched all day for an agency willing to give (not sell) a bag. Late in the day, I found one. The pastor secured a nurse, and she prepared to attach the bag. But the man was shy and didn't want to be alone, undressed in front of a female nurse. Because we did become close that day, he insisted I hold his hand. So there I was: close-range, breathing stench, and upfront watching a procedure I really didn't want to know about.

"Who am I?" Sometimes God commands us to do **what seems the impossible**. In my case, it was to handle the colostomy bag crisis and get to know this man. If He had commanded me to do this on my first day of volunteering, I would've walked away and found a more comfortable means to serve Him. But He didn't. Like Moses, He prepared me – one step at a time, each day giving me harder tasks in His name. So on that particular day, He knew I could *handle it.*

"Who are you?" Today at work or where you volunteer, you'll be like Moses. God will command you to do **what seems the impossible**. You won't want to. The "stench" of the task may be great. You'll be afraid to fail. Like Moses, you will question His call – hoping He changes His mind or calls someone else to step in.

But today, He knows you are capable. He's prepared you. At His command, you will do **what seems the impossible**. You will *handle it*!

Prayer

Father God, give me strength to respond. You are preparing me for something. When You command me to do **what seems the impossible**, let me not ask "Who am I?" I know who You are, and that's all that matters. In Your Son's name, I pray. Amen.

James D. Slack

Week 22, Day 3

sow from the heart condition

Reading

2 Corinthians 9:6(b)-7 [ESV] whoever sows sparingly will also reap sparingly, and whoever sows bountifully will also reap bountifully. Each one must give as he has decided in his heart, not reluctantly or under compulsion, for God loves a cheerful giver.

Reflection

In the modern world, we are blessed to have medical technology that keeps us living longer. This is especially true with cardiology. Advancements help people with heart conditions in a wide variety of ways from cholesterol medications to stents to bypass surgery.

Yet there is another kind of heart condition that affects everyone, even those who are in the best physical health. God has given you a *spiritual heart condition*. It is without blockage. He expects you and me to give our best from that heart in all we do. He warns us of the consequences of giving less – of doing things reluctantly or because we have to. If we go through the motions when we sow, we certainly will reap sparingly. God wants you and me to give cheerfully, voluntarily, and enthusiastically – in all dimensions of our walk with Jesus.

How is your spiritual heart condition at work? *It is without blockage.* So are you giving freely, voluntarily, and enthusiastically from that heart?

At work today, **sow from the heart condition** He has given you. Reap bountifully.

Prayer

Lord, today at work, help me give all I have from my heart because I work for You. In Your name, I pray. Amen.

Chris Summers

Week 22, Day 4

do not be troubled

Reading

John 14:27 [KJV] Peace I leave with you, my peace I give unto you: not as the world giveth, give I unto you. Let not your heart be troubled, neither let it be afraid.

1 Peter 3:14-15 [KJV] But and if ye suffer for righteousness' sake, happy are ye: and be not afraid of their terror, neither be troubled; But sanctify the Lord God in your hearts: and be ready always to give an answer to every man that asketh you a reason of the hope that is in you with meekness and fear.

Reflection

In areas of my country, fledgling churches can no longer meet in public schools. Military chaplains are forced out for taking stands on the principles of God. One local government is trying to censor pastors' sermons. Some private businesses, owned by Christians, are penalized for taking stands on sin. Modern society is attacking the only moral standard – His Word.

All this is troubling, and it is easy to spiral into the dark abyss of hopelessness. The temporal takes our eyes off the eternal. The horizontal variables take our attention from our vertical relationship with the heavenly Father. This affects our capacity to be *Christ Workers.*

But the trials and persecutions of this present age are no different than ages past. And our Savior has not forgotten us. He remains the One who calms our troubled hearts and provides the peace that only an eternal perspective can provide. A perspective and hope He has asked us to share with others – even in the midst of adversity – especially when our faith is under siege.

So today at work – **do not be troubled**. It doesn't matter if you're a *Christ Worker* at a fledgling church or at a school that no longer lets churches use its vacant rooms on Sundays or at a government agency that questions sermons or at a private enterprise standing for Christ. In your work, mitigate the challenges presented by the horizontal, and share the hope of Christ.

At work today, **do not be troubled**. Focus on the peace only He can bring – and share it!

Prayer

Abba Father, in the name of Jesus, I pray. I ask for courage on this workday. I ask for Your peace upon my heart as I reach into the darkness with the hope of the Gospel. Help me keep my eternal focus upon Your word and promises. Use me to be a voice to those troubled by the cares of this world. Amen.

Bill Dudley

Week 22, Day 5

as you water others

Reading

Proverbs 11:25(b) [KJV] and he that watereth shall be watered also himself.

Reflection

My great grandmother had a very large garden. Each time I spent the night, she gave me the job of watering it – taking several hours to soak the corn, green beans, tomatoes, and sweet potatoes. I was young, and watering the garden was not my favorite thing to do at her house.

But my great grandmother taught me a lot about watering – much more than helping to give a bountiful crop of vegetables to my family. She also taught me that, with a giving heart, you would be watered **as you water others**.

Now that I have given my life to Jesus, I go out of my way to water others and show them how much I am watered in return.

Today at work, as Jesus waters you with His love, healing, joy, peace, strength, grace, and kindness – water others with the same. And **as you water others**, Jesus will water you even more. Like my great grandmother's garden, the crops you harvest will be bountiful!

Prayer

Father, in the name of Jesus, I pray. Thank You for sending me so much water! Continue to create in me a giving heart as I will water others as You water me. Amen.

Jimmy Davis, Jr.

Week 23, Day 1

Love less like others expect

Reading

1 Corinthians 13:4-7 [ESV] Love is patient and kind; love does not envy or boast; it is not arrogant or rude. It does not insist on its own way; it is not irritable or resentful; it does not rejoice at wrongdoing, but rejoices with the truth. Love bears all things, believes all things, hopes all things, endures all things.

1 John 4:8 [ESV] Anyone who does not love does not know God, because God is love.

Reflection

Workplace love – two words that usually don't go hand-in-hand. And I don't mean "affairs" but rather <u>Christian</u> love – the kind of love shown because we know God. For me, it seems so much easier just to show, well, indifference at work. On a good day, perhaps loyalty and accountability. Sometimes it's too easy to let anger and hatred pop up. But unconditional love? Unbounded love? Infinite love? I feel safer showing that kind of love anywhere <u>but</u> in the workplace.

Yet God gives me no excuse <u>not</u> to love – including in my workplace. And I've learned that Christian love is not mine to give. I am merely the channel through which God loves others – even coworkers and supervisors.

So today at work, *pass the love of Christ* to those around you. It's risky; I know, and there is always that one coworker who will reject His love and ridicule you behind your back. But that's OK. **Love less like others expect** and more like God commands. After all, Jesus died for you and your faults – all because of His great love for <u>you</u>.

Love is His tool to shape your life – even the hours you spend at work. So today, shrink your fears, swallow your pride, and *pass the love of Christ*. Approach that one hardened soul who may reject His love but who needs His love the most. **Love less like others expect**.

Prayer

Mighty God, without love I am nothing. Give me courage to set aside my envy, pride, and arrogance. Give me strength not to fall into indifference or settle for loyalty and accountability. Guide me away from anger and hatred. Instead, flood my heart with Your unconditional, unconventional, and unbelievable love for those who need it most. In Your Son's name, I pray. Amen.

Stephanie Van Straten

Week 23, Day 2

catch your breath

Reading

Psalm 34:18 [MSG] If your heart is broken, you'll find God right there; if you're kicked in the gut, He'll help you **catch your breath**.

Reflection

A close friend recently lost his 22-year old son. "My baby's dead" was all he could say. Unless you've been through it, there's no way anyone can understand the gut-wrenching pain induced by the loss of one's child.

No one, that is, but God. He lost His only son. Remember?

How many times do we read today's scripture and feel warm thoughts about our God as the Healer of broken hearts? Plenty. But this verse is so much stronger than just a warm reassurance. He supports us as our knees buckle. He breathes air into our lungs when sobbing and anxiety robs us of breath. He carries us through the worst times with one absolute guarantee – He'll never leave us to grieve or face any trial alone.

Today at work, pray you don't get that phone call about the death of a loved-one. But still, you will face a difficult situation. After all, what is more challenging than public service? You may have to choose whom to lay-off or what programs to discontinue. Your own job may be on the line. Or the project deadline is now, and the internet is down. Or perhaps your job may lead you face-to-face with death. Whatever happens, know this: there's nothing that God cannot help you handle. It can be terrible out there; I know, but He will help you **catch your breath**.

He calls you a *Christ Worker* because He wants you to serve others as He wants them served – despite <u>or perhaps because</u> of what's coming your way today.

So, just as my friend found in the loss of his son, God is right there for you, too. And He's gone through more than you can ever imagine. So He understands your pain and anxiety.

Today and tomorrow and the next day, too, He will help you **catch your breath**!

Prayer

Father, help me catch my breath. Today I bring You my sorrows, my worries, and all my doubts. Take them in Your hands and ease my condition. In return, give me the blessing of showing others how a *Christ Worker* is truly called by You! In Jesus' name, I pray. Amen.

Anne-Marie Amiel

Week 23, Day 3

He's gardening you

Reading

Mark 4:30-32 [NIRV] Again Jesus said, "What can we say God's kingdom is like? What story can we use to explain it? It is like a mustard seed, which is the smallest seed planted in the ground. But when you plant the seed, it grows. It becomes the largest of all garden plants. Its branches are so big that birds can rest in its shade."

Reflection

It's easy to feel small and unimportant. Houston is a huge city, and when I first moved here, I definitely felt that way. I had no real friends or family in the area. The nature of my job is entrepreneurial, and there are days when I'm out of the office. I kept wondering whether anyone would notice when I didn't show up. If I got hurt or sick, how long would it take someone to miss me? When would coworkers realize something was wrong?

So at first, I felt like a mustard seed that had just been planted. No roots. No evidence of existence. No worldly, tangible purpose. And, to make matters worse, the devil kept me thinking I wasn't good enough for this calling. You see, I forgot I had a Gardener.

It's taken about a year in my new work setting, but now I have good friends. I've laid more groundwork, experienced small amounts of success, and don't usually get that feeling of being small and unimportant. And the Lord has shown me that I am worthy of His calling – that I am growing into the *Christ Worker* He needs me to be – on and off the soccer field where I coach. And He confirms, in so many ways, that He is my Gardener and not just my Planter!

Perhaps you're starting a new job. You might now live in a strange town or work in a different organization. You, too, may feel rootless and have no evidence of purpose. No sense of calling.

Today at work, know that God planted your mustard seed right where He wants it. Jesus knows you are there and what you need to glorify Him. At this very moment, **He's gardening you**!

So keep growing! You are designed to be a mighty tree of destiny. You have purpose in His kingdom. He didn't plant you to be small and unimportant. That is why **He's gardening you**!

Prayer

Planter, Gardener, Father – thank You for planting Your tiny seeds in me. You are my Gardener, and I feel me growing each day. I hear Your calling, Father. Let me glorify You in this workday as Your seeds continue to grow. In Your Son's name, I pray. Amen.

Kathryn Saunders

Week 23, Day 4

take a chance and lead with love

Reading

1 Corinthians 13:13(b) [NKJV] but the greatest of these is love.

Reflection

Ah, it's springtime in my country, and *love is in the air* – and so are weddings. Wherever you live in the world, spring seems to be the season when beautiful gardens are filled with pastors and priests reciting this particular scripture to loving brides and grooms.

While used in weddings, this verse is also relevant in the workplace. I mean, as a *Christ Worker*, shouldn't I abide by love with my teammates and associates? Because love is the greatest value, shouldn't you and I bring love into where we work? And, when we do, shouldn't we use it to do more than simply increase the bottom line? After all, love also means to have a stake in the lives of those entrusted to us.

I know love is easier said than done in the workplace. Love means you can't lose patience. When saying "no," you must say it with love, not vengeance or indifference. And you can't be arrogant or provocative. Perhaps most challenging, you can't keep score as to wrongs suffered. You just have to let it go and live to work together another day.

To bring love into the equation is difficult but well worth the effort in the workplace. Marriages fail for lack of it, and there are more job resignations, terminations, and agency closings than there are divorces. So, if love is key to the "workplace" of marriage, it's also key to success in other settings – including that place where you're paid to spend most of your time.

Today at work, **take a chance and lead with love**. Doesn't matter if you are the supervisor or the junior person on staff. And who knows, maybe that springtime feeling of *love is in the air* will hold true throughout all the seasons – even the darkest of winters!

So yes, at work today, **take a chance and lead with love**.

Prayer

Father, thank You for the opportunity to serve Your purposes. Today help me abide by love with everyone I serve and all my coworkers and supervisors. In the mighty name of Your Son, my Lord and Savior, Jesus Christ, I pray today. Amen.

David Boisselle

Week 23, Day 5

let your attitude match your message

Reading

Romans 15:18 [NLT] Yet I dare not boast about anything except what Christ has done through me, bringing the Gentiles to God by my message and by the way I worked among them.

Reflection

My job on Life Row is a hall runner. I am permitted out of my cell, and I pass out food trays and juice to my brothers. On hot days, I give them a cup of ice so they can cool down a bit. I also stop by each cell for talk and fellowship.

Some of the brothers are Christian, and some are not. I try to treat them all the same. I try to love them the same. I try to show the same compassion to each, the same mercy to each, and the same forgiveness.

Sometimes, that's not easy to do. The heat in the cells is no different from the heat in the hallways, and everyone gets a little cranky. Sometimes, it's me, and sometimes, it's a brother in a cell. Regardless, I need to make adjustments, every now and then, to keep my attitude in line with my message.

All of us have different kinds of jobs, and we are around different kinds of people. But your attitude should never hinder brothers and sisters coming to God. When it does, it matters not who is at fault – you need to make an adjustment.

Today at work, as Jesus works in you, **let your attitude match your message**. Only then can those around you truly be served.

Prayer

Father, in the name of Jesus, I pray. As I work among Christians and non-Christians, continue to work on me and through me so my attitude won't hurt the message You plant inside my heart. Amen.

Jimmy Davis, Jr.

Week 24, Day 1

a burnt bridge

Reading

Galatians 6:9 [KJV] And let us not be weary in well doing: for in due season we shall reap, if we faint not.

Reflection

"Don't burn your bridges" is an idiom in my country that warns about being caustic or unprofessional with individuals you may need favors from in the future. In earlier years, I didn't heed that wisdom, and I felt the negative effects of burning a bridge or two. Later, as I became a Christian, I also realized that **a burnt bridge** hinders my ability to speak into an individual's life about Christ.

Once when talking to a group of peers, I got the opportunity to present the Gospel and was instantly confronted by someone who knew me much earlier in my Christian walk. He quickly recalled an email where I was not so professional and certainly not so Christian. God gave me the grace to be able, in front of the other men, to confess my fault and ask for forgiveness. I then used that moment as a doorway to show why we all need Christ.

While this situation turned out well, there are others in my professional career where I may never get the opportunity to right the wrong or to rebuild **a burnt bridge**. I have to remember just one flippant word or action taints my reputation as a Christian. Even worse, that one stupid act of ignoring the Gospel and reacting in my flesh *taints the reputation of Jesus Christ.*

As a *Christ Worker*, each workday you can impact someone's life by doing well in being His example. That coworker you dislike may one day be ready to hear the Gospel. The supervisor, who rubs you wrong, may be watching to see how you react to pressure. That citizen, searching for an empathic someone, may forever be changed by how you speak. In due season, blessings come if you do not faint in the face of adversity.

At work today, don't taint Christ with **a burnt bridge.** Build and do not burn!

Prayer

Father, give me wisdom and strength to be Your instrument of love to others. Through Christ, let me speak grace into coworkers just as You speak grace into me. May You receive all the glory for what You work in and through me. In Jesus' name, I say Amen!!!

Bill Dudley

Week 24, Day 2

always a gut check time

Reading

Luke 10:33 [NIV] But a Samaritan, as he traveled, came where the man was; and when he saw him, he took pity on him.

1 Samuel 16:7(b) [NIV] People look at the outward appearance, but the LORD looks at the heart.

Reflection

When you walk into a social services building, you see people suffering. Hurting from something. Bleeding from emotional wounds. Having physical needs that require attention. Broken families with broken hearts. The same is true when you walk into a court building or a building that houses homeless. You see people hurting on the streets. The hurt is real.

It's a challenge being a public servant, but it's an even greater challenge being a *Christian* public servant – a *Christ Worker*. Constant interaction with the wounded and broken can wear you down. Toward the end of the day, do you really want to come by another person desperate for help?

With each encounter, it's **always a gut check time**. Will you take the comfortable path – the easy one that leads quickly to the day's end? After all, no one will probably know if you do. And, if someone does, you can always rationalize why you did less than you could.

Or will you pay the price? Will you get your hands dirty one more time? Will you invest sweat and time? Will you forget fatigue and do some more heavy lifting?

Today at work, remember the Samaritan. Be the Samaritan. Remember how God judges you. You have a choice: make the world a bit colder by not giving? Or use time and energy to help and, thereby, make Jesus proud.

You know there's **always a gut check time**. At work today, what will you do?

Prayer

Lord, please give me the strength to see the need in others and take Your love to the hurting. In Your name, I pray. Amen.

Gary E. Roberts

Week 24, Day 3

steps are ordered by the Lord

Reading

Psalm 37:23(a) [NKJV] The steps of a *good* man are ordered by the LORD

Luke 23:26 [NKJV] Now as they led Him away, they laid hold of a certain man, Simon a Cyrenian, who was coming from the country, and on him they laid the cross that he might bear *it* after Jesus.

Matthew 16:24(b)-25 [NKJV] If anyone wishes to come after Me, he must deny himself, and take up his cross and follow Me. For whoever wishes to save his life will lose it; but whoever loses his life for My sake will find it.

Reflection

Ever wonder how you and I end up in unenviable situations? I often do. You may be thrust into the midst of coworkers arguing because one did not receive the promotion. I may receive a late night call about the death of a coworker's spouse or child. We may be supervisors given the task of telling a subordinate he's fired. You or I may have to respond to a citizen who will not get all the assistance needed to make it through the month with dignity.

As a *Christ Worker*, how are you supposed to react?

When Jesus carried the cross with the weight of our sins and the sins of the world, even He received help from Simon. I wonder if Simon thought, in retrospect, that his steps were the result of God's command – even though he was forced by soldiers to carry that cross.

Fact is *Christ Workers* have a duty to lift up the cross that others bear. And like Simon, that is why we find ourselves in very unenviable situations. Yes, the *Christ Worker's* **steps are ordered by the Lord**.

So you <u>are</u> in the right place in the right time. The question is Are you willing to lift and carry someone's cross?

Today at work, know your **steps are ordered by the Lord**. Walk, run, and react accordingly!

Prayer

Father God, I pray in Your Son's name that I may never be blind to the needs of others. Please allow me to have the strength to carry my own cross and to help others at the appropriate time by also lifting up their crosses. May I do this for love of You and in remembrance of the greatest gift bestowed upon me: Your Son's willingness to give His life for my sake. Amen!

Stephen Pincus

Week 24, Day 4

impossible to deny Christ

Reading

John 3:1-2 (NKJV) There was a man of the Pharisees named Nicodemus, a ruler of the Jews. This man came to Jesus by night and said to Him, "Rabbi, we know that You are a teacher come from God; for no one can do these signs that You do unless God is with him."

John 8:13 (NKJV) The Pharisees therefore said to Him, "You bear witness of Yourself; Your witness is not true."

John 19:39 (NKJV) And Nicodemus, who at first came to Jesus by night, also came, bringing a mixture of myrrh and aloes, about a hundred pounds.

Reflection

I've always been amazed at the dishonesty of the Pharisees in scripture. They knew Jesus came from God, and yet they persecuted Him. Their job was to show their people the way to God, and yet they knowingly rejected God's own Gift to the world. With few exceptions, like Nicodemus who became a follower of Christ, the Pharisees knew Him but denied Him.

Today you and I face *workplace Pharisees* – coworkers who surely must know He is Lord but still deny Him. A few are like Nicodemus, but so many more choose to remain completely dishonest. They know we are Christians and may even recognize us as good people, but they knowingly choose to treat us as an evil that must be purged.

How you react to their persecution will determine whether your testimony bears fruit. So be careful. Use Christ-like actions when it comes to that workplace Pharisee sitting next to you. Let that coworker see Christ shine through you.

Today at work, make it difficult for others to be dishonest about Christ. In fact, make it **impossible to deny Christ**. You never know how far your testimony of actions will take someone – even to the point of becoming a believer like Nicodemus!

Prayer

Lord, help me be like You. I want everyone at work to know You are in me. Use me in letting them know You are their God. Let them come to know You as

Savior. And, when they persecute me, let me rejoice because they knowingly rejected You first. In Your name, I pray. Amen.

Kevin J. Cooney

Week 24, Day 5

God notices misery

Reading

Genesis 29:32(a) [NLT] So Leah became pregnant and gave birth to a son. She named him Reuben, for she said, the Lord has noticed my misery

Reflection

A friend shared with me that she was in the wrong relationship, and God had revealed to her that she should leave. But she didn't obey God. Not only did the relationship with that guy fail, her relationship with God also fell apart. She did not value that **God notices misery** – including her misery. Instead, she valued more the wrong relationship she was in.

We all love many things. Many times we value the wrong things. We get comfortable in our sin. Before you know it, misery sets in, and you don't know why. It may be because of an intimate relationship that is wrong or something else at home is not right. It may be some kind of misery you bring to work. Or maybe it's work misery you take home.

Doesn't matter! Just value that **God notices misery** – especially your misery. Submit when He provides a solution. Be obedient when He calls you for change. Or will you be like my friend and just ignore God because you value that wrong thing in your life?

At work and at home, know that **God notices misery** – especially yours, especially today.

Prayer

Father, in the name of Jesus, I pray. Thank You for noticing me in my misery. Let me always have a grateful heart to appreciate Your calling and Your solution. Let me always be obedient to Your voice and Your command. Amen.

Jimmy Davis, Jr.

Week 25, Day 1

do His chores

Reading

John 14:15 [ESV] If you love me, you will keep my commandments.

1 John 5:3(b) [ESV] And his commandments are not burdensome.

Reflection

I took my mother for granted when I was growing up. She cared for me and protected me. With such a good mother, you'd think I would've done the chores she asked of me. But, like most children, I didn't want to do chores. I didn't understand why I had to do them and why she was upset.

When I grew a little older, my sister helped me understand. I should do Mom's chores because it is one way I can show her my love. And I found her chores were not that burdensome. And, just as I did chores for my mom on Earth, I learned I must do them for my Father in heaven.

As an adult, I see many Christians persecuted because they **do His chores** as He asks. Ridicule follows following His rules. Mockery accompanies obedience to Christ and His commandments. They laugh as we obey Someone we've never even seen, and they bet we do so out of fear.

They don't understand God loves you and me so much – yesterday, today, and tomorrow – that He sacrificed His Son for us. Now God asks you and me to follow His commandments and words – to **do His chores** – not out of fear but because it is one way to show God our love.

Today at work, it might be hard to **do His chores** – the tasks of love, honesty, selflessness, and patience sometimes don't fit well in the current business models of efficiency and bottom lines. And stress can tempt you to wonder why it's important to obey Him at <u>any</u> particular moment.

But don't be tempted! No, today, follow the instructions of your Father, and do so out of love. If you **do His chores** as He asks, they will not be burdensome!

Prayer

Heavenly Father, I know You have done so much for me despite my sin and doubt. Today at work, let my love for You flow through my obedience of Your commandments. In Your Son's name, I pray. Amen.

Brock Wolitarsky

Week 25, Day 2

a mountain can surely move

Reading

Matthew 21:21(b)-22 (NLT) if you have faith and don't doubt, you can do things like this and much more. You can even say to this mountain, "May you be lifted up and thrown into the sea," and it will happen. You can pray for anything, and if you have faith, you will receive it.

Reflection

In Greek, the words "doubt" and "belief" are closely tied. Doubt means to separate from belief, and belief means to trust in someone other than yourself. Doubt is hard to get rid of, and belief is hard to gain. But Jesus warns us not to separate from God. He calls us to place all our trust in Him. In doing so, *belief removes doubt*.

But don't you ever feel uncertain? I think all believers do at times. For me, it happens at night while I lay awake. I don't know when my future will arrive. You might feel uncertain about the future of your children because you are without work. You may feel uncertain about keeping the job you have. If you lose it, then what?

Uncertainty doesn't mean doubt. The uncertain believer continues to pray while the doubter gives up on faith. The trick is not to let uncertainty turn into doubt. The trick is to maintain faith.

So today, it's OK to feel uncertain about finding work or keeping a job. You don't know <u>when</u> the mountain will be moved. Just continue to trust in our Lord completely. Do so with audacity. Pray mightily against all odds. The wait for His answer may be long, but if you have faith, **a mountain can surely move**.

If you have faith, **a mountain can surely move**.

Prayer

Dear God, limit my uncertainty and never let it fester into doubt. You know my worries. They don't really matter because I trust in You with audacity. I pray mightily in Your name. My belief will never let You go. In Your Son's name, I pray. Amen.

Gregory Hunt

Week 25, Day 3

the heavenly outcome of work

Reading

Psalm 39:4 [NKJV] Lord make me to know my end, and what is the measure of my days, that I may know how frail I am.

Romans 14:12 [NKJV] So then each of us shall give account of himself to God.

Reflection

Some days, I feel like the detail work never ends. I finish the paperwork for one project, and there's another project waiting. I end one phone call, and the phone starts ringing again. At the very moment I begin to remember the spiritual, I'm swamped once more with the *immediacy of worldly detail*.

It's easy to rationalize the purpose of life as revolving around a zillion worldly details. And, since work consumes nearly one-third of life, it's easy to let the worldly detail of work keep focus from **the heavenly outcome of work**. And that, my friend, is embarrassing.

God's time is precious, and He can take it back any moment. When that happens, we'll have to account to God. Were you overwhelmed by worldly detail, especially at work? Was I too busy to remember **the heavenly outcome of work**?

You're right; worldly detail is important. Agencies could not function without it. The people we serve would be hurt if worldly detail was ignored. The media would justifiably attack if it sensed detail was neglected. And, frankly, we all would lose our jobs.

But, as a *Christ Worker*, keep perspective. Remember the people you serve need more hope and comfort than what is afforded just by worldly detail. Talk directly and frequently with God about that detail. Glorify Him always as you work through that detail. Do not forget why that detail is needed by Him. Just *don't get swamped by the detail*.

Nothing today is more important than **the heavenly outcome of work** as you go about doing its worldly detail. At your Great Accounting, you want to show your work-life was more than a ton of worldly paperwork and phone calls having nothing to do with His glory and His Kingdom.

A zillion worldly details simply won't cut it.

Prayer

Lord, help me. I get so caught up with worldly detail. I measure my worth with all the wrong tools and measures. Everything on this earth will fade to dust. Help me keep my eyes fixed on Your goals and not get swept away in worldly tasks. In Your name, I pray. Amen.

Angela Arbitter

Week 25, Day 4

motivation, delivery, and timing matter

Reading

Galatians 4:16 [GNT] have I become your enemy by telling you the truth?

Reflection

The Bible is full of statements about truth. It teaches we should never tell a lie – not even a white lie. Yet it also reminds us truth-telling is complicated. The truth can hurt and do damage. You can end up on someone's bad side by telling the truth. I mean, do you tell a friend the new hairstyle looks terrible? Or, for as long as possible, do you try to avoid the consequences of that particular truth? And naturally, you tell your children they'll receive Christmas gifts. But do you try to avoid the truth about that one thing they won't find under the tree? With children and adults – **motivation, delivery, and timing matter** when it comes to the truth.

The same is true in the workplace. There are times to tell the truth – and face the consequences for telling the truth. And you may be in trouble for telling the truth. You may admit an error. You might address a touchy situation with a colleague. You may have to confront an unwelcome truth with a supervisor. Because the truth can hurt and do damage – **motivation, delivery, and timing matter** in the workplace.

Today at work, may God help you know not only what to say but *how and when to say it*. Remember: **motivation, delivery, and timing matter**. When it comes to truth-telling, they matter a lot.

Prayer

Father God, I don't want to be divisive in what I say. Please help me always live and work as an agent of truth and righteousness. Help me know when to be discreet and when I need to be bold. Help me be a truth-teller – never a liar or a gossiper. But help me also find the limits of what must be shared and known. Keep my motives pure. In Your Son's name, I pray. Amen.

Eric Patterson

Week 25, Day 5

the meal of sharing something greater

Reading

1 Corinthians 10:31 [NLT] So whether you eat or drink, or whatever you do, do it all for the glory of God.

John 6:35(b) [NLT] I am the bread of life.

Reflection

Last week, two correctional officers blessed me. They gave me some of their lunch. It was Chinese food, and I have never tasted Chinese food before. It was really good! Chinese rice with chopped-up beef and duck sauce and soy sauce poured over everything. I was dancing in my cell eating that Chinese food!

The officers stood at the bars and watched my joy. But, while eating the food covered with those sauces, I gave them a meal, too. I took the opportunity to share the gospel. Turned out all three of us were hungry for more than Chinese food – we were hungry for *the bread of life*. And, receiving it, our hearts were also dancing!

At work, you are going to eat a meal. Depending on when you work, it may be breakfast, lunch, or dinner. Why not share some of it with those around you? It might be Chinese food, but it could be just a bologna sandwich. Someone may take joy in having a part of your meal, but then again, that person may not want any of it. It does not matter. Give them **the meal of sharing something greater** – something more filling than Chinese food or a bologna sandwich – share *the bread of life*.

Today at work, glorify God in what you eat. Give someone **the meal of sharing something greater**. And your hearts will be dancing!

Prayer

Father, in the name of Jesus, I pray. Thank You for *the bread of life*. It is a meal fit for a follower of a king! Let me share it with someone today. May my heart dance in Your glory. Amen.

Jimmy Davis, Jr.

Week 26, Day 1

show love instead

Reading

Luke 6:27(b) [NKJV] Love your enemies, do good to those who hate you

Ephesians 4:32 [NKJV] And be kind to one another, tenderhearted, forgiving one another, even as God in Christ forgave you.

Reflection

You've heard the motto *kill them with kindness*. Well, a friend did just that when faced with a difficult workplace situation. Each day, a coworker made a point to criticize everything she did. To top it off, this coworker was a Christian – at least, she wore a cross and had a bible on her desk. This coworker could never find anything positive to say about my friend's work, let alone a Christian word of support or fellowship.

Do you work with someone like that? What are you doing about it?

My friend kept brushing off the harsh words, and even more frustrating for this coworker, she decided to **show love instead**. Each day, she prayed for this coworker, and she presented forgiveness for such unchristian behavior. Finally, the coworker found no fun in the torment.

Business models have transformed many public and nonprofit work settings. Some changes are good, but those models can replace *kill them with kindness* with just *kill them*. And, even on a good workday, it's difficult to love one who wants you to have a bad workday.

My friend could have grieved. And, if her job were on the line, I supposed she would have filed a complaint. But in the meantime, she opted for God's help, not the help of a supervisor.

As a *Christ Worker*, make every effort to **show love instead**. Yes, love the one who hates you. Walk in kindness, tenderness, and forgiveness – as Christ does for you. It's going to be rough, but you are His ambassador in the hard times as well as the good times. Your actions under workplace fire can cause a positive shift in others.

So at work today, **show love instead**. Do so at every turn. Coworkers and those you serve will see God in you. And change will surely be nearer!

Prayer

Lord, on this workday, help me love the unloving, be tenderhearted to the cold-hearted, and forgive the unforgiving – the way You act toward me each day. In Your name, I pray. Amen.

Phoenecia Hill

Week 26, Day 2

nothing but the truth

Reading

Matthew 5:37 [ESV] Let what you say be simply 'Yes' or 'No'; anything more than this comes from evil.

Reflection

Answer *yes or no*. As a child, this is what my mother demanded to find out if I had done my chores. Too often, my answers were full of double-talk and excuses. Now as an adult, I realize they were lies.

You know, we encourage public servants and leaders in business and law to tell the truth – **nothing but the truth**. But nowadays we find more and more answers filled with *double-talk*. Even in our own work, excuses cover our tracks, and little white lies leave out part of the truth. We respond childishly – trying to avoid getting in trouble and seeking ways to manufacture a clear conscious. So we find excuses for late projects. We see double-talk in the misdirection of agencies. Silence replaces spoken truth when leaders of organizations make dreadful mistakes.

In today's world, it's OK to do that. I mean, it's not really lying, is it?

Today at work, stand up and answer with responsibility and honesty. Tell **nothing but the truth**. Let the glory of God shine in the integrity of your heart. Become one who can be trusted for a straight answer – with *neither double-talk nor excuse*.

Yes, today at work, tell **nothing but the truth**. Use His strength to answer simply *yes or no*. Anything else comes from evil.

Prayer

Heavenly Father, guide my words today, and lead me to honor You with simple truths. In Your Son's name, I pray. Amen.

Brock Wolitarsky

Week 26, Day 3

with spiritual eyes

Reading

I Samuel 17:17-19 [CJB] Yishai said to David his son, "Please take your brothers five bushels of this roasted grain and these ten loaves of bread; hurry, and carry them to your brothers at the camp. Also bring these ten cheeses to their field officer. Find out if your brothers are well, and bring back some token from them. Sha'ul and your brothers, with all the army of Isra'el, are in the Elah Valley, fighting the P'lishtim."

Reflection

I'm blessed with a job that allows me to live and work in Israel!

The best benefit is being able to visit many biblical sites – like the time I stood on the hill where the Philistines camped, across the Elah Valley where the Israelites waited. What struck me, as I stood there, was how David was just a young teenager who was asked to do *a simple task*: deliver food and report back on the well-being of his brothers.

But when he saw Goliath and heard the challenge, he viewed the situation differently – **with spiritual eyes**. And you know the rest of the story. David rose to the challenge and killed Goliath but not in any manner Saul or either army expected.

How many times in your job are you asked to do *a simple task*?

Do you see that task from a human view, or do you look **with spiritual eyes** when there may be a larger challenge to conquer? To our human eyes it may seem daunting, but through faith in God, you can rise to any task He requires.

Today at work, be like David. View the task **with spiritual eyes**. And be amazed at what you can conquer!

Prayer

Lord, You are a great and wonderful God! Thank You for caring for me and sustaining me in my body, home, and workplace. Help me see things **with spiritual eyes**, and guide me to assist in situations where another may only see difficulty. In Your name, I pray. Amen.

Andy Scharein
(Disclaimer: the views expressed are the author's and do not represent his employer.)

Week 26, Day 4

still enough

Reading

Psalm 46:10(a) [KJV] Be still and know that I am God...

Reflection

How often do we approach work or learning with *stillness*? Yesterday I did, and as a result, I witnessed true blessings.

Engrossed by the topic presented in class, break time too easily appeared. But instead of wandering randomly, students chose to continue the conversation with their professor. The afternoon was beautiful as we walked across the campus lawn and the training of intellect continued. The uniqueness of our walk was its *stillness* – students spoke not one word. But we listened and hung on to every soft word spoken by the professor.

Surprisingly, the professor led us to a car. There, a best friend of 13 years waited. The resemblance was identifiable between human and hound. For both: a life full of work, a life full of passion, a life due honor and respect – honor for the years spent in faith and loyalty to each and their respective life tasks. This professor talked to the dog, with love of heart, before putting him back into the car. They needed each other, but both were pleased to share this quiet moment with students before returning to class.

As we walked back across the lawn, I felt the spirit of God embrace and touch my heart. Did the other students feel what I felt? Did our professor even know the tribute that God had just orchestrated for us that day? A declaration that *God is here* – in the calm passion of classroom discussion, in the beauty of a campus, in the quiet of learning during that walk, in the caring between human and hound, and in the compassion between professor and student. *God is truly here* if we only remain **still enough** to realize His quiet blessings.

Today at work, be **still enough** so Jesus can show Himself through the many quiet miracles of the day – those things that transpire but once and are gone forever. Be **still enough** to allow God's spirit and presence to work in your workday.

Yes, today be **still enough** to witness the love He so freely shows and gives – so you, too, can attest that *God is truly here*!

<u>Prayer</u>

Father, in the fray of work and classes, help me be **still enough** to know You are God and You are truly here! In Your Son's name, I pray. Amen.

Tracie M. Beller

Week 26, Day 5

shine out but not on

Reading

Psalm 100:2 [HCSB] Serve the Lord with gladness; come before Him with joyful songs.

2 Corinthians 4:6; 10:17 [HCSB] For God who said, "Let light shine out of darkness," has shone in our hearts to give the light of the knowledge of God's glory in the face of Jesus Christ... So the one who boasts must boast in the Lord.

Reflection

The other day a brother stopped me in the yard. At the end of our talk, I asked him to pray for me. He looked at me like I was strange. Of all the men on Life Row, he thought I would be the last one ever to need prayer. To this brother, I am always so cheerful and confident. I serve the Lord with strength and gladness. I praise my Lord with joyful songs. So this brother could not imagine me having trouble in my Walk.

He is wrong, and his words did not let me sleep that night.

Do my gladness and joy make me look like I am boasting about myself? Do I come across as the Christian who never has any problems here on Life Row?

Sometimes, shining the light can give the wrong effect. It can blind a brother seeking a way out of the darkness. It can prevent others from helping me in my own darkness.

I am now more watchful. I do not want others to think of me as "perfect" or boastful.

Today at work and throughout the weekend, don't let anyone see your light for Christ as a light for yourself. Just let the light **shine out but not on**. If you don't, it will be helpful to no one living in darkness – including those times when you live in darkness, too.

Today let the light **shine out but not on**. It shines only for the glory of Christ.

Prayer

Father in the name of Jesus, I pray. Shine through me but let others never think You are shining on me. The glory is Yours and Yours alone. Amen.

Jimmy Davis, Jr.

Week 27, Day 1

a hotdog, a spare rib, or even buttered popcorn

Reading

John 6:35(b) [NKJV] I am the bread of life. He who comes to Me shall never hunger, and he who believes in Me shall never thirst.

Reflection

Well, it's the first day of the workweek, and I'm still thinking about the weekend. I had a good time, and I guess I ate a lot of food. Went to a baseball game and ate hotdogs. Went to a great restaurant and had spare ribs. Went to a movie and had my share of buttered popcorn.

Yes, I guess I ate a lot of food over the weekend! But I also ate something much more important – something much more satisfying – *the Bread of Life.*

You see, life consists of food that goes beyond the physical. There is the food specifically intended for your soul. And true nourishment for the soul comes from our Creator and Him alone. It does not come from **a hotdog, a spare rib, or even buttered popcorn.**

And while you may attempt to fill your soul-hunger with other types of spiritual food, it will never be as satisfying and complete as Jesus living inside you.

So as this workweek begins, be glad you had a great weekend that included some really good food. And, who knows – today's lunch may include **a hotdog, a spare rib, or even buttered popcorn**. That's fine. But it will not get you to eternity. That kind of food comes from Him, not a baseball game, a restaurant, or a movie theater. It comes only from Him.

So stay alive, my friend! Find the break time to eat more than **a hotdog, a spare rib, or even buttered popcorn**. Pray, read the Word, and fellowship with Jesus and His saints.

And at work today, you will not hunger.

Prayer

Lord, fill me with the Bread of Life throughout this workday. I do not want to hunger. In your Name, I pray. Amen.

Chris Summers

Week 27, Day 2

highlight the beauty

Reading

1 Peter 3:3-4 [ESV] Do not let your adorning be external—the braiding of hair and the putting on of gold jewelry, or the clothing you wear— but let your adorning be the hidden person of the heart with the imperishable beauty of a gentle and quiet spirit, which in God's sight is very precious.

Reflection

Today I pulled over to take a photograph of the beautiful trees bursting with color overflowing onto the road beneath them. I drive this road to and from work every day just like others, but how many actually notice the beauty of God's creation as they pass by?

Too often, we get caught in the habit of living-in-extremes – work desperately hard for five days and on Saturday pay attention to the enjoyable aspects of life. The reality is this: as *Christ Workers*, we have the opportunity to **highlight the beauty** so often missed by those who just focus on their destination.

Beauty is less about perfectly planned outings and more about appreciating the everyday miracles our Creator sets before you. Regardless of what happens, there is beauty to be discovered.

So take a moment to **highlight the beauty** Christ places within you – love of God, love of others, a gentle heart, a peaceful spirit. Share that beauty with the rest of His creation, letting all know how much He loves them, too.

And today at work, **highlight the beauty** in your environment – the people you come in contact with, what is said, and the work that is done. As long as you know your Creator is above and give Him all the glory, everything that surrounds you will be exactly as He wants it.

Yes, **highlight the beauty** everywhere – even on that road to and from work. And then take comfort knowing it's all His beauty.

Prayer

Lord, here I am; now send me. Let me be the light that glorifies the miracles easily missed. Thank You for the beauty You blessed me with and the guidance I would be so lost without. In Jesus' name, I pray. Amen.

Stephanie Van Straten

Week 27, Day 3

seems more impossible than not

Reading

Luke 24:2 [NIV] They found the stone rolled away from the tomb

Jeremiah 29:11(b) [NIV] plans to give you hope and a future

Philippians 4:13(a) [NIV] I can do all this through him

Reflection

Nothing seems as impossible as Jesus rising from the dead and rolling away the heavy stone that kept Him entombed. But God had a plan for the life of Jesus – how He would teach people then and now – how He would touch their hearts then and now – and how He would give His life for the forgiveness of all sins then and now.

And God has a plan for your life, too. That includes a plan for your job and career. A plan that removes the heavy stone, offers you His work, and allows you to serve others and Him.

But that doesn't mean it will all be easy. You know today will present struggles and doubts. That difficult coworker. Your overbearing boss. The never-ending project. And the rude citizen you are trying to serve. Yes, work often **seems more impossible than not**. Sometimes you just want to stay in bed and hide under the covers – like a tomb with a heavy stone keeping all out.

When work **seems more impossible than not**, keep your faith in Jesus! He has a plan – at work and in your life. You can come out of your tomb because all things are possible – but only through Him. And the same Jesus, who died and rose again, is with you at work – today! The God who removed the heavy stone from Jesus' tomb has already done the same for you!

So today at work, remember Jesus rose to be with you. And the heavy stone is already gone.

Prayer

God, I thank You for giving me Your only son. I thank You for making the impossible possible and for being with me during my hardest times. In Your Son's name, I pray. Amen.

Christopher Sean Meconnahey

Week 27, Day 4

and don't be afraid

Reading

Isaiah 55-9 [NIV] As the heavens are higher than the earth, so are my ways higher than your ways and my thoughts than your thoughts.

Psalm 56:3-4(b) [NIV] When I am afraid, I put my trust in you... What can mere mortals do to me?

Reflection

We all know the workplace environment can be quite stressful. It's easy to get nervous and even fearful when, for instance, a new mayor has a different agenda – or a new department head turns into the ultimate micromanager. Then there's the irritable citizen willing to go to the top because, no matter how hard you try, he doesn't like the outcome. Worse yet, what if there's another reduction-in-force? What if you get demoted or fired?

You know the stress and fear I'm talking about?

Things at work may not go right despite your best efforts. And, when bad things happen, it's easy to wonder if God is working on your behalf. But as a *Christ Worker*, you're called to trust Him – even in the midst of workplace storms – even when career doors slam shut.

And don't be afraid. His ways are higher than your ways! He has something good or better for you – in that same workplace or in another. And He's trying to teach you something. What appears to be drastic is a way for Him to get you refocused – on His ways. You may not understand – you don't have to understand. All you need do is just trust God completely **and don't be afraid**. When mere mortals upset your apple cart, remember God is still on your side. And He will use the situation to bring you closer to Him.

So as you start this workweek – trust God completely, **and don't be afraid**. When something happens, pray up that situation. Place all circumstances in His loving hands. And remember *His ways are higher than your ways* – always.

Yes today at work, seek His ways with all of your heart. And when things go badly – trust God completely, **and don't be afraid**. After all, the heavens are higher than the earth, and He is the One in total control of every outcome.

And you belong to Him.

Prayer

Dear heavenly Father, I thank and praise You with all of my heart, for protecting me <u>always</u> – especially when I am afraid. Help me know and trust You in every situation regardless of the outcome. Help me understand You are in control and Your ways are higher than mine. In Jesus' name, I pray. Amen.

Wendy Standorf

Week 27, Day 5

don't abuse God's freedom

Reading

Galatians 5:13 [MSG] It is absolutely clear that God has called you to a free life. Just make sure that you don't use this freedom as an excuse to do whatever you want to do and destroy your freedom. Rather, use your freedom to serve one another in love; that's how freedom grows.

Reflection

One day last month, I lost my cool. I got frustrated with a brother. A correctional officer heard me and asked if I was OK. I told him I was, but he knew better. And so he repeated, "No! Look at me. A-r-e y-o-u OK?"

As the correctional officer walked away, I got back in the right spirit. When I saw him again, I apologized. I also apologized to the brother who I shouted at.

You see, God has granted me a lot of freedom here on Life Row. I am trusted. Others depend on me. I even minister to the correctional officers. And so gradually my freedoms have grown. Oh, I know it's still prison, but I am graced with so many blessings from the privileges I have.

Yet there I stood – using this freedom as an excuse to get mad and shout at a brother. And then using it to be annoyed with a correctional officer who was only showing concern over me. My actions and attitude could have destroyed my freedom.

Your freedom is found in every aspect of your life. And you might act like me sometimes, taking your freedom for granted and using it to hurt someone. This can happen in your home, I know, and it can also happen where you spend most of your time each day – at work.

So at work today, be careful and **don't abuse God's freedom**. You might lose it. Instead, use the freedom God gives you to serve – not hurt – someone else.

Yes, **don't abuse God's freedom**. Use it to serve, not hurt.

And watch how He lets that freedom grow!

Prayer

Father, in the name of Jesus, I pray. Thank You for Your unfailing grace toward me. Forgive me when I abuse Your freedom. Help me use it to help others. Amen.

Jimmy Davis, Jr.

Week 28, Day 1

yelling and shouting

Reading

Mark 15:13 [NIV; MSG] "Crucify him!" they shouted... They yelled, "Nail him to a cross!"

Reflection

I am told in my country we used to love public executions. They were the entertainment event of the 18th and 19th centuries – kind of like the Super Bowl or the World Cup today. The day of the hanging, thousands began to gather hoping for a show and possibly a souvenir – a strand of the noose, rips of the shirt, or a shoe cast off at the jerk of the neck. The execution day often began in church where the pastor strongly condemned the doomed person. Then a procession to the hanging tree – with the condemned leading the way. And all along the way, people were **yelling and shouting**, enjoying the spectacle.

It was no different with the execution of Jesus, except His was bloodier and much more painful. Yet the crowd was still there – **yelling and shouting** – wanting to be entertained. Perhaps seeking a souvenir. Watching with family and friends.

Today we're much more "civilized." When actually executing someone, it's done in ways so the condemned cannot hear the **yelling and shouting**. When we *symbolically* execute someone – like at work or in our private lives – the **yelling and shouting** usually comes in quiet forms of whispers, glances, and gossip.

It's easy to get caught up in the process. It's easy to get caught up in the event and think not about consequence. Just as in Jesus' time, we like the show of something public. We seek a souvenir. And yes, we don't mind **yelling and shouting** in "civilized" ways.

Today, at work and in your private life, think twice about **yelling and shouting** at someone's misfortunate. They may deserve it, or they may not. Either way, before you start **yelling and shouting**, think about what Jesus heard. Think about what He felt.

Prayer

Father God, I grieve at what Jesus heard and felt amidst those wanting entertainment. Give me strength to remember Your son the next time I get the urge to be part of the crowd. It is in His name that I pray. Amen.

Bill Dudley

Week 28, Day 2

forget self-help

Reading

Ecclesiastes 9:17-18 [NIV] The quiet words of the wise are more to be heeded than the shouts of a ruler of fools. Wisdom is better than weapons of war, but one sinner destroys much good.

Proverbs 14:12 [NIV] There is a way that seems right to a man, but in the end it leads to death.

Reflection

We live in a self-help society where people preach their personal version of wisdom. From books that fill the stores to the coworker who has a solution to every problem, this day-and-age is obsessed with self-fixing problems. Yet despite this abundance of "supposed wisdom," families and businesses fail. Sin abounds, and the next social experiment looks to "fix" *you*.

Today do you have a tough decision to make? About a task or project? About a coworker, supervisor, or subordinate? About how to confront a situation? Or perhaps you must make a decision about your own job or career.

Will "self-help" really suffice?

When it comes to wisdom, **forget self-help**. Only God's word contains wisdom and conveys the responsibility to exercise this wisdom in your everyday world. Only God's wisdom is long-lasting – it's been there since the beginning and will be there until the end of time. And it works.

So when seeking wisdom in the workplace, remember the source. Is it you? Some faddish book? A manual created by committee? Or is it something more lasting? As the Giver of eternal wisdom, God will *help you out* in His trusted way.

As this workday begins, remember only He has the age-tested wisdom to lead you down the right path. Rely upon God's wisdom, and discern solutions beyond your own ability!

Yes, today and each workday, **forget self-help**. Only He can help you out!

Prayer

Lord, You bless me with Your wisdom. Even though it appears foolish to the world, help me to rely solely upon You for my direction. In Your name, I pray. Amen.

Jonathan Lantz

Week 28, Day 3

faithful in all He does

Reading

Psalm 33:4 [NIV] For the word of the Lord is right and true; he is **faithful in all he does.**

Galatians 6:9 [NIV] Let us not become weary in doing good, for at the proper time we will reap a harvest if we do not give up.

Reflection

I left the job. It wasn't easy; I loved my job, but the work environment was too much to take. High stress. Drama. Taking work stressors home to my family. Yes, it was too much for me.

So I put in numerous applications. I knew God had other plans for me. You see, I study His word and have faith in His word. And with each application, I prayed for God to strengthen me and to give me the ability to deal with everything.

And God provided! He gave me strength to come to work every day with a smile despite the stress. And eventually, He provided me with a new job. Not an ideal job, but a new job. One without the drama and stress. And it was easy to take the job because when God opens a door, you walk through it. So while I remain unsure of where my path will take me next, I am certain God will never steer me in the wrong direction. And so far, I am loving my new job!

If you feel like it's time to seek a new job, don't do it on your own. Faith in God means faith in His word. Go to His word, pray about it, and see where He leads you. Do not become weary, and know He is **faithful in all He does**!

Prayer

Thank You for guiding me, Lord. Thank You for Your faithfulness to me. Help me to continue to make You the center of my journey. I work for You, Lord. Help me in doing Your will. In Your name, I pray. Amen.

Logan Dickens

Week 28, Day 4

approved in His sight

Reading

Matthew 6:3-4 [NKJV] But when you do a charitable deed, do not let your left hand know what your right hand is doing, that your charitable deed may be in secret; and your Father who sees in secret will Himself reward you openly.

Matthew 20:26-28 [NKJV] Yet it shall not be so among you; but whoever desires to become great among you, let him be your servant. And whoever desires to be first among you, let him be your slave – just as the son of man did not come to be served, but to serve, and to give His life a ransom for many.

Reflection

Let's face it; it's not easy being a servant. And it's really difficult being a *Christ Worker* – a *servant leader*. We are mocked by a public unaware that business principles must be balanced with (and sometimes sacrificed for) compassion and charity. We are ridiculed by political leaders who don't understand the meaning of *servanthood.*

Yes, most citizens barely acknowledge your servant leadership. Fewer still show any kind of appreciation. And that hurts even more when you go "above and beyond" to serve someone.

Yet your servant leadership is commendable before God – it is **approved in His sight** – for He sees what others fail to acknowledge or appreciate. He sees you as humbly serving His needs and the needs of His people.

So today at work, quietly remain a *Christ Worker*. Secretively be steadfast in your servanthood. No need to boast about your charitable deeds. Your heavenly Father already finds you **approved in His sight** – for what you do for His flock, in His workplace, in His world.

Yes, today at work, know you are **approved in His sight**. He secretly sees what you are doing. And He will reward you in eternal ways.

Prayer

Father, thank You for the opportunity to serve Your purposes. Help me follow Your Son, Jesus, who knew that being a servant leader is not easy. Give me strength to persevere despite a lack of appreciation and commendation in my workplace, secure in the knowledge that You provide the ultimate oversight of my life. In the mighty name of Your Son, my Lord and Savior, Jesus Christ, I pray today. Amen.

David Boisselle

Week 28, Day 5

let all things die

Reading

Romans 5:8 [NIV] But God showed his great love for us by sending Christ to die for us while we were still sinners.

Reflection

For a long time, I was so selfish I could not show love to my family. I could not share any peace with my mother. No hope or joy or even encouragement for my sisters. But that was before the blood of Jesus. Now I show love to my family – bountiful love – the love of Christ.

You see, it took a long time for me to die – a strange word coming from a man on Life Row. But something inside me had to die before I could show the love of Christ. And for me, that thing was my selfishness.

What needs to die in you? Shame? Regret? Envy? Judgement? Anger? Hatred? Bigotry? Fear? Control? Unforgiveness? Or do you have the same affliction I once had – selfishness?

Do these things die in church only to be resurrected at home? Do they die at home but reappear at work?

It is difficult, but just **let all things die** that keep you from showing the love of Christ.

Don't bring them to work, and don't take them home. Bury them in an unmarked grave.

Just **let all things die**.

Prayer

Father, in the name of Jesus, I pray. Thank You for Your unfailing love for me. The love You show through Your Son's blood shows me how to live and share it with others. Amen.

Jimmy Davis, Jr.

Week 29, Day 1

a fool by comparison

Reading

I Corinthians 3:18-19(a) [NKJV] Let no one deceive himself. If anyone among you seems to be wise in this age, let him become a fool that he may become wise. For the wisdom of this world is foolishness with God.

James 1:5 [NKJV] If any of you lacks wisdom, let him ask of God, who gives to all liberally and without reproach, and it will be given to him.

Reflection

The world views some occupations as filled with really smart people holding such titles as doctor, lawyer, or professor. While many of them avoid the *arrogance of title*, some do not. They believe lofty titles make them special like Old Testament kings. And they won't admit their own foolishness.

You don't have to look far into other professions to see what can happen from the *arrogance of title*. Regardless of occupation, people devise their own loftiness. Arrogance can come from gaining the title of group leader, unit head, or supervisor – as much as from titles like doctor, lawyer, or professor.

Do you see this in your own workplace? Does IQ skyrocket simply because of title?

Now, I'm not suggesting a flat-line organization. And Jesus had the title of Rabbi. But scripture reminds we are not on par with Jesus! And we are not fooling God – even if we fool the world around us. His wisdom proves each of us **a fool by comparison**.

As a *Christ Worker*, confess your wisdom is limited. Reject the arrogance of title. Proclaim you are **a fool by comparison**. Invite the God of the universe to come into your workplace and shed His wisdom upon you.

At work today, humbly ask for His wisdom and let others see you as **a fool by comparison**.

Prayer

Lord, You give wisdom. All I need do is ask for it. So I am asking You today to grant me Your wisdom in all I do and say, especially in decisions I make that can bless those whom I serve. In Your name, I pray. Amen.

Kevin J. Cooney

Week 29, Day 2

ointment of healing

Reading

Proverbs 17:22 [KJV] A merry heart doeth good like a medicine: but a broken spirit drieth the bones.

Philippians 4:4 [KJV] Rejoice in the Lord always; again I say rejoice.

Reflection

The media is fixed on the negative with stories of wickedness, sadness, and sorrow every time you turn on the TV. No wonder we see a multitude of broken spirits in our world. At times, my dry bones need a *mitigating influence*. And at home, that influence comes via my 5-month old daughter. When I walk into her presence, she smiles so brightly that it soothes any sorrow inflicted upon my soul. A good medicine to my heart, she truly is an **ointment of healing**.

At work, God positions you and me to be that same kind of **ointment of healing** – a mitigating influence on coworkers and the citizens we serve. Competition, the pressures of deadlines, and the demand for excellence lead to criticism and burnout. Workplace rumors lead to broken spirits. But as *Christ Workers*, we have the ability to change the hearts of others by displaying the joy of the LORD, His encouragement, and His empowerment.

Today be an **ointment of healing** in your workplace. Show His mitigating influence!

Prayer

Father, through Your Spirit, may my intentions focus on Your grace and blessing. Empower me to be an **ointment of healing** to those sickened by the influence of this world in my workplace. Use me to direct their gaze towards Your Son, the Lord Jesus. Glory and praise to You, and in Your Son's name, I pray. Amen.

Bill Dudley

Week 29, Day 3

the only thing you need to remember

Reading

Exodus: 13:3(b) [KJV] Remember this day, in which ye came out from Egypt, out of the house of bondage; for by strength of hand the Lord brought you out from this place.

Reflection

The older I get, the harder it is to remember everything. Oh, I try to compensate with lists: things to do, people to contact, issues to verify, resources to locate. These lists go on and on. In fact, I'm guilty of making lists of lists. And wouldn't you know, sometimes I forget where I place my lists!

Ever happen to you? If not, wait a decade! And in the meantime, consider the old Connie Smith gospel lyrics "Remember I'm human and humans forget; so remind me, remind me dear Lord" that were sung back in the day. Eventually, it rings true for all of us!

As you and I make plans at work – set goals, apply mission statements, propose projects – we may forget things. But let's just roll back the curtain of memory to look at the strength of the Lord's hand that brought us where we are. Let's remember He brought you and me out of bondage. We may forget how to deliver a lost list, but let's never forget Who delivered us!

Today you may serve a young, immature man reaping the consequences of his actions. Or you may serve an older woman victimized by difficult circumstances. As you serve, **the only thing you need to remember** is that, by the grace of God, you are rescued from bondage.

So *serve victoriously* in your workplace – *serve as a freed slave* committed to your Lord – the One who delivered you from bondage for a purpose. And that purpose is to serve Him victoriously in bringing others out of their own bondage.

Young or old, He delivered you – and that's **the only thing you need to remember**. Whatever else you forget, it'll be OK.

Prayer

Dear Lord, remind me of where You brought me from and where I could have been. Open my eyes to see where You are working today, and give me the strength to be Your faithful servant – Your freed slave! In the name of Jesus, I pray! Amen.

Debra Neal

Week 29, Day 4

you lack nothing

Reading

Psalm 23 [NIV] The LORD is my shepherd, I lack nothing. He makes me lie down in green pastures, he leads me beside quiet waters, he refreshes my soul. He guides me along the right paths for his name's sake. Even though I walk through the darkest valley, I will fear no evil, for you are with me; your rod and your staff, they comfort me. You prepare a table before me in the presence of my enemies. You anoint my head with oil; my cup overflows. Surely your goodness and love will follow me all the days of my life, and I will dwell in the house of the LORD forever.

Reflection

This may be the worst workweek of your life. Or perhaps that was last week. Or it could be next week. Responsible to change what is beyond your control. Interpersonal problems. Anxiety about another reduction-in-force. The job interview did not go well. The job interview went splendidly, yet still no phone call. Wait and worry – draining your energy. Wondering what you lack that others have.

As a *Christ Worker*, know **you lack nothing**. Our Lord is refreshing your soul right this moment. Feel Him? Feel His oil anointing your head? In the midst of all things going wrong, or could go wrong, is your cup not overflowing? It's true; **you lack nothing**.

Surely His goodness and love follow you throughout this particular workday as well as the next workday and all the ones that follow. Surely you dwell in His house – even in your wretched workplace.

So if this workweek is the darkest valley, He remains with you. And **you lack nothing**.

Prayer

My Heavenly Father, I thank You for refreshing my soul. I will be Your instrument in refreshing the souls of others in my daily Walk at work. Praise be to You! In Your Son's name, I pray. Amen.

Lyse-Ann Lacourse

Week 29, Day 5

you will be strong

Reading

2 Corinthians 12:10 [KJV] Therefore I take pleasure in infirmities, in reproaches, in necessities, in persecutions, in distresses for Christ's sake: for when I am weak, then am I strong.

Reflection

Last weekend I worked at a Kairos Prison Ministry event here on Life Row. I served homemade cookies, coffee, and soft drinks to 14 selected brothers and 8 free-world men. I also served the wonderful homemade meals this ministry brings to Life Row – so we were all very blessed!

But I had to serve a couple of brothers who persecuted me in the past. To be honest, I wanted to be weak – for my sake – and give them only the <u>impression</u> of me being strong. I could have gotten even for all the persecution by treating them differently than the rest. I could have given them less soft drinks in their cups, or I could have run out of sugar and powdered cream for their coffee. I could have made sure they got fewer cookies – and more of the ones that weren't their favorite. Oh, I could have given everyone second helpings of the homemade meals – only to run out before I got to their plates.

Surely, they would have recognized I was flexing my muscles.

But instead, I chose to be strong – not for their sake, nor for mine. So all weekend, I blessed them with the very <u>best</u> service I could give, and I was so very blessed in return. At first, those brothers thought I was being weak – humble because of what they did to me. But they soon got it: my weakness made me strong – *for Christ's sake.*

At work, do you ever find yourself in a similar situation? You have a chance to get even. Do you use your weakness for your own sake? Or do you surrender your weakness for His strength?

Today at work –don't fight back, and don't seek revenge. It's only when you are weak that **you will be strong** – strong *for Christ's sake.*

Prayer

Father, in the name of Jesus, I pray. Keep my mind on kingdom thoughts. I want to be strong – not for my sake but for Your Son's sake. It is only when I am weakest that I am able to share Your awesome love with others. Amen.
Jimmy Davis, Jr.

Week 30, Day 1

connect with the Father

Reading

Luke 5:16 (NIV) But Jesus often withdrew to lonely places and prayed

Reflection

The alarm buzzes. Your eyes open. It's another day. Your thoughts start racing overall thinking of what you have to do today. You make mental lists, and before you're out of bed, you're at work. You work eight hours, maybe more, and then head home to take care of other tasks. Go to bed, and then it starts all over again.

Life is busy! Sometimes it feels like there simply is no time for Bible study, prayer, and reflection. But we have to remind ourselves not one of us has ever held a job that is more important than the work Jesus did. His earthly ministry was the most significant task that ever has been performed on the earth. Yet, even He still took time to get away to **connect with the Father**.

If Jesus saw the need to break away from the busyness of life, then why shouldn't we do so also? Today, even if it means skipping lunch or staying up a few minutes past your bedtime, take time to **connect with the Father**. You may not feel like you have time to, but the truth is, you can't afford not to. Let's imitate Jesus' example.

Amid the chaos of your day, take a little time to withdraw and **connect with the Father**. You will definitely have a better day!

Prayer

Father, life can be so hectic and chaotic. In the rush of every day, I sometimes get caught up in the business of everyday life. Please give me the grace and strength to deal with all that comes my way. More importantly, though, let me remember to withdraw and connect with You each and every day through prayer. In Jesus' name I pray. Amen!

Hannah Shoop

Week 30, Day 2

think in a godly manner

Reading

Psalm 139:3(b)-4 [HCSB] You are aware of all my ways. Before a word is on my tongue, You know all about it, Lord.

Reflection

Sometimes it's so difficult to respond in a godly manner – let alone **think in a godly manner**. Today you may have a dispute with a coworker. Are you charged with waging battle with another agency unit? Perhaps you will be called in by your supervisor to talk about your performance or behavior. Are you that supervisor who has to discipline an uncooperative subordinate? Could be you're confronted with a citizen blaming you for the world's problems.

Today at work, it will be rough. But as hard as it can be, don't just talk in a godly manner – **think in a godly manner**. After all, He is aware of all your ways – *even those unspoken.*

Prayer

Dear Lord, help me act and **think in a godly manner**. I know You are watching me in all ways. But I also know Your love and mercy will guide me in all ways. So it is in Your name, I pray. Amen.

Chris Summers

Week 30, Day 3

delivery is everything

Reading

Proverbs 25:15 [ERV] With patience, you can make anyone change their thinking, even a ruler. Gentle speech is very powerful.

Reflection

I'm sure you've experienced the pain of trying to convince a stubborn supervisor to change a standard operating procedure. His response can sometimes be cautious. Then again, it may even be suspicious or defensive – despite your argument that modification will add either efficiency or effectiveness.

You'll make several attempts to change his mind but to no avail. You may question the rationale for the original procedure, and you might even ridicule it. But you never know who came up with it, nor the reasons for making it "standard." To suggest an alternative way of doing things, well ... may be viewed as an insult to the intelligence of those who built the procedure in the first place. And your supervisor might have had a part in it.

Remember **delivery is everything**. And scripture reminds us that *gentle speech is best*. With gentle speech, you can complement the current way of doing things and validate your supervisor's perspective. In that way, you might remove the defensiveness and make way for an open mind about your proposed modification.

Today at work, remember: **delivery is everything**. *Gentle speech is best*!

Prayer

Lord, give me a gentle tongue and a humble spirit as I propose changes in my work environment. Let my words be viewed as positive suggestions, and let no one take offense. In Your name, I pray. Amen.

Joycelyn Biggs

Week 30, Day 4

audacious faith

Reading

Mark 9:23(b) [NIV] Anything is possible if a person believes.

Reflection

My supervisor often tasks me with things that are, well, largely important. I tend to question my own ability to accomplish these tasks. Do I really have the skills to get the job done? How can my supervisor trust me so much?

The ability to trust someone takes a significant amount of faith. It's risky, and perhaps in some situations, **audacious faith** is needed. The ability to accomplish a difficult task also takes a significant amount of faith. Risky, it too requires **audacious faith**.

As a *Christ Worker*, God wants you to be audacious in your belief. To boldly proclaim God is with you on that project. So let **audacious faith** radiate from within! Trust in God's ability in your work and the work of others. Let yourself and others show how limitless our God is in your workplace!

Have **audacious faith** in completing all tasks. You will glorify God!

Prayer

Lord, You are Sovereign. You are more powerful than any worldly strength. Let me have **audacious faith** that allows Your limitless power to be active in my work life. Let Your will be done in my workplace for I am Your hands and feet. In Your Son's name, I pray. Amen.

Angela Arbitter

Week 30, Day 5

not to sell out

Reading

1 Kings 21:20 [NLT] "So, my enemy, you have found me!" Ahab exclaimed to Elijah. "Yes," Elijah answered, "I have come because you have sold yourself to what is evil in the LORD's sight."

Reflection

The other day, two brothers were about to fight in the yard. Others just stood by and said nothing to calm the situation. I guess most were scared, and some just wanted to see a fight. Like Ahab, each of them sold themselves to what is evil.

It's difficult **not to sell out** to evil. And there's a lot of selling out going on in this world. It happens in many ways. Remaining silent when someone is mistreated. Looking the other way when someone is bullied. Doing nothing when injustice occurs. Waiting to see what happens when someone's need for arrogance and control takes over.

And we all sell out at times. I do. But not on that day!

On that particular day, a couple of brothers from my church joined me in convincing those two brothers **not to sell out** to evil. *We were like Elijah*! As the brothers circled with clenched fists, we asked them if what they were about to do was pleasing in the Lord's sight. We claimed each had courage **not to sell out** like they were about to. We asked the same of the brothers watching. And we continued until their fists opened and the watching brothers were ashamed. What could have been ugly turned pleasing to our Lord.

Going to work, at work, and after work – *be like Elijah*! Today have courage **not to sell out.** When you see mistreatment, bullying, and injustice – don't wait to be found like Ahab. No, b*e like Elijah*! It's what's pleasing to our Lord.

In His sight, have courage **not to sell out.**

Prayer

Father, in the name of Jesus, I pray. Thank You for helping me be bold in not allowing evil to prevail. Thank You for giving me courage **not to sell out.** Amen.

Jimmy Davis, Jr.

Week 31, Day 1

believe, trust, and turn

Reading

Ephesians 1:19-20 [NLT] I also pray that you will understand the incredible greatness of God's power for us who believe him. This is the same mighty power that raised Christ from the dead and seated him in the place of honor at God's right hand in the heavenly realms.

Reflection

Have you ever had someone in your office who you can't seem to encourage? I recently had an appointment with a constituent who felt defeated by the system – defeated even though she was trying to do good. After my initial attempt to ease her mind, I recognized I wasn't very effective.

With a quick but silent prayer for guidance, I took a different angle to explain to this citizen how everything was working in her favor. I encouraged her to believe all things happen for a reason. And if she trusts God, her good actions will be rewarded later. While she wished things hadn't happened as they had, she left my office with a greater understanding and peace about her current situation and her future.

I, too, walked away with something. I remembered that my power comes from God. But my power only comes when I **believe, trust, and turn** to Him. Only then can I set a course that favors Him and have greater power to do His work.

So today as you begin your work week – **believe, trust, and turn** to God.

You will be a more powerful *Christ Worker*!

Prayer

Lord, Your power is awesome! I thank You for using me as Your vessel and working through me to share an encouraging word. I pray You will continue to remind me of Your power and allow me to have an attitude reflecting Your power in my workday. In Your name, I pray. Amen.

Deanna Alexander

Week 31, Day 2

such a despicable boss

Reading

Proverbs 16:12 [VOICE] When kings commit evil, it is despicable, because their thrones should be built on justice.

Philippians 2:3 [VOICE] Don't let selfishness and prideful agendas take over. Embrace true humility, and lift your heads to extend love to others.

Reflection

Last night I received a disturbing email from someone I mentor. Just a year ago, she was so excited about her first job. But things went south pretty quickly, and my friend is angry.

Seems her boss is bad. He favors some workers but not all. He keeps needed information from those he doesn't like. In an ostensibly collegial setting, he angers quickly against those who raise questions. He protects the ones "on his side" but not those he deems as "against him."

I tried to explain some people make despicable leaders. And sometimes every boss has a bad day. And a few bosses become despicable due to circumstance. And justice is always a casualty.

Scripture suggests leadership requires justice – even in the workplace. But you know; the toughest thing is not a supervisor who forgets or rejects that principle. No. The toughest thing is having to work with **such a despicable boss** in ways *pleasing to Christ*. And that means, despite the temptation, no worker can please the Lord through agendas of anger and getting even.

That's what I told my young, angry friend. She can't change the boss. But she can stay away from a prideful and selfish hidden agenda laced with anger and paybacks. For her sake, my friend must follow Christ: embrace humility and show His love to **such a despicable boss**.

Do you have a boss like hers? If so, don't plot ways to retaliate against injustices.

Today at work, just be humble. Lift your head to extend love, not anger. For **such a despicable boss** truly needs the love of Christ.

And Christ's love leads all to justice – even **such a despicable boss**!

Prayer

Father God, thank You for allowing me to mentor. Help me set the example by raising my head to extend Your love – regardless of who has forgotten to build his workplace throne on justice. Help me help others do the same. In Your Son's name, I pray. Amen.

James D. Slack

Week 31, Day 3

watches you and is watching over you

Reading

Psalm 121:5 [NLT] The LORD himself watches over you! The LORD stands beside you as your protective shade.

Matthew 10:29(b) [NLT] But not a single sparrow can fall to the ground without your Father knowing it.

Reflection

It's easy to get caught in an *iPhone birdcage* – you know; a picture or video is taken, an e-mail or tweet is sent, and now the whole world watches. Nothing is private. Everything can be recorded and forwarded – and you can't fly out of that cage once you're caught.

This is nothing new for Christians. After all, we've always lived in a sort of birdcage – one constructed by Him. He is always watching us and expecting us to act with radical integrity – since everything we see, say, and do reflect not just ourselves but also our faith and our Lord.

Yet in His birdcage, He is not just watching us. He is watching over us. Even when we make mistakes, He shades us with His protection. We belong to Him – He loves and forgives us – and that's why we are at home where He places us.

So when others land in their iPhone birdcages, do not join them. Our Lord already **watches you and is watching over you**. He knows what you are doing, but He also knows what is being done to you by this world. Just represent Him well, and be comforted by His protective shading. Walk the walk of faith. If He knows when a sparrow falls to the ground, He knows when you are in need of His help and guidance. He knows when you are tempted.

As you go to and from work today, fear not the photos and videos, e-mails and tweets you won't be a part of. After all, you don't live in their birdcage.

You already live in a place chosen by Him – where He **watches you and watches over you**. And that's a blessed place to dwell!

Prayer

Dear Lord, You are watching me and watching over me all the time in everything I do. Help me live in such a way that everything I do can be laid bare before You and my coworkers. Help me be a witness to Your goodness and grace in all that I do. In Your name, I pray. Amen.

Mary Manjikian

Week 31, Day 4

a teachful way

Reading

James 3:1(b) [NIV] we who teach will be judged more strictly.

Jeremiah 33:3 [NIV] Call to me and I will answer you and tell you great and unsearchable things you do not know.

Reflection

I heard God's calling for many years before I agreed to be a teacher. I thought for sure His call was for someone else – certainly not me. And, frankly, I was afraid. It's one thing to be taught but to teach someone else? That's an awesome responsibility, and I did not want to be judged so strictly. But once I heeded God's calling, I felt a new kind of peace.

As good public servants, so many of us "teach." If you supervise, you teach. If you train apprentices, you teach. If you're an informal mentor to a new coworker, you teach. When an intern asks for advice, you teach. If you volunteer to help a nonprofit, chances are you teach someone something.

I have found that teaching is never a question of knowing more than anyone else; it's a process of finding, well, **a teachful way** of explaining what you have learned. And this means the standards are higher for you and me.

As a *Christ Worker*, you and I also teach in another way. We are obligated to share the Gospel – including at work. Yet there is a sacred responsibility not to lead others astray when it comes to the Good News. And God is always calling you and me to be *His teacher*.

So today at work, work at being *His teacher*. In addition to helping others find workplace knowledge, find **a teachful way** to show them the Good News of Jesus Christ. Yes, you will be held at a higher standard, but you will also feel great peace in following His calling.

Don't wait many years before you heed God's calling to teach. Today at work, find **a teachful way** to show His ways!

Prayer

Lord, I pray for wisdom and the ability to help my students learn to love learning and to love You. Help me find **a teachful way** to lead them to You. In Your name, I pray. Amen.

Stan Best

Week 31, Day 5

you step up

Reading

Daniel 11:32 [HSCB] With flattery he will corrupt those who act wickedly toward the covenant, but the people who know their God will be strong and take action.

Psalm 75:6-7 [HCSB] Exaltation does not come from the east, the west, or the desert, for God is the Judge: He brings down one and exalts another.

Reflection

Yesterday, a talk with a brother led to bad-mouthing another brother. Does this happen to you? At work, is there someone who bad-mouths another coworker? It happens when the one being bad-mouthed is not around. And it is always about the past, never the future.

What do you do when someone bad-mouths another?

I stopped the brother. I reminded him that when God promotes someone no one could hinder him – except himself. I said, "I see how God is changing your heart and how you deserve to be promoted by God." But I also told him, "When you judge someone else, you see only the past – and if you judge your brother's past, God might just bring you down – for God is working in the heart of that brother you're bad-mouthing."

So the bad-mouthing stopped, and I pray he will see all of his brothers from God's point of view. He needs to be strong and take action against those who don't quite know God. He must be strong and take action against himself when he is tempted so he will know God better.

At work today, someone will bad-mouth another. Perhaps you will bad-mouth someone. Be strong and take action. Affirm God is at work. Find a way to say, even if it is to you, *only God promotes and only God brings down.*

If **you step up**, others will know your God. If **you step up** against yourself, you will also know your God a little better!

Prayer

Father, in the name of Jesus, I pray. Thank You for giving me a new heart to see Your sons and daughters as You see them – worthy of Your exaltation. Give me strength to affirm and not to judge. Let me see their future and not their past as You see my future and not my past. Amen.

Jimmy Davis, Jr.

Week 32, Day 1

no matter how many NO's you endure

Reading

Luke 1:37 [KJV] For with God nothing shall be impossible

Reflection

Not qualified. Thank you for your application, but we've selected a more experienced candidate. There were many applicants, and unfortunately, you were not chosen. At this time, we are no longer filling this position.

You ever run smack into these words?

If you're like me, I bet you've applied for what seemed to be a dream job. You thought you had all the skills, education, and talents necessary to get that job. But the answer was no! And perhaps you continue to be overlooked in the job search. And perhaps you're getting to the point of thinking "I'm so tired of hearing no; I give up!"

As a *Christ Worker*, it's OK to have these emotions – to want to quit and not apply for the next job. But just remember: God will not leave you nor forsake you. And **no matter how many NO's you endure**, He has a *yes* waiting on you!

So keep striving for success in and outside of the workplace. Don't stop looking for His dream job for you. Go to God in prayer of faith, not desperation, and continue to work towards the purpose He has set for your life.

Count on it. Yes, **no matter how many NO's you endure**, He has a *yes* waiting on you.

Prayer

Lord, I come to You now thanking You for each rejection, for every "not qualified," and for all those denials. I know that, through You, all things are possible. Everything You do to me is for the betterment of me. And so in Your name, I continue to pray in faith, not desperation. Amen.

Tammy Robinson

Week 32, Day 2

never be a double

Reading

Matthew 11:18-19; 33 [NKJV] For John came neither eating nor drinking, and they say, 'He has a demon.' The Son of Man came eating and drinking, and they say, 'Look, a glutton and a winebibber, a friend of tax collectors and sinners!' But wisdom is justified by her children... But seek first the kingdom of God and His righteousness, and all these things shall be added to you.

Reflection

Reading my course evaluations, I came upon the following comment: "He is biased against Republicans." I was surprised and concerned until I read the next student's comment: "He is biased against Democrats." Obviously, both students claim I have a double standard.

It was a proud moment for me in that I knew I was doing my job right – challenging my students equally to think about their beliefs in a fair manner – even though these two students only heard what they did not want to hear. There was no way to please both of them at the same time. If I had tried to please one, I would have done a disservice to the other. But by focusing on teaching my students to think about their beliefs, I was doing my job correctly – despite claims of a double standard.

The world looks at Christians in the same way – through the lens of a double standard. In fact, the natural desire to please everyone and be accepted by the world causes some Christians to conform to the world's expectations. They forget just Who they should be trying to please.

It's nice to know that Jesus was accused of having a double standard. So was John the Baptist. Both were condemned for their opposite behaviors in serving our Lord. And every practicing Christian since that time is vulnerable to such condemnation.

As a *Christ Worker*, focus on pleasing God when you do the mission you are called to do. Don't worry about claims against you since you <u>are</u> a child of Wisdom. Remember He is calling you to be His representative with all whom you meet.

Today at work, just focus on pleasing Him. Then there will **never be a double standard** worth worrying about!

Prayer

Lord, help me be like You in everything I do and say. Let everyone see You, not me, in my professional life. Help me not try to please those around me – but to be measured only by my service to You. In Your name, I pray. Amen.

Kevin J. Cooney

Week 32, Day 3

face it with God

Reading

Romans 5:3-5 [ESV] Not only that, but we rejoice in our sufferings, knowing that suffering produces endurance, and endurance produces character, and character produces hope, and hope does not put us to shame, because God's love has been poured into our hearts through the Holy Spirit who has been given to us.

Reflection

We suffer in this world, and we wonder why. God warns you and I <u>will</u> hurt. But He also assures we will gain from the pain – and He promises we will <u>never</u> be put to shame by it. God's love is poured into our hearts to help with the suffering.

Are you suffering today? Are you letting the world dictate the pain you feel? Or have you invited the Holy Spirit to accompany your journey through all the hurt? And have you thanked God for the many times He has seen you through past sufferings?

God never said this particular day will be a carefree stroll. Not before work, not during work, and not after work. But the stroll you take will never be by yourself.

So as you step into this workday, **face it with God**. Let happiness and gratitude overcome the pain. He is right next to you! Allow Him to shine through you – even in the darkest situation.

Whatever happens today at work, whatever baggage you bring to work – you <u>can</u> **face it with God**. He <u>is</u> with you.

Prayer

Lord, thank You for blessing me abundantly – especially in times of pain! Forgive me for getting too involved in worldly matters to appreciate You being by my side – always. Come with me today, Lord, as You and I conquer my hurt together. In Your name, I pray. Amen.

Stephanie Van Straten

Week 32, Day 4

know the people you work with

Reading

1 Thessalonians 5:11-13 [KJV] Wherefore comfort yourselves together, and edify one another, even as also ye do, and we beseech you, brethren, to know them which labor among you, and are over you in the Lord, and admonish you, and to esteem them very highly in love for their work's sake. And be at peace among yourselves.

Reflection

The toughest challenge any leader faces is to develop and sustain an authentic relationship with subordinates. (Even the word "subordinate" sounds distant, doesn't it?) We get busy and end up not knowing what's going on in the lives of workers. That lack of authentic relationship encourages contempt and jealousy. It also means less productivity. A mentor once told me "Most conflicts are not institutional; they are personal within an institutional context." Believe me if you can mitigate personal conflicts, you solve most workplace problems.

The best way, then, to have peace within the workplace is to **know the people you work with** – just like you know Jesus. As a *Christ Worker*, you can't truly have an authentic relationship with others unless you have an authentic relationship with Christ. Our Lord gives the needed wisdom to have peaceful relationships. So to **know the people you work with**, you must first know Christ. Then you must take Christ to work with you each day.

Today get to **know the people you work with**. Do so through Christ. And be at peace.

Prayer

Lord, help me this day to take the time to reach out to those I labor with. Help me speak into their lives with the life I am leading for You. Give me an attentive ear to those I need to hear, and use me to bring Your peace as I labor for Your glory. In Your name, I pray. Amen.

Bill Dudley

Week 32, Day 5

stolen goods hidden there

Reading

Joshua 7:22(b) [NLT] ... They ran to the tent and found the **stolen goods hidden there**...

Luke 15:20(b) [KJV] ... But when he was yet a great way off, his father saw him and had compassion and ran and fell on his neck and kissed him.

Reflection

When I first came to Life Row, it was really death row. I was a *great way off* from the Father. I didn't know it, but I was. I traveled here all by myself. He did not leave me, but I certainly left Him. Oh, I would come back now and then just to show Him I was doing fine by myself. But I would not stay. You see, I left Him for foolish earthly reasons. And then I found myself in a place surely He could never find and surely He wanted no part of. When I was at my lowest, I never thought the Father would run to me, fall on my neck, and kiss me.

But several brothers on Life Row knew different. They found **stolen goods hidden there** in my heart. Compassion. Love. Forgiveness. Righteousness. Salvation. All hidden deep inside. They knew the Owner of the property and knew His Father would show compassion in greeting the thief. Over time, these beloved brothers convinced me to surrender what belonged to Jesus, and when I did, I was no longer *a great way off*.

Someone you know has **stolen goods hidden there** – deep inside the heart. A coworker. A citizen you serve. Maybe it's you. *A great way off* from the Father – wasting on death row. Waking up on death row. Going to work on death row. Returning home to death row. Not even realizing Life Row is just a prayer away.

Today at work, be like my beloved brothers on Life Row. Find a way to help that person with **stolen goods hidden there** in the heart. Believe me; Life Row is not *a great way off*.

Prayer

Father, in the name of Jesus, I pray. Thank You for loving me even after I stole so much from You. Thank You for opening my eyes to the stolen goods hidden in each man and woman You create. Thank You for taking me from death row to Life Row. Thank You for never being a great way off. Amen.

Jimmy Davis, Jr.

Week 33, Day 1

born into different cloth

Reading

Isaiah 61:10(b) [NIV] For he has clothed me with garments of salvation and arrayed me in a robe of his righteousness

Philippians 1:27(a) [NIV] Whatever happens, conduct yourselves in a manner worthy of the gospel of Christ

Reflection

There are times at work when things don't go right. A supervisor requests the impossible – knowing he has you to blame. A coworker neglects <u>again</u> an important part of the task – and she knows she will get away with it – <u>again</u>. It's easy to let anger into your heart. The question is what would Jesus want you to do?

The words of Isaiah and Paul are reminders of what Christ expects of you and me. We are clothed in garments of salvation and robes of righteousness. Truly we are **born into different cloth**. And we must act as such.

If you are offended or wronged at work, people will watch how you respond. Especially because you are a *Christ Worker*, they want to see your true nature. Today let them see Christ in you and nothing else.

Today let them truly see you are **born into different cloth**.

Prayer

Lord, thank You for reminding me that I have no choice. I must reflect You and Your Word because I am wrapped in garments of salvation and robes of righteousness. I must reflect You in all things and in all situations. Today at work, I know You will give me courage and strength to do so. In Your name, I pray. Amen.

Gilbert O. Craven

Week 33, Day 2

our Lord detests lying lips

Reading

Proverbs 12:19, 22 [NIV] Truthful lips endure forever, but a lying tongue lasts only a moment... The Lord detests lying lips, but he delights in people who are trustworthy.

Reflection

Growing up, children who told "stories" – lies – were punished by having their mouths washed out with a bar of soup. Did it happen to you? I confess; it happened to me once or twice. But we were just kids, not adults. As we grew older, we learned **our Lord detests lying lips**.

But for some public service leaders today – adults! – truth seems to escape them. Worst yet, there is no judgment from the public or the media. Lying seems an accepted practice, regardless of the workplace, and the ability to rationalize is almost a qualification on the job description. So we turn our heads. We do not call them out when lies are told. We let it go when rationalization is heard. And those with lying lips become emboldened.

As *Christ Workers*, we are the only testimony some people see and hear. We need to pray for strength to question the actions and motives of those who make claims.

In your workplace and mine, we need to watch our steps and our words. We are too old for that bar of soap but never too old to remember **our Lord detests lying lips**.

Prayer

Lord, give me a love so deep I never lead others astray by my actions or words. In Jesus' name, I pray. Amen.

R. Gary Allen

Week 33, Day 3

don't let work get in the way

Reading

Proverbs 3:5-6 [NIV] Trust in the Lord with all your heart and lean not on your own understanding; in all your ways submit to him, and he will make your paths straight.

Reflection

I admit it. I've drifted away from God. I've allowed my own agenda to interfere in God's plan for myself and my life. I haven't trusted in the Lord because the farther I drift from Him, the more I exert my own will.

Fact is life can get in the way of my relationship with God. Fact is *work also gets in the way.*

But the fact is every single day I need to reach out to Him and engage Him. Just like a plant, without nurturing, my relationship with God does not grow. Without effort, it dies.

What efforts are needed by you today? What ways can you grow in your relationship with God?

Whatever is needed to grow in Christ, **don't let work get in the way.**

Don't drift!

Prayer

Dear God, thank You so much for not giving up on me. For loving me even when I drift far from You. Help me crave You and Your word. Help me renew our relationship even when I am weak and tired – when it is so easy to brush it off until tomorrow. I want to seek You today – only You. I want to seek You forever. In Your Son's name, I pray. Amen.

Jessica Kay

Week 33, Day 4

leave the rest up to Him

Reading

1 Corinthians 3:6-9 [NIV] I planted the seed, Apollos watered it, but God has been making it grow. So neither the one who plants nor the one who waters is anything, but only God, who makes things grow. The one who plants and the one who waters have one purpose, and they will each be rewarded according to their own labor. For we are co-workers in God's service; you are God's field, God's building.

Reflection

Some days at work seem less productive than others. Often we work at planting or watering, but sometimes we get discouraged when setbacks occur. Impatience seems the only thing that grows when we don't see the immediate impact of what should happen.

Recently I visited Romania on a mission project. There I was reminded that God is always at work, and our job is to serve faithfully – and **leave the rest up to Him**. Where my team once started a Bible School, now you see a church and a local pastor shining light into this Roma village. In a difficult environment, others watered what my team planted, and God continues His work in that field.

So as you go about today's tasks at work, do not get discouraged. Realize you and your associates are actually coworkers in His field, not just yours. You have parts to play, so just do your job well. Remember only God can make your project or community grow.

So as frustrating as it may be, **leave the rest up to Him**.

Prayer

Dear God, on this particular workday, help me remain diligent in my tasks. When I face adversity, help me recognize my labor is not in vain and You will bless the seeds I plant. Bless the efforts of my team as we serve as Your co-workers for our community – in ways that bring honor and glory only to You. In Christ's name, I pray. Amen.

Lou Lassiter

Week 33, Day 5

Happy Birthday

Reading

John 3:3(b) [NLT] Jesus replied, "I tell you the truth, unless you are born again, you cannot see the Kingdom of God."

Psalm 107:2 [NLT] Has the LORD redeemed you? Then speak out! Tell others he has redeemed you from your enemies.

Reflection

Happy Birthday!

My brothers said that to me after I was *born again* here on Life Row. I didn't know what they meant until I realized my life was anew. Just thinking about it makes me want to celebrate! Me – I was redeemed by our Lord. Redeemed from my enemies (including the old me) – He chose to redeem me! And today another brother on Life Row is renewed by His redemption. Now, he can see the Kingdom of God! So we celebrate another birthday here on Life Row!

I know in some churches being born again isn't talked about. And I know some Christians feel awkward about it. Being born again happens so many different ways. Sometimes the Holy Spirit enters at a single moment, and you just know something's different. For others, redemption is a process – so gradual that you may not realize what's happening. And yet, while His birthday Gift of Redemption arrives differently into each heart, it still brings renewal into every heart.

But scripture requires us to speak up about it. We need to wish every Christian a **Happy Birthday!** For this day truly is new only through His redemption.

Today at work, wish a brother or sister **Happy Birthday!** Find a way to speak about your own redemption. You don't need to preach about it, but you can talk about it. You can bring it up when someone asks how you are doing. You can bring it up at lunch. You can bring it up with the coworker next to you who might just see the Kingdom of God for the first time!

And **Happy Birthday** from Life Row!

Prayer

Father, in the name of Jesus, I pray. Thank You for my new birthday! Thank You for letting me see Your Kingdom. Let me celebrate my new birthday every day of my life! Let me share Your Kingdom with those who cannot see. Let me celebrate it with those who do see. Amen.

Jimmy Davis, Jr.

Week 34, Day 1

pause and look

Reading

1 Chronicles 29:17(a); 5:20 [NIV] I know, my God, that you test the heart and are pleased with integrity... They were helping in fighting them, and God delivered the Hagrites and all their allies into their hands, because they cried out to him during battle. He answered their prayers, because they trusted in him.

Isaiah 30:15(b) [NIV] In repentance and rest is your salvation, in quietness and trust is your strength.

Reflection

One of the greatest lessons I've learned throughout my career is that there will always be slumps, lulls, and even dark times. That can often be difficult to accept especially when we feel confident we are in the place God intended for us or in that position we prayed long and hard for – believing it was that "dream job." Or maybe you're in a different predicament – maybe you're between jobs or waiting on a much-needed change or an open door.

Regardless of where your day-to-day falls on the spectrum of job satisfaction, remember that in the most perfect of situations *there will still be bad days*. Likewise, in the darkest times, there will be good days. As the saying goes, "God is God in the valley and on the mountaintop." But because of His faithfulness, He makes all aspects of your life perfect!

When you face those trying times, those long hours, those situations that make you complain "this is not what I signed up for" – remember His grace is sufficient in our weakness. When praying and asking for a way out – or deliverance from whatever antagonist you face – just **pause and look** for the His sustaining grace. Just **pause and look** for His sustaining grace that brings you through the situation. Just **pause and look** for His sustaining grace that works for His glory...and for your good.

So today at work, know *there will still be bad days*. But proclaim your trust in His strength. Then just **pause and look**.

Prayer

Thank You, Father, for Your blessings – seen and unseen. Thank You for the knowledge, wisdom, and skills you've blessed me with to do the job set before me. Lord, forgive me for losing sight of You and becoming inundated with circumstance. Remind me of Your grace that carries me always. Help me work and lead with integrity and Christ-like character and to be Your light that is needed in places I don't even realize are dark. In Jesus' name, I pray. Amen.

Christie Brown

Week 34, Day 2

wait and watch with one another

Reading

Matthew 26:40(b) [NIV] Could you men not keep watch with me for one hour?

Reflection

Sitting in a health clinic waiting room, I noticed a young person clearly distressed. I did not know if she was waiting to take tests or for test results. I did not know if the worry was about herself or someone she loved. But I did see she was anxious, and she was alone. Worse yet, I could feel she felt alone.

So I took a risk. I moved my seat next to her. I did not intervene or interfere, but I did want my presence known. I prayed the Holy Spirit would accompany me.

You know; as *Christ Workers*, we try to do good. So you and I will usually locate a resource to address the hungry or the sick or the broken. Physical problems are troublesome, yet you can find something to help. But what happens when you witness a broken soul? A soul so scared that it knows not what to do. A soul so frightened that it forgets Who is waiting and watching. What do you do about the *unseen brokenness*?

So I sat next to her and prayed silently. She noticed me – and perhaps much more. She talked a little, and I listened mostly. With tears in my eyes, I began to apologize to this broken young lady for not being able to ease her pain. It was then she whispered I was "meeting her deepest, darkest need" – just by waiting with her and watching over her for what soon became the unbelievably horrific news that changed her life forever.

You know; as our Lord was about to face the most horrific fate of the cross, all He wanted was for His disciples to wait and watch with Him. I learned today He still wants His disciples to **wait and watch with one another**.

At work today, remember it's not just the physical that requires attention. Do not neglect the *unseen brokenness* of those you encounter. Please, **wait and watch with one another**.

Prayer

Dear Heavenly Father, grant me the strength and energy to wait and watch with the broken souls You place in my path on this side of eternity. In the name of Jesus, I pray! Amen.

Debra Neal

Week 34, Day 3

carry the hurting to Him

Reading

Romans 12:15 [NIV] Be happy with those who are happy, and weep with those who weep.

Reflection

It's easy to be joyful when everything goes well at work. When your coworkers are like a well-oiled machine accomplishing every task on time and under budget, there are smiles all around. Unfortunately, that never lasts.

As a *Christ Worker*, you might feel false pressure to fix everything. But many with whom you come in contact will suffer tragedy in their lives, and you cannot fix that! You can mourn with them, but only God will do the fixing – that's His job, not yours. All you can do is to help **carry the hurting to Him**.

Today at work, remember it is not your helping hands that count in fixing tragedy. Sure, you can do some things, but the only real power you have in your hands is the power to raise them in prayer.

Today **carry the hurting to Him**. God will do the fixing.

Prayer

Lord, I thank You for Your helping hands. Continue to remind me that the only power in my hands is the power to lift the hurting up to you in prayer. In Your name, I pray. Amen.

Stan Best

Week 34, Day 4

whispered in your ear

Reading

Matthew 5:3 [MSG] You're blessed when you're at the end of your rope. With less of you there is more of God and his rule.

Reflection

Well, sometime during this week it will happen. Perhaps it will happen today. Maybe it's happening this very second: that moment when you *reach the end of your rope!*

As a *Christ Worker*, you know any day may be filled with negativity and hurt. From the citizen lowering himself to the level of a "customer" – forgetting he has more "rights" as a citizen than privileges as a "customer." From the coworker who refuses to co-work. From the boss who doesn't believe you or doesn't believe in you.

Yes, it's easy to slip into a cavern of despair. And when you finally reach the end of your rope, you feel so alone – so ashamed of wasting time and effort for so long. You wonder why did I ever invest my life in a career of helping people?

When you reach the end of your rope, remember what God **whispered in your ear** some time back. He wants you to serve others, but He wants you to be weak and vulnerable in serving. He wants less of you so there can be more of Him in the process and product of serving. And He wants you to remember what a blessing it is to have had that **whispered in your ear**. Oh my, to be *God's chosen servant* – and have had that **whispered in your ear** – *by Him*!!

So when you feel the last ragged edge of the rope running through your fingers, remember this: *Christ Workers* are not the takers in this world; we are the givers – givers in His glory. Personal riches and fame pass away – God's service lives forever.

Today at work, remember what was **whispered in your ear** – you are chosen by Him! Then let God extend that rope a little farther – so you can make it through even this workday!

Prayer

Father in Heaven, You know only too well how I like to be in control. When I feel out of control, I am lost and alone. Help me this day to focus on what I know to be true: that You are in control, and You will lift me up out of my deepest cavern so that I can mirror the joy and truth that is You. Today, Father, let there be more of You and less of me. In Jesus' name, I pray. Amen.

Anne-Marie Amiel

Week 34, Day 5

the brother serving trays

Reading

Psalm 101:2 [CEB] I want to study the way of integrity.

Reflection

Before I gave my life to Jesus, I saw something that left me shocked. A brother on Life Row was serving meal trays to the men in their cells. At one cell, the brother inside did not like the meal – or maybe he was just angry about something else and blamed the food. He cussed **the brother serving trays** and said disrespectful things. He threw back the tray leaving nothing to eat. The abuse was so bad **the brother serving trays** walked away from the cell.

About ten minutes later, he came back, and the brother inside apologized. But that wasn't what shocked me. No, it was how **the brother serving trays** responded. He said, "Why, I don't know what you're talking about. I'm sure you're hungry, so *would you like my tray?*"

Now, that's true integrity. He ignored the insult, stayed above the fray, and showed mercy.

I did not understand it at the time, but that response by **the brother serving trays** led me to work on my own integrity. He became my spiritual mentor and was instrumental in showing me *the integrity of Jesus*, my Savior.

Studying *the integrity of Jesus* is important because you and I never know when we will face a moment or situation that calls for it. If His integrity does not show, we hinder others from knowing Jesus.

As a *Christ Worker*, you are always **the brother serving trays** – in one way or another. Today at work, when faced with a difficult person or difficult situation – show His integrity.

You may have to walk away for a moment. But then come back. Show His integrity, and offer your tray.

Prayer

Father in the name of Jesus, I pray. Continue to give a teachable heart so I can show others Your integrity through my decisions. May I always bring praise to Your Son. Amen.

Jimmy Davis, Jr.

Week 35, Day 1

keep pushing through

Reading

Genesis 50:20 [NLT] You intended to harm me, but God intended it all for good. He brought me to this position so I could save the lives of many people.

Matthew 6:15 [NLT] If you forgive those who sin against you, your heavenly Father will forgive you. But if you refuse to forgive others, your Father will not forgive your sins.

Reflection

A close friend is called to do work that is not the easiest. Often she ends the day questioning why she is challenged with overload, disrespect, and constant disappointment from those in her difficult work environment. She goes home unforgiving. I'm sure you can relate!

But God has called her to this place at this time, so she is prone to **keep pushing through** – trying to find His way around the resistance, His way to confront complaint, and His way to find forgiveness in her heart. And slowly, God is making her bad situation good.

I know God can make your work situation good. All you need do is **keep pushing through** the day. In the midst of waiting for good, let your heart not be deceived. Let bad intentions of others not dictate how you reveal God's light to those who may not know Christ.

As *Christ Workers*, we do not always get the easiest jobs. But when you and I serve in accordance to God's will, we have the most rewarding job.

So do not give up hope. Continue to tame your thoughts and actions. And forgive – forgive as He forgives you! Just trust God enough to bring good out of a bad situation.

Yes, today at work, **keep pushing through**! God does change bad into good.

Prayer

Dear Heavenly Father, strip from me everything that is not like You. Let me exercise forgiveness as quickly as I ask You for forgiveness. I trust You, so I know evil will not prevail over Your intentions. In Jesus' name, I pray. Amen.

LaShonda Garnes

Week 35, Day 2

that second look

Reading

James 3:2 [ESV] For we all stumble in many ways. And if anyone does not stumble in what he says, he is a perfect man, able also to bridle his whole body.

1 Peter 5:6-7 [ESV] Humble yourselves, therefore, under the mighty hand of God so that at the proper time he may exalt you, casting all your anxieties on him, because he cares for you.

Reflection

Have you ever completed a task and went back to it later and wondered what happened? Perhaps no one else noticed, but it wasn't your best work. Far from it! What was going on with you that day? You wonder; was I distracted? Did I not care? Was I just bored?

You know a hiccup can wreak havoc if you allow it. Or a daydream can take you places you're not supposed to be. Regardless, you must stay on track or damage can be done.

As *Christ Workers*, we've been placed in positions to do our best work. And, frankly, you and I always have the ability to check twice before signing off on a task. Let's take **that second look**, find the mistake, correct it, and move on. Let our thoughts not run away.

When mistakes are made, acknowledge them and cast all anxiety onto our Father. He recognizes that you will stumble at times. But He expects you to try your best – always.

So today at work, take **that second look** before signing off on a task. And rejoice for the blessing of working under the Hand of God!

Prayer

Father God, even though I may stumble, You are right there to help me. I thank You, Lord! In Your Son's name, I pray. Amen.

Erica Everette

Week 35, Day 3

remember to be patient

Reading

Isaiah 40:31 [NIV] Yet those who wait for the LORD Will gain new strength; They will mount up with wings like eagles, They will run and not get tired, They will walk and not become weary.

Reflection

As I waited in a very long line at the airport yesterday, I became aggravated at the slow pace of the security officials. It appeared they were not concerned with my urgency. Now I know; they do the same thing methodically, and they face more than a handful of impatient travelers like me. But that did not remove my frustration, not one bit!

Then I noticed they were performing their jobs with smiles and courtesy. It was taking a long time to get cleared, but they were being very patient with the hurried people in line. They were patient with me and my bad looks!

And this reminded me that I need to be patient with those around me. After all, a little patience goes a long way in making everyone's day just a bit better!

At work today, **remember to be patient** – to those you serve and to your coworkers. At work today, **remember to be patient** with our Lord. Things are not working on your time schedule, only on His time schedule.

So *set the example* at work. Set His example!

Prayer

Dear God, please give me strength to have patience with those around me. Help me to set the example today at work. In Jesus' name, I pray. Amen.

Adam Schenkel

Week 35, Day 4

He always responds with faith

Reading

Matthew 11:2-4 [NIV] When John, who was in prison, heard about the deeds of the Messiah, he sent his disciples to ask him, "Are you the one who is to come, or should we expect someone else?" Jesus replied, "Go back and report to John what you hear and see"

Reflection

As a young man working my way through the initial third of my life, *doubt has been my constant companion*. Doubt began early; for me, it was kindergarten. I doubted whether my fellow classmates would like me. As an adult, I doubt whether I have the necessary elements to become "successful" in a competitive world. My spiritual life is not void of doubt either. Am I following God's plan for my life?

A preacher once told me that doubt isn't necessarily a bad thing because its existence provides for the existence of its opposite: faith. So when John the Baptist doubted who Christ was, Jesus responded with faith.

As a *Christ Worker*, it's OK to doubt His calling. It will ultimately lead to a stronger faith once the doubt is answered. When answering Christ's calling for your life and career, doubt will exist, and difficult decisions will have to be made. Just remember that others have doubted, and **He always responds with faith**.

Today at work, doubt will surely rise – but **He always responds with faith.**

Prayer

Lord, I am a doubter and find myself overwhelmed at times. I need Your guidance and vision. As I go to work today, ease my doubts – turn them into solid faith based on Your foundation. It is in Your name that I pray – without a doubt! Amen.

Joseph N. Harrell, III

Week 35, Day 5

tears from the soul

Reading

Psalm 84:5-6 [HCSB] Happy are the people whose strength is in You, whose hearts are set on pilgrimage. As they pass through the Valley of Baca, they make it a source of spring water; even the autumn rain will cover it with blessings.

Reflection

The Valley of Baca means the Valley of Tears. I am in a place called prison where so many brothers cry out from their souls with tears – Help Me! Love me! Forgive me! Listen to me!

So many of us ignore their **tears from the soul** – including Christians on the inside and Christians on the outside. But if we all, as the Body of Christ, trust in His strength and set our hearts right, we can be the source of spring water and cover them with God's blessings.

This I know for scripture says it's so.

You are not in prison, but you may find yourself in the Valley of Baca. There may be a coworker or citizen who is in the Valley of Tears. Today at work, don't be blind to **tears from the soul**. Don't be deaf to the crying.

Today be that source of spring water and blessings. Yes, be that autumn rain.

Prayer

Father, in the name of Jesus, I pray. Forgive me for all the times I pass through the Valley of Baca and focus only on my own desires. Let me hear the crying. Let me respond to all **tears from the soul**. Strengthen me so I can be the vessel You can use and put on display. Amen.

Jimmy Davis, Jr.

Week 36, Day 1

Jesus heals best

Reading

Jeremiah 30:17(a) (NLT) "I will give you back your health and heal your wounds," says the Lord.

Matthew 10:8(a)(c) (NLT) Heal the sick… Give as freely as you have received!

Reflection

Too many times, I've cared for patients with hearts no longer willing to live – hearts without the muscle to beat. But when I see the patient unexplainably improve, I'm always excited.

In the medical world, we use words like "hardiness" and "resilience" to help explain why some people heal and others do not. But I know it's much more than that. Those who recover best generally have loved-ones nearby. When you matter to someone, it makes a difference. In my career, I've found the power of medicine is most effective when it is joined with the power of love. *Healing really does require love.*

In times of healing, the most powerful kind of love is the love of Jesus. Sure, secular love and even atheist love can help. But even before I became a practicing Christian, my experience told me the love of **Jesus heals best**.

Your workplace may not be like mine. Your career path quite different. But you deal with people needing healing. That coworker who lost a loved-one. The citizen who is depressed. The colleague with cancer. The supervisor with broken bones. Like His disciples, Jesus sends you and me out each day to heal through His love – to give freely His love just like we've freely received His love. He sends us out with *a most powerful medicine* – knowing the love of **Jesus heals best**.

You've been healed through His love many times. Haven't you? Won't you give freely as He has given to you? It's really quite simple: the love of **Jesus heals best**.

Prayer

Lord, show me how to heal. Remind me that Your love will be my most powerful medicine – it will help all other medications work more effectively. Today give me courage to bring Your love to those in need of some kind of healing. In Your name, I pray. Amen.

Patricia Baum

Week 36, Day 2

the arrogance of the day

Reading

Psalms 8:3-5 [NIV] When I consider your heavens, the work of your fingers, the moon and the stars, which you have set in place, what is mankind that you are mindful of them, human beings that you care for them? You have made them a little lower than the angels and crowned them with glory and honor.

Reflection

In today's world, it's way too easy to view situations with arrogance – as "us versus them." This includes the workplace – when we deal with others. Whatever position a coworker takes, it's easy to perceive it <u>wrong</u> simply because you or I disagree with it. It's easy to assume superiority when a coworker's opinion differs from ours. Yes, it's easy to get caught up in **the arrogance of the day** – even for *Christ Workers* like us.

Yet our Lord expects much more from you and me – and something much more basic.

Remember those two *Christ Workers* in 1968 and what they did on Christmas Eve? Orbiting the moon, the Apollo 8 astronauts delivered a message to the world. Given all the human-made technology around them, their message could've been about misguided patriotism, pretentious pride of national know-how, or arrogance of cold-war "us versus them" comparisons. But it wasn't. Instead, they marveled at <u>His</u> creation, shared <u>His</u> bible verses, and reminded everyone on earth that we are <u>His</u>.

Now if you and I do the same this workday – if we forget "us versus them" and see all people as His people – *just like those two astronauts* did, we can avoid **the arrogance of the day**.

It's up to you as a *Christ Worker*. Will you spend this workday in a manner that treasures others regardless of the differences you may have with them? Will you be like those two astronauts and see the commonality in all humans? Will you see all in the image and likeness of our Creator? Will you acknowledge He crowns all with glory and honor?

Yes, as this workweek continues, be just like those two astronauts. Forget "us versus them." Avoid **the arrogance of the day**.

And, just like those two astronauts, what a wonderful view you will have!

Prayer

Lord, help me see with Your eyes, not mine. Let me not fuss with the petty differences of the day. Since You do not make junk, help me not get caught up in arrogance and misguided pride. Let me be mindful that each brother and sister is crowned by You with glory and honor. I ask this in Your name. Amen.

Stan Best

Week 36, Day 3

do that one small thing

Reading

Ephesians 4:32(a) [NIV] Be kind and compassionate to one another

Romans 14:8 [NIV] If we live, we live for the Lord; and if we die, we die for the Lord. So, whether we live or die, we belong to the Lord.

Reflection

Have you ever meant to do something for someone but then became sidetracked and forgot? And you eventually remember, but it's "too late" because you missed your chance. Well, that happened to me.

A couple of months ago, my little girl was having a conversation on her play phone with the lady I employed for over three years as a house cleaner. We let her go because my daughter started preschool, and we had to cut back on expenses. My daughter was "telling" our former cleaning lady just how much she missed her. It was so sweet; I took a video of the "conversation" and was going to send it to her. But I got busy with my own work and forgot to text it.

Well, today I received a phone call from our former cleaning lady. Her sister died unexpectedly, and to my surprise, I was the first person she called. How much she must have thought of me. How little I had been thinking of her. And I couldn't help but see how my pointless "busyness" prevented me from doing something nice for her some time back. I mean; was I really so busy I couldn't take a moment to text a video? Was I really too busy to **do that one small thing**?

At work today, be kind and compassionate to someone. Take time to do something nice for a coworker or citizen you serve. You know what I'm talking about. Yes, **do that one small thing** that will make someone smile. That will make someone know you care. Don't worry about the busyness of the moment. It'll still be there when you're through. And at the end of the day, all that matters is how you live and die for the Lord.

Yes, don't miss your chance. Today take time to **do that one small thing** for someone at work. Because you both belong to the Lord.

Prayer

Lord, thank You for reminding me to really sweat the small stuff of doing something nice for someone today. It is the small stuff – that act of kindness and compassion – that will be remembered – by someone and by You. So please help me stay focused on what's really important for You and not my own busyness. In Your name, I pray. Amen.

Maureen Bereznak

Week 36, Day 4

unlovely in the eyes of some

Reading

Matthew 5:44(b) [NKJV] love your enemies, bless those who curse you, do good to those who hate you, and pray for those who spitefully use you and persecute you.

Reflection

Where I work, we use a lot of volunteers. While all help out of love, they can become **unlovely in the eyes of some**. A few volunteers are slow, and others do their work way too quickly. And there are times when one can just get in the way.

Not long ago, a volunteer caused a major spill. A full-time staff member cleaned it up, but out of fatigue and frustration, he loudly complained about the "nuisance" who created the mess. The young volunteer overheard and broke into tears.

Now I happen to have a godly relationship with this young volunteer, so I quietly reminded her she was there to serve Christ through serving others. To do this, she needed to show a kind of love that would surpass being **unlovely in the eyes of some**. She had to bless the coworker who cursed her. She had to do good to him because he mistreated her. Then we prayed for this guy who deemed her a nuisance.

Well, she humbly approached that irritated employee and asked for forgiveness. She confessed she was sloppy and careless. She then asked for his guidance so she could do better in the future. Before the shift was over, her unloveliness disappeared!

Even you and I can be subject to ugly behavior in the workplace. And being **unlovely in the eyes of some** may not be controllable – despite your efforts. But you can remove the unloveliness by blessing that coworker who just cursed you. By loving that supervisor who despises you. By asking for guidance from the associate who really doesn't want you around. By praying for the one who hates you.

And when you have done this for His sake, truly you are a *Christ Worker*.

Prayer

Lord, when faced with hate, help me love. In Your name, I pray. Amen.

Katherine Zasadny

Week 36, Day 5

because that person is Jesus

Reading

Matthew 25:40(b) [MSG] Whenever you did one of these things to someone overlooked or ignored, that was me – you did it to me.

Reflection

You and I have the same job. My workplace may be a little different than yours, but we serve the same purpose in our work – as we do in our private lives. We serve God. And our job commands us to treat each person as special **because that person is Jesus.**

Fact is we are all overlooked and ignored. We all have worldly hurt and shame. This is true for the brothers on Life Row, and it is true for free-world brothers who visit. And the correctional officers feel the loneliness of hurt and shame no less than the person working next to you.

But God takes time to treat you and me as *special*. In fact, He wants to visit with you every second of the day. He sees His son in each of us. And if He can see Jesus in the likes of me, why can't you see Jesus in everyone you meet? Too busy? Too embarrassed? Too *what*???

Today at work, join me in doing His work. Visit with Jesus. He isn't hard to find. Just look into the heart of the person working next to you. Look into the eyes of each citizen you serve today. Look beyond the hurt and shame – the hidden loneliness – and there you will find Jesus.

Yes, today treat as special the person next to you – **because that person is Jesus.** Visit with the citizen you serve – **because that person is Jesus**. Attend to the needs of each person you meet. Love the overlooked and ignored.

Do so because it is His job for you. Do so **because that person is Jesus**.

Prayer

Father, in the name of Jesus, I pray. Thank You for visiting with this overlooked and ignored sinner. Thank You for showing this sinner how to love and follow Your son. Thank You for allowing this sinner to visit with Your son as I treat special the person next to me. Amen.

Jimmy Davis, Jr.

Week 37, Day 1

doors to His need

Reading

Psalm 16:11(a) [NLT] You will show me the way of life

Jeremiah 29:11(a) [NLT] For I know the plans I have for you

Matthew 4:19 [NLT] Come, follow me, and I will show you how to fish for people!

Reflection

A friend called about his job. Oh, he loves his current job – working for a Christian organization. While he vents about workplace problems, he quickly remembers the many blessings he receives. It's like being year-round at a *Christian vacation park*. He says practicing Christianity is quite easy there, but he wonders if it's a little too easy. And that is his dilemma.

Does God want him to stay? Or is it time to get back to work in the secular world? Was he there to get refreshed? Or did God give him this job as a permanent reward?

I told him I didn't know. I mean certainly, coworkers in a Christian setting need God and the support of the Body of Christ as much as coworkers in secular settings. And there are fish to catch for Him – even in the most holy of places!

Yet there are fish in every workplace, and perhaps the **doors to His need** are wider elsewhere.

Well, after much prayer, my friend believes the vacation is over. It's time to get back into His trenches and do His work. He has decided to follow Him someplace else – someplace where God will surely open new **doors to His need**. It won't be as spiritually safe, but Jesus never said to follow Him only where it's safe!

Today at work, you may be struggling. Does God want you to stay, or does He need you to venture out? What are the consequences? What are the rewards, if any, in staying or going?

Today at work, pray and know He will show you the way. He has a plan for you, and it always involves following Him. Just make sure you are walking through the **doors to His need** and not just gateways to your own opportunity. Yes, whether you stay or go, make sure you're walking through the **doors to His need**.

Prayer

Father God, let me always follow You. Show me the doors through which you need me to walk. In Your Son's name, I pray. Amen.

James D. Slack

Week 37, Day 2

the process of discipline

Reading

Hebrews 12:11 [NIV] No discipline seems pleasant at the time, but painful. Later on, however, it produces a harvest of righteousness and peace for those who have been trained by it.

Proverbs 12:1 [NIV] Whoever loves discipline, loves knowledge, but he who hates reproof is stupid.

Reflection

I was saved at a young age, but as I grew older, I wandered away from my faith. I was en route to self-destruct. By age 17, my dad was writing me letters at least twice a week attempting to correct my destructive behavior through harsh, loving words of discipline. It made me angry. I did not want the accountability. I wanted to remain stupidly sinful.

The letters provoked no change within me. But what did have a huge impact was my dad stopping after work at a florist shop and buying me a beautiful daisy – every day – for four months! What kind of daughter could stay mad at a dad like that? What kind of daughter could continue hurting a father who loved her that much? Not this daughter.

Now, discipline is sometimes required in the workplace. Every person is a sinner, by nature and choice. The issue is not our sin but how we deal with sin and **the process of discipline.** As *Christ Workers*, we have a duty to provide loving discipline – never a pleasant process, but a necessary, corrective process. Yes, **the process of discipline** molds our behavior. How we go about the process makes all the difference.

So today at work, do not be intimidated when disciplinary action is required. Just use **the process of discipline** that He wants you to use. And remember loving discipline produces a harvest of righteousness and peace for those trained by it.

So at work today, give critique and discipline in a way that increases knowledge, understanding, and correction in the workplace. And do so always with Him in mind.

Prayer

Lord, thank You for allowing me to be capable of change and reformation. You are a God that makes all things new. Help me view the discipline process as a means to maturity and correction – as a way to glorify You. In Your Son's name, I pray. Amen.

Angela Arbitter

Week 37, Day 3

tendency for memory lapse

Readings

John 14:26 [ESV] But the Helper, the Holy Spirit, whom the Father will send in my name, he will teach you all things and bring to your remembrance all that I have said to you.

Reflection

I know this guy who *prays* for his coworkers on Sunday and then preys on his coworkers the rest of the week. He never remembers Christ's command to love others. He is a child of God, but he has no memory of being so at work. So throughout the workweek, he plays all sorts of games

Truth is, we all have short memories on some things, and now and then, we all forget Christ's commandments. Sometimes we even take our **tendency for memory lapse** to the office – just like that guy I know.

Well, God has a solution for our **tendency for memory lapse**. He provides the Holy Spirit, who, if we listen, is there to remind us of who we are and to Whom we belong.

Today at work, listen and learn from your Helper. Don't leave home without Him in the car, and don't make a decision without Him being in your heart. And in all situations, bring your remembrance to bear on all that He teaches.

Prayer

Dear Lord, thank You for my Helper. Today at work, let me not forget the lessons You teach. Let me practice each lesson in Your glory. In Your name, I pray. Amen.

Loren M. Crone

Week 37, Day 4

His work where we work

Readings

Deuteronomy 30:19-20 [NLT] Today I have given you the choice between life and death, between blessings and curses. Now I call on heaven and earth to witness the choice you make. Oh, that you would choose life, so that you and your descendants might live! You can make this choice by loving the LORD your God, obeying him, and committing yourself firmly to him. This is the key to your life. And if you love and obey the LORD, you will live long....

Reflection

I have a confession to make; I struggle constantly at work to be the light that Christ wants me to be. I ask myself questions like: Should I allow the actions of others to dictate my reaction? Should I use my spiritual beliefs to encourage coworkers? Should I tell someone I am praying for them? Should I tell someone about Christ at work or remain silent and only demonstrate my faith through my actions and attitude?

This choice was brought home to me the other day when I saw a worker explode at their coworker for a simple mistake. It was a mistake, a careless mistake that would cost everyone time. In my heart, I thought of how I would have reacted in my office or should react if guided by the Spirit. Ultimately my choice is between being obedient to the Holy Spirit or caving in to the whims and fears of my flesh. And you know what? Choice, obedience, and commitment are all matters of the heart. They speak about our love of God and our love relationship with His Son.

I know; you don't have to tell me we should never deny Him; however, there are just so many temptations at work to be silent in both word and deed – so many excuses to avoid serving our Lord. The fact remains He needs us in our places of work so that He can do **His work where we work**.

So what's your choice? Heaven and Earth are watching and waiting for our decision. Will you serve Him today in your place of work? Will you be a *Christ Worker?*

Prayer

Heavenly Father, thank You for giving me the ability and strength to choose You at work. Help me never to deny You and to always be an example of You to all whom I meet. In Jesus' name, I pray. Amen.

LaShonda Garnes

Week 37, Day 5

not to hit back

Reading

Romans 12:17-19 [MSG] Don't hit back; discover beauty in everyone. If you've got it in you, get along with everybody. Don't insist on getting even; that's not for you to do. "I'll do the judging," says God. "I'll take care of it."

Reflection

The way I was raised – not by my mother or a father but by misguided people – there was one old rule: *always get even*. And my life went downhill because of it.

Well, that rule still shackled me when I came to Life Row. I escaped only when I gave my life to Jesus. And in here, now being free, Jesus put in my heart a desire to share the Gospel with everyone – inmate and officer alike.

But first, Jesus had to teach me **not to hit back**. He had to teach me to stop feeling like the world was out to get me and I had to get even. Jesus had to teach me to see the beauty in everyone, including those who do me wrong. Yes, He had to teach me **not to hit back** so I could see from God's perspective. And God has shown me so many wonderful things here on Life Row because I discovered the beauty in everyone.

At work today, you may deal with people who are misguided. Hurt. Abused. Neglected. Angry. They may be citizens or coworkers or supervisors. Some will want to get even with the world by disrespecting you and disrupting your day. And you will be tempted to get back at them.

Ah, but don't get even. Don't get shackled by that old rule. Remember God is the judge, not you or me. As a *Christ Worker*, it is your job to discover the beauty – His beauty – in each person – especially in those who view you with misguided hate.

Today, it is your job **not to hit back**. Don't worry about anything else. God will take care of it.

Prayer

Father, in the name of Jesus, I pray. Thank You for overlooking my wrong and seeing my beauty. Lord, you see beauty in even the likes of me! Let me do the same for others throughout this day. Let me retaliate with nothing but Your love so I can see Your beauty. Amen.

Jimmy Davis, Jr.

Week 38, Day 1

correct with love

Reading

Isaiah 35:3-4 [NIV] Strengthen the feeble hands, steady the knees that give way; say to those with fearful hearts, "Be strong, do not fear; your God will come, he will come with vengeance; with divine retribution he will come to save you."

Reflection

Like you, I must work with others to correct errors. Sometimes the mistakes are major, but quite often they are not. In fact, the little things require the most attention. Large or small, it's so easy to become angry or frustrated with the thoughtless mistakes of those around me. My natural reaction is to make them suffer for their mistakes, whether by publicly reprimanding them or by simply letting them continue to fail. But these options accomplish nothing. When I rely upon *the instincts of the flesh*, I always disappoint myself.

As a *Christ Worker*, I have a higher responsibility to those who are under my charge. Don't you? Not only must we lead, we must also serve those we lead. We must help one other succeed – not by overlooking mistakes and sweeping them under the rug. No, we are bound to a much higher standard – to **correct with love.**

One day, we will stand before His throne of glory and will answer to God, our Just Judge. Therefore, as *Christ Workers*, we must strive today to glorify Him at work in the ways we handle every situation. And this means we have to **correct with love.**

So, as you go to work this week, seek to strengthen coworkers. By your example, point them toward the kingdom of God. Throw away frustration. Cast aside anger. Remember the sacrifice Jesus made for you. Instead of the instincts of the flesh, **correct with love.**

Prayer

God, You fill my life with many good things. I am richly blessed by Your grace. You brought me to a place where I have influence over others. Help me to love these people and to serve them daily as You would have me do. Please start this work in my heart today. I ask this in Jesus' name. Amen.

Jonathan Lantz

Week 38, Day 2

a simple display of faith

Reading

2 *Corinthians* [KJV] 1:12 [NKJV] For our rejoicing is this, the testimony of our conscience, that in simplicity and godly sincerity, not with fleshly wisdom, but by the grace of God, we have had our conversation in the world, and more abundantly to you-ward.

Reflection

I think sometimes we like to complicate the message of the Gospel and also make the methods of sharing the Gospel too complex. I am all for programs which help to encourage people to witness. Yet sometimes **a simple display of faith** is all that is required to share the message.

In all my training in preaching and evangelism, I have found *one simple tool* (not taught or learned in any formal class or program) that has been very effective. I put a bible verse on my license plate, and that verse serves as an accountability tool. Believe me, knowing those *simple symbols* were displayed on my truck kept me in line during many temptations towards road rage. I also found that people, even unbelievers, look up the verse just to find out what it says. No matter what their intent is for looking it up, they read the word. How awesome is that?

That *simple set of letters and numbers* stamped onto a piece of metal – my license plate – opened the door of unexpected fellowship in my workplace.

Just today, a man that I had seen but not met before walked up and asked about the bible verse on my license plate. This man was an immigrant saved out of a heavy Islamic and Hindi background. He shared the vision God had given him and how it changed his life. We had passed each other during busy times over the years but had not really talked. A *simple bible verse* brought us together. A *simple message* had given us both a hope and a heritage we now shared. While we talked and shared our testimony, numerous others close by heard the exchange and the gospel.

Today at work, in what *simple ways* will God use you? What *simple sign* of being a *Christ Worker* will you display? Look for the opportunities God presents to show His love in your workplace. What coworker, citizen, or passerby is struggling today and just needs an encouraging word from you? A *simple word of encouragement* could change that person's entire day.

Now, go share His love through **a simple display of faith**! After all, it's really not that complex.

<u>Prayer</u>

Lord, use me this day to be Your instrument of love and encouragement. Give me wisdom and grace to simply share Your wonderful message of hope. May You be glorified in all I do. In Jesus' name, I pray. Amen!

Bill Dudley

Week 38, Day 3

giving your best is not optional

Reading

Galatians 6:9 [NIV] Let us not become weary in doing good, for at the proper time we will reap a harvest if we do not give up.

Reflection

As *Christ Workers*, giving and serving is a foundational element of our spiritual job description. The giving part is still not easy, especially when we are squeezed for time and our energy is limited. We all have a home and personal life. When the children are sick, the recent car repairs break the budget, we have an argument with our spouse, the boss is never satisfied, and the stack of work orders never seems to end – our "love tank" can run on empty.

How can we refill and get back our zest for serving others?

In these times, remember this: **giving your best is not optional** – not in life and not in the workplace. You need to make a choice to love others, in spite of how you feel. The answer is to call on the Lord in prayer for the will to serve and then ask for the strength to do your job with excellence.

At work today, you can make excuses – but when you humble yourself and call upon the Lord, He will answer and guide you through the deep waters. He will remind you that **giving your best is not optional** – for Him and for those you serve.

Prayer

Lord, help me to love others in spite of how I feel and what I am thinking. Change my heart, knowing that You will never test or tempt me beyond my ability to endure. Thank You, Lord, for filling my tank with Your eternal love. In Your name, I pray. Amen.

Gary E. Roberts

Week 38, Day 4

a good Christian marriage

Reading

Matthew 19:8(b) [NIV] Moses permitted divorce only as a concession to your hard hearts, but it was not what God had originally intended.

Reflection

Statistics show many marriages today will end in divorce, but this is not what God intended. The fact that a marriage will end today doesn't mean it is sudden death. Marriages begin to die at the first glance at a stranger or the first flirt with someone we know. The dying begins with a fantasy. It continues because few desire to truly practice what it takes to have **a good Christian marriage**. Fewer still are willing to remind others – and to show them – what it takes to keep **a good Christian marriage**.

Now don't get me wrong – if there is abuse and danger in the relationship, a Christian should get out for it is not the kind of relationship God intended. If the relationship is not based on abuse and danger, the marriage may be able to be saved. However, the tendency is just to give up. Even more, the tendency is to celebrate the death of that marriage. Too many people view divorce as a liberating social event.

You probably know a coworker who is experiencing marital troubles. As a *Christ Worker*, find ways to help that coworker find ways to heal what was once **a good Christian marriage**. Show them that a good marriage is based on love, trust, and respect for one another. Show them a marriage is a reflection of the relationship the Lord has with His people. And if God is willing, such a marriage can be healed.

So today at work, do all that you can to support that coworker, but do all you can to save **a good Christian marriage**.

And the first thing you can do is to show what **a good Christian marriage** looks like in your own life – in your own workplace!

Prayer

Lord, each day in front of my coworkers, help me live the example as a spouse in **a good Christian marriage**. Provide me the words to encourage others to give their own marriage another good Christian try. In all things, Thy will be done. And in Your name, I pray. Amen.

Stan Best

Week 38, Day 5

and just do what you can

Reading

Matthew 10:41-42 [MSG] ... This is a large work I've called you into, but don't be overwhelmed by it. It's best to start small. Give a cool cup of water to someone who is thirsty, for instance. The smallest act of giving or receiving makes you a true apprentice. You won't lose out on a thing.

Reflection

You must have heard. A hateful man in my country murdered some brothers and sisters while they were worshiping our Lord. What happened in that South Carolina church affected everyone around the world. It affected me and the brothers on Life Row. It's so easy to be overwhelmed with the evil surrounding us when destruction like that happens.

But right after those murders, something on TV made me smile. Two brothers in a supermarket decided to pay for the groceries of total strangers. Now imagine that! In the wake of such hatred in Charleston, two people in that same city chose not to be overwhelmed by evil. Instead, they did what they could and remained faithful to what God put in their hearts.

It doesn't take devastation like murder for you and me to become overwhelmed by the problems in this world. I know; so many things seem to make it impossible to do God's work. Yet if you take the day easy – if you start small **and just do what you can** – you will be a true apprentice of our Lord – like those two men in the grocery store. Like those dear brothers and sisters who died praying for their own murderer.

Today at work, a lot will happen to get you overwhelmed. You know that's true. Why should today be different than any other day?

So in your workplace, start small **and just do what you can**. You are His apprentice, and as He says, you won't lose out on a thing!

Prayer

Father, in the name of Jesus, I pray. Refresh me so I won't get overwhelmed with the evil in my world. Refresh me so I won't forget Your faithfulness to me. Refresh me today, Father, so I can give Your son's love, grace, and mercy to all I meet – in small but important ways. Amen.

Jimmy Davis, Jr.

Week 39, Day 1

good but not God

Reading

Proverbs 3:5 [ESV] Trust in the LORD with all your heart; and lean not to your own understanding

Reflection

I am a former stockbroker and pageant queen. I am a daughter of an alcoholic. I am also a homeschooling mom and, in my country, a "southern" woman. I am headstrong. And, for most of my 48 years on this earth, I loved making my own money and having my own life – and doing things the way I designed. And my beloved husband and I have made a good life for our children.

No, I did not consult God about most things. I figured He was busy with bigger problems.

But I was still searching for my calling – my big splash in the world. And somehow, I missed the part about *really trusting God in everything* – not just the convenient things, like Sunday mornings or whether I really need to eat the entire box of Thin Mint cookies in one sitting. But really trusting Him with the important things, like what I am supposed to do in the world. No, He was not my career consultant at all.

You know sometimes a really good decision may not be God's decision. Hmm... **good but not God**. Let that sink in – after all, if you're like me, it's a difficult concept to grasp.

So I'm trying something new. I surrendered my stubborn heart and started really trusting God in everything. Now I am leaning on His understanding, not mine. And, with much prayer, He is leading me toward a calling where He needs me.

And guess what? My family continues to have a good life. And, most importantly, I have learned **good but not God** is simply not good enough!

What about you? Are you leading the show – in your life? Your career-path? Your job? Is it family and spouse who chart your course? You need their input, naturally, but where is God in your equation? Is He central? Quintessential? Are you really trusting Him in everything?

Before you go to work today, surrender to Him. Lean on His understanding, not yours. And you will find **good but not God** is no longer good enough!

Prayer

Lord, I pray that I make career decisions by trusting in You – with every ounce of strength, mind, body, and heart You give me. Help me accomplish Your Will in every decision – big and small – when I speak with a coworker, influence a policy, or touch another's heart and direction. In Your name, I pray. Amen.

Valerie Steele-Clearman

Week 39, Day 2

let's do this day together

Reading

Psalm 5:3 [NIV] In the morning, LORD, you hear my voice; in the morning I lay my requests before you and wait expectantly.

Reflection

Every morning my exuberant Labrador retriever is peering through the patio blinds to see if I'm headed out for my morning coffee and game of tennis-ball-fetch. I'm always so disappointed to tell him I have to go to work or, even worse, to be in such a rush to not have time to play for even a few minutes. The disappointment on his face is apparent, yet he just sits down and waits until I come home in the evening – hoping he'll get his time.

If you're not a dog fan, this may seem ridiculous. But I truly believe our Heavenly Father shares the sentiment. His faithfulness is new EACH day; morning by morning His mercies we see! Yet each and every day we are anxious, confused, and even worried by so many things.

I challenge you to examine your routine. Have you become so busy getting ready for work that instead of spending a few minutes with the One who grants unending peace, joy, and rest – you pick up the very thing that fuels the feelings of anxiety, confusion, and worry? In His presence is fullness of joy, and at His right hand are pleasures forevermore. Life will still happen, day in and day out. But to sense his presence – from the first step out of bed til the lamp clicks off at night – is to walk and rest in assurance that He knows you need to make it through another day and will provide 100 times over.

The way you choose to start the workday is directly connected to the way your day progresses and ends. Don't get me wrong; I'm not always off to the best of starts either. Life is busy. Work is busy. My iPhone taunts me the minute the alarm goes on and says "look at me, look at me."

But in the morning, before work, the Lord is waiting to hear your voice. He's waiting on you to say "good morning, Father, **let's do this day together**."

Prayer

Good morning, Father, **let's do this day together**. Forgive me for becoming so busy that I forget to acknowledge the blessing of another day You've given me. Another day to spend in Your presence. Another day to shine Your light to those who don't even realize they need it. You know my worries. They are many. But my worries about the workday are nothing too great for You. Give me Your peace as I fix my mind on You. In Your Son's name, I pray. Amen.

Christie Brown

Week 39, Day 3

an even greater responsibility

Reading

Proverbs 20:4 [ESV] The sluggard does not plow in the autumn; he will seek at harvest and have nothing.

Colossians 3:23 [ESV] Whatever you do, work heartily, as for the Lord and not for men.

Reflection

Yesterday was a very stressful workday. Oh, not because of what I had to do but how I chose to do it. Rather than attacking my tasks methodically and judiciously, I dallied until suddenly I was overwhelmed and frustrated. Realizing I had wasted precious time, I had to rush through my work without giving it the proper attention and detail it deserved.

Why do I always seem to overestimate the time available and underestimate the magnitude of the task? In essence, why do I procrastinate? Upon reflection, the answer became very clear: I am selfish. I want to do what my heart desires rather than what my duties require. In the end, I put myself above those to whom I owe my best effort.

But it stops today!

As a *Christ Worker*, I have an obligation to perform my work duties to the best of my abilities – and **an even greater responsibility** to honor and serve God in the process. When I delay what should be accomplished now, I fail to serve Him best.

At work today, why not join me? Don't be selfish. No one may be looking, and perhaps no one really cares. But He is looking, and He does care.

So remember today you may be able to slide by, but don't. You have **an even greater responsibility** – to honor and serve God.

Prayer

Dear Lord, help me to accomplish my work tasks with diligence and urgency and not wait until the last minute. Give me strength and courage not to act selfishly and dishonor You. In Your name, I pray. Amen.

Paul Theroux

Week 39, Day 4

define success as He does

Reading

Matthew 25:21(b) [KJV] Well done, thou good and faithful servant

Reflection

How do you define success?

You and I sometimes pay lip service to the values of being a *Christ Worker*. We go through the motions and don't give it our "all" when it comes to truly finding remedy for clients, agency, and the public-at-large. We go through the motions of pleasing Christ.

You know Christ challenges us every day to **define success as He does**: getting the job completely done for His sake, to His satisfaction, and for His glory. It means going that extra step or mile as a *Christ Worker*.

And sometimes we fail Him.

Today at work, do not fail Him. Be the *Christ Worker*. Go that extra step or mile to please Him. Your reward will come when He says *"well done good and faithful servant."*

Yes, today at work, **define success as He does**.

Prayer

Lord, let me please You in my workplace in all my activities. Help me gather the courage to trust You for my rewards. In Your name, I pray. Amen.

Gary E. Roberts

Week 39, Day 5

no matter how people respond

Reading

1 Timothy 1:12 [NIV] I thank Christ Jesus our Lord, who has given me strength, that he considered me trustworthy, appointing me to his service.

Reflection

This whole week has gone terribly. I felt so undervalued and unappreciated. I felt like I was surrounded only by selfish and ungrateful brothers. Brothers who care only about their needs – never my needs. Brothers I could never please.

I am sure you have them around you, too. Perhaps in your family, but certainly where you work. You know the type – people who want nothing more than to drain you completely.

But today I read this verse, and the Light went on! All week long, I was wrong!! I was the selfish one – the ungrateful one. It was I who was undervaluing and unappreciative. You see, all week long I felt it was my service – not His service.

As Christians, Jesus places us in every kind of trying situation. He does so because He trusts us. He appoints you and me to do His service. He strengthens us to glorify Him.

So I finally got it. It doesn't matter if I feel undervalued and unappreciated. It doesn't matter if I feel like I am being drained completely. What matters is me making my Lord valued and appreciated. What matters is me raising up my Lord!

Today at work, remember Jesus appoints you. Because you are a *Christ Worker*, He trusts you. He strengthens you. He counts on you. You and you alone!

So do His service **no matter how people respond**. Don't worry about your feelings, and don't fret about those who want to drain you completely.

Yes, just do His service - **no matter how people respond**. It is His response that counts.

Prayer

Father, in the name of Jesus, I pray. Thank You for all You do for me and through me. During the next week, keep reminding me to do Your Service, to bring fruit and glory to Your name. Amen.

Jimmy Davis, Jr.

Week 40, Day 1

forgive those who trespass

Reading

Matthew 6:9(b)-13 [NAB] Our Father who art in heaven, hallowed be thy name. Thy kingdom come. Thy will be done, on earth as it is in heaven. Give us this day our daily bread, and forgive us our trespasses, as we forgive those who trespass against us, and lead us not into temptation, but deliver us from evil.

Reflection

What a beautiful prayer that gives praise to our Creator and direction to our actions. But the problem comes at the part where we proclaim "as we **forgive those who trespass** against us." Now I suppose most workplaces have a resident misanthrope, but a friend called last night to talk about a coworker named "Susan."

Susan revels in making office life harder than it needs to be. She has anger issues, and she pronounces daily her non-belief in God. Susan especially strikes out at coworkers who try to live by faith – and that includes my friend.

After years of being screamed at and deliberately embarrassed by this coworker, my friend continues having trouble praying those words – **forgive those who trespass**. And yet God keeps nudging her. At worship, she now swallows hard and visualizes Susan as she recites the Lord's Prayer. Then my friend prays that God will forgive her for feeling so negative about that coworker. My friend even repeats **forgive those who trespass** in the elevator before work.

I pray my friend will see a miracle today at work, but I know all things happen in God's time. For me, the small miracle is that my friend no longer wishes Susan ill.

At work today, I'm sure you have a "Susan" hanging around – doing everything to make the day miserable for everyone. You can't wish that coworker away – you can't send her to another job in another town. No, like my friend, all you can do is **forgive those who trespass** against you.

If you **forgive those who trespass**, at least your day will not be as miserable as that coworker!

Prayer

Loving Father, remind me daily that You provide me with this job and, through it, the abundance necessary to take care of my family. Let me focus on doing my best for the constituents in my city who come through my office for help. Let me not engage in unpleasant office politics. Let me forgive the ones who are burdened with bitter situations unknown to me. Let the Holy Spirit choose my words in all situations, and let Your compassion and truth guide my actions throughout this workday. I pray in Jesus' name. Amen.

Patricia A. Maley

Week 40, Day 2

loving the unlovable

Reading

John 13:35 [NKJV] By this all will know that you are My disciples, if you have love for one another.

Reflection

As a complaints commissioner, I encounter dissatisfied citizens over the phone. Last week, I dealt with someone who verbally attacked me and threatened to come to my workplace with a baseball bat – yes, we play baseball in Canada!

The temptation is to treat these unloving people just as they treat you. You know, "an eye for an eye." But I did not do that. Although he seemed unlovable, I chose to *love*. I chose to pray under my breath for a satisfactory resolution to the conflict. Eventually calm returned, and God reminded me that love-in-action means **loving the unlovable.**

Later the customer actually showed up in our office (without the bat), and I quickly asked God for strength as I remembered the threats and venom. I put God's word into action. I began **loving the unlovable.**

In each workday, you run into the unlovable. The coworker with that attitude. The citizen demanding complicated needs be met "immediately." The supervisor who knows what's already on your desk yet throws another project into your basket. It's so easy to let your feelings and perceptions determine who you love.

It doesn't take much effort to love the good colleague and the polite citizen. But as a *Christ Worker*, your job is to demonstrate His love to all, even the disgruntled, the unpleasant, and the arrogant.

So today, show true love-in-action by **loving the unlovable**.

After all, isn't that what He does toward you?

Prayer

Father, I pray You will help me demonstrate Your love to others at work – those who are easy to love and those who are hard to love. Today may I be an effective witness of You and everything about You. In Your Son's name, I pray. Amen.

Suzanne Denis

Week 40, Day 3

remove the X

Reading

2 *Corinthians* 12:9(a) [NLT] Each time he said, "My grace is all you need."

James 4:6(a) [NLT] And he gives grace generously.

Romans 5:8 [NLT] But God showed his great love for us by sending Christ to die for us while we were still sinners.

Reflection

Recently I met an Acadian-Canadian woman whose ancestors, like many others, were expelled from Nova Scotia in the 18th century. Her last name is Devereaux. I asked her why some Acadians spell that last name with an X at the end and others spell it without that X. She said folklore has it that a long time ago an unwed girl got pregnant, and a priest put the X at the end of her name – as a "scarlet letter" to mark her family for generations.

Wow, what a price to pay for a sin!

Although my last name does not end in X, I've done things deserving of a scarlet letter. I'm sure you have, too. So you and I should be thankful – very thankful – for a God and Savior who extends unconditional grace. For a Lord who, regardless of folklore and the spelling of last names, continues to **remove the X** from our lives.

And you and I must do the same for others by offering grace and the forgiveness that comes with it. What is grace? Grace is being thankful, generous, patient, content, joyful, forgiving, sympathetic, and kind. It's God's *sufficient living gift* to us – and we must pass it on to others.

So today at work, **remove the X** from anyone who has offended you. Show kindness. Show forgiveness. And remember your Lord continues to **remove the X** from you.

At work today, do the same for others. Extend grace to one and all!

Prayer

Lord, You shine Your face upon me and are gracious to me. As You are to me, let me be to all whom I meet today and with all whom I meet each day. Let me glorify You by living my life fully in the grace You bestow on me. In Your name, I pray. Amen.

Matt Whitman

Week 40, Day 4

grace to give

Reading

Exodus 34:6(c)-7(b) [NLT] The God of compassion and mercy! I am slow to anger and filled with unfailing love and faithfulness...But I do not excuse the guilty.

2 Corinthians 6:1 [NLT] As God's partners, we beg you not to accept this marvelous gift of God's kindness and then ignore it.

Reflection

I know you don't want to hear this, but we must not receive God's grace in vain!

When I ignore His grace, I become guilty of reacting with frustration, disappointment, and criticism. Coworkers learn not to expect grace from me. They may then hide the truth from me, making positive changes even more difficult and increasing the chances of making the same mistakes twice.

But when I show grace as God has shown me, completely undeserved and unmerited grace, others are more likely to be truthful. They will seek my forgiveness and spiritual support when they make mistakes. They can then move forward with freedom to openly share what they have learned and perhaps prevent someone else from making the same mistake. All this happens when I remember that I receive His **grace to give** to others.

Now, isn't that the kind of workplace God wants?

Today at work, remember you can't control the behaviors and attitudes of others and fear doesn't really work in controlling circumstances. But you can control your own reactions! Just be grace-filled. That's the way He responds to your mistakes, so use Him as your model in responding to others. If you do that, you will create a nurturing work environment. You will create a place where people feel free to make mistakes, learn from those mistakes, and avoid repeating previous mistakes.

So today and every day, don't receive God's grace in vain! Use it to build a workplace filled with learning. A workplace filled with forgiveness. A workplace filled with His **grace to give** to others.

Yes, give His **grace to others**, and things will go a lot better this workweek. A <u>lot</u> better!

Prayer

Dear Father, help me to be more like You in all that I think and do. Thank You for the grace You show to me. Please help me show grace to others. In Your Son's name, I pray. Amen.

Martha Smith

Week 40, Day 5

hold up the hands

Reading

Exodus 17:12(b) [HCSB] Then Aaron and Hur supported his hands, one on one side and one on the other so that his hands remained steady until the sun went down.

Reflection

A spiritual mentor of mine was having a pretty rough week. So God put it on my heart to encourage him. I told him that when he gets so stressed-out that he can't do something, I will do it for him. When he gets so tired that he can't think, I will do the thinking for him. When he gets so fearful that he can't even pray for himself, I will do the praying for him.

Well, that afternoon he came to my cell and thanked me for holding up his hands – giving him strength – just like Aaron and Hur held up the hands of Moses. And like Moses, my brother could now make it through the day.

You know, there is someone around you who is very tired. Stressed out. Upset. Fearful. That brother may not be able to think or to do. That sister may not even be able to pray.

Is it the coworker sitting right next to you? In the next office? Down the hallway?

Are you willing to **hold up the hands** of that particular someone today – not just for a moment but *until the sun goes down*? Make that person's workday just a little easier?

Today at work, **hold up the hands** of the one who needs your strength. Do it in glory to God. Hold them up high – like Arron and Hur did for Moses.

Yes, **hold up the hands** until the sun goes down. Hold them up high like Jesus holds yours.

Prayer

Father, in the name of Jesus, I pray. Continue to move my heart with compassion so I can be a steady support to others to advance Your Kingdom. Amen.

Jimmy Davis, Jr

Week 41, Day 1

far scarier than a heart attack

Reading

John 16:33(b) [NLT] Here on earth you will have many trials and sorrows. But take heart, because I have overcome the world.

Reflection

Twenty years ago, I felt it. Now my wife and I just got to church. (We started attending regularly since He gave us two babies. But while my wife and toddlers were in Sunday school, I read the newspaper in the car. You see, on Sundays, I was just going through the motions. And my conduct reflected that throughout the week.)

But on that day, I felt it. A strange acid indigestion. Not in pain, but I had to buy some antacids or go to the hospital. As I drove, for some reason, I chose the hospital. Only after I arrived, did the heart attack take place.

A heart attack is scary and brings on many trials and sorrows. For me, two toddlers seeing daddy on a gurney. Rehab and months of not having strength to carry my babies. The constant battle of keeping weight off. And always worrying about what might happen to my family.

But that heart attack transformed my life. God saved me that day – and started to save me for eternity. And each day after, *He gave me use*. Not everything changed at once, but I knew then I work for Him. And while I still struggle, especially in my job and career, I know one simple fact: not working for Him is **far scarier than a heart attack**.

So it's been two decades, and each day I try to be a better *Christ Worker*. Somedays I fail. It's not easy, and each day, I have to *take heart* to stay on His path.

At work today, I hope you don't have a heart attack. It's scary. But you will have trials and sorrows today – handling a situation – responding to a coworker or citizen – you know what's going on and you know what and how you do. It's easy to mess up, so do yourself a favor.

Today at work, know He is overcoming your world and your workplace. Understand you need to *take heart* to stay on His path. Accept you need to work for Him – not yourself, nor anyone else.

And remember not working for Him is **far scarier than a heart attack**.

Prayer

Father God, You blessed me with my heart attack. Through it, You made me realize You. Good days and bad days don't matter; I know I work for You. In Your Son's name, I pray. Amen.

James D. Slack

Week 41, Day 2

hear His whisper

Reading

Deuteronomy 31:8 [NIV] The Lord himself goes before you and will be with you; he will never leave you nor forsake you. Do not be afraid; do not be discouraged.

Reflection

When my son was born, I planned not to seek a professional job away from family – until he was at least school-age. But things happen, and when he was barely out of diapers, I received a phone call with a job offer. After much prayer, I accepted the position. So my son and I moved away from family and everything that brought comfort and security.

As you might expect, the new location left me with no immediate support system. And the demands of my new position left me little time to create one. I began to feel very discouraged.

But as the darkness of lonesomeness crept in, I started to **hear His whispers**. "Don't be afraid. I'm at your side. I called you here, didn't I? I'm not going to forsake you or your little boy."

Have you ever left the comfort of familiarity for a door He opened?

As a *Christ Worker,* God provides you with career opportunities so you can use the gifts and talents He needs where He needs them. Sometimes this requires you to walk through the valley of uncertainty and loneliness. But when that happens, just **hear His whispers** – know He is with you.

Today at work, challenges and opportunities may come in many forms. Too much work. An unreasonable boss. A disagreeable coworker. An irate citizen. God probably wants you to stay put and do His work where you. But then again, He may need you to take a new position far away from family and friends. Whether he wants you to stay or go, you may feel so all alone in following Him.

Whatever the challenge, just stop and **hear His whisper**. Know He is with you. Dedicate the challenge as an opportunity to serve His glory.

Yes, at work today, **hear His whisper**. He's not leaving you, nor is He forsaking you!

Prayer

Father God, I thank You for challenges and growth opportunities. Allow me to always remember, in the midst of everything, You are here. Help me hear Your whispers when I feel alone or discouraged. Let the challenges I face help me to become a better servant. Let me keep my focus on You and be sensitive to Your voice. I ask this in Jesus' name. Amen.

Erica Everette

Week 41, Day 3

cannot run well without Him

Reading

Hebrews 12:1-2 [ESV] Therefore, since we are surrounded by so great a cloud of witnesses, let us also lay aside every weight, and sin which clings so closely, and let us run with endurance the race that is set before us, looking to Jesus, the founder and perfecter of our faith, who for the joy that was set before him endured the cross, despising the shame, and is seated at the right hand of the throne of God.

Reflection

I recently attended my country's national collegiate cross-country championships. Over 500 men and women ran, including my son who ran for the winning team. The men on his team averaged just under 30 minutes for the 10,000-meter race – a true testament to their dedication and endurance.

I've watched my son run for the past nine years and know the tremendous dedication he has for his sport and team. In each race, he is motivated to endure all obstacles and conditions so he can run the best time possible for himself and his team.

Watching my son's championship caused me to reflect on my own dedication and endurance for running the race set before me – including in the workplace. God requires me to pursue excellence in my job while remaining a faithful servant of Jesus Christ. As a *Christ Worker*, I **cannot run well without Him**. To serve others requires dedication only to Him and endurance only for Him.

Now, you don't have to be a cross-country champion to know your position in your own race. At work today, realize you **cannot run well without Him**. So dedicate yourself only to Him and serve with endurance only for Him.

Only to Him and only for Him. Today at work, win the race with Him!

Prayer

Dear Lord, help me always keep my eyes fixed on You and run the race that You have set before me. Today let me win by glorifying You. There will be trials, I know. But grant me the strength and perseverance to endure those trials set before me so I might serve You through my service to others. In Jesus' name, I pray. Amen.

Paul Theroux

Week 41, Day 4

help from a God-given gift

Reading

Romans 12:5-8 [NIV] so in Christ we, though many, form one body, and each members belongs to all the others. We have different gifts, according to the grace given to each of us. If your gift is to prophesying, the prophesy in accordance with your faith; if it is serving, then serve; if it is teaching, then teach; if it is to encourage, then give encouragement; if it is giving, then give generously; if it is to lead, do it diligently; if it is to show mercy, do it cheerfully.

Reflection

A couple of days ago, a coworker experienced a cardiac event here in the office. As a volunteer firefighter and emergency medical technician, I quickly assessed his vital signs and symptoms. I alerted 911 for immediate transport to the hospital. Fortunately, he reached the emergency room and was treated without major complications.

The next day many stopped by my cubical to thank me for taking care of our coworker. His supervisor even went to my supervisor to inform him of the great job I did and how professional I was in getting this man to the hospital.

But while all the accolades were nice, that was not why I did what I did. God gifted me to become a firefighter and emergency medical technician – a gift few are given.

You know our Lord gives everyone gifts and talents, and He expects everyone to use these gifts to further the Kingdom.

So what gift has God given you? Do you acknowledge that gift? Do you use it to serve others? How about in your workplace? You might think He's given you no gifts or that your God-given gifts are minor. But you're wrong. God doesn't neglect, and all gifts are important!

Today at work, someone could use **help from a God-given gift** you have.

And **help from a God-given gift** could mean the world to that person in need.

Prayer

Father, You give gifts through the Holy Spirit. Guide me and everyone to use the gifts bestowed to help those in need. Let my gifts, and the gifts of others, be a blessing to someone and always a praise to You. In Your Son's name, I pray. Amen.

John F. Long, Jr.

Week 41, Day 5

really hurting Jesus

Reading

Acts 9:4 [NLT] He fell to the ground and heard a voice saying to him, "Saul! Saul! Why are you persecuting me?"

Reflection

These past few weeks have been very troublesome where I live and work. A riot and a strike – all in the general population section, not on Life Row. But this has meant a lockdown for everyone, including Life Row. And any lockdown means no visitation by loved-ones. And, as if that were not enough, yesterday there was an execution.

All this places great strain on the correctional officers. The strike means the officers have to do the work normally done by the brothers in general population. Cooking. Serving the food. Cleaning. Maintenance. Toilet repairs. Electrical repairs. And a lockdown places even more stress on the officers – the food now has to be served to each cell. And the men and women on the execution team – well let's just say they don't look forward to what they have to do.

What's going on here reminds me of scripture. You see, Saul thought he was hurting people when he was **really hurting Jesus**. This is what the rioters and strikers in general population believe – that they are hurting the correctional officers. And some men being executed try to hurt the officers. But in fact, when a man on Life Row tries to hurt someone through blame, he is **really hurting Jesus**. We all know this.

So for the past several weeks, the Church here on Life Row has found ways to bless the correctional officers. We know we could make their day miserable, but we'd be **really hurting Jesus**. So we send them scriptures of encouragement. We pass notes of love down the row to them. And guess what? The correctional officers feel that love, and their day is slightly easier.

Today at work, do not try to hurt others. Don't persecute your coworker. Oh, you may have reason to do so, but don't. Just don't. Like Saul and the brothers in my prison's general population, all you'd be doing is **really hurting Jesus**.

And at work today, is <u>that</u> what you really want to do?

Prayer

Father, in the name of Jesus, I pray. Thank you for removing the scales off my eyes so I won't persecute you in any way. Amen.

Jimmy Davis, Jr.

Week 42, Day 1

be gentle to all

Reading

2 Timothy 2:24 [KJV] And the servant of the LORD must not strive; but be gentle unto all men, apt to teach, patient, in meekness instructing those that oppose themselves.

Reflection

I love God's word, yet my flesh fights against some of His commands, such as "don't strive." My flesh wants to honk the horn – yell and scream at the "nice" young man who just cut me off in traffic and almost caused me to wreck. So I pray to calm myself. But just after the Spirit calms me, a lady almost runs over me in the parking lot. I want to shout, "Hey, lady! Stop texting and pay attention to who you're hitting!" More prayer is needed to calm me down.

I know the Word says **be gentle to all**, but that's really hard to do throughout the day.

In moments of conflict, I must remember that those same people – who I may want to seek retribution for their misdeeds – are immortal souls that God has placed in my path to teach and instruct in meekness. And you know *meekness is not weakness*. Meekness is a controlled spirit, willing to put emotions in check while trying to speak wisdom into the lives of others through the infinite power of the Holy Spirit. It is tough to **be gentle to all** and speak truth without invoking fleshly responses. However, with the power of the Spirit, you and I can be the servant He wants us to be.

As a *Christ Worker*, you have the unique opportunity to be a voice of calm at work. You have the opportunity to remain meek in the midst of workplace tasks that stress even the calmest of individuals. Who will you teach and instruct with gentleness? Who will tempt you to "strive" at them today?

At work today, **be gentle to all**. Remember *meekness is not weakness*.

Prayer

Father, use me today to be the difference in the lives of others. As I listen to Your gentle voice, may I be the gentle voice of hope to the special souls You allow me to encounter this day. Through Your Spirit, empower me to glorify You this day and **be gentle to all**. In Your Son's name, I pray. Amen.

Bill Dudley

Week 42, Day 2

being a team player

Reading

1 Corinthians 3: 12-13 [KJV] Now if anyone builds on this foundation *with* gold, silver, precious stones, wood, hay, straw, each one's work will become clear; for the Day will declare it, because it will be revealed by fire; and the fire will test each one's work, of what sort it is.

Reflection

Success is a value assessment that is subjective in application. Even when objective standards are used for measurement, success is perspective-based. On one level, you and I pay lip service to the values of Christ – that our success is based upon the good we do for our coworkers and the citizens we serve. But when I awake at night, mulling over the issues of the workday, my own mind is drawn to the personal indicators of success. In many cases, you and I are like basketball players concerned more about his points-per-game than being a team player.

How do you define success? Is it a more impressive job title? A bigger office? That promotion?

Christ challenges you every day to "die to the self" and find ways of **being His team player** – playing defense and passing over the shot to a coworker in better position. It's true; **being His team player** may not move you up the fast-track, but you will receive the important reward from our Coach and Team Owner.

Today at work, are you **being His team player** and encouraging subordinates and coworkers to excel even when you could accomplish the tasking and receive the credit yourself? Are you supportive of the supervisor you have disagreements with? Has the cause of Christ been enhanced by your presence at work today?

Yes, **being His team player** ain't easy, but the Win is precious and eternal.

Prayer

Lord, enable me to be Your team player and make the hard sacrifices to make my agency truly successful. Help me to esteem others greater than myself as I work today and serve both coworkers and citizens. In Your name, I pray. Amen.

Gary E. Roberts

Week 42, Day 3

who's my Daddy

Reading

Psalm 34:2 [HCSB] I will boast in the Lord; the humble will hear and be glad.

Reflection

Back when I just a little boy, I would say things like: "My daddy is better than your daddy." Or "My daddy is stronger than your daddy." Or "My daddy can beat-up your daddy."

Yes, we like to boast about our "daddies" – whether our worldly fathers are great or not, we want others to think well of them because they are a part of us.

So why don't we boast about our heavenly "Daddy" in the same way?

God wants you and me to go to Him with the simplicity of a child – and what better way to do so than to boast in Him like a child boasts? We know our Heavenly Father is better than any other. We know He is stronger than anything we fear. We know He is greater than every opponent we face. We know God's team is superior to all other teams in the universe.

So as this workday begins, remember **who's my Daddy?** Find ways to tell coworkers and citizens just how strong He is in your life and how He can beat up anything going wrong in their lives. Above all, boast that He can protect them against the Evil One.

Yes, today ask yourself **who's my Daddy**? Boast in Him by the way you live that answer! Let others be glad your Daddy is the strongest!

Prayer

My Father in Heaven, thank You for being the best, the strongest, and the Only One I can always rely on to protect me. I ask You for strength and courage to boast in You – today and every day of my life. Let others hear and be glad! In Jesus' name, I pray. Amen.

Chris Summers

Week 42, Day 4

that quiet click of the latch

Reading

2 Corinthians 4:8-10 [ESV] We are afflicted in every way, but not crushed; perplexed, but not driven to despair; persecuted, but not forsaken; struck down, but not destroyed; always carrying in the body the death of Jesus, so that the life of Jesus may also be manifested in our bodies.

Jeremiah 29:11(a) [ESV] for I know the plans I have for you

John 10:9(a) [ESV] I am the door.

Reflection

I've been a *Christ Worker* my entire adult life. I served in the U.S. Navy for 10 years. I was a law enforcement officer for nearly 20 years. I've been a public school teacher for the last 9 years. And I have been a state senator for the past 4 years.

But I lost my primary race recently. I have to admit; I feel struck down.

When one door closes, another opens. But right now it's hard to hear anything other than the slam of the closing door. Yet I know – *if I rely on the power of Jesus* – I will soon hear **that quiet click of the latch** opening the new door. And it will be His door!

Have you had a major setback in your job or career? Didn't get that promotion? Lost an election? Been fired? I bet you feel afflicted, perplexed, persecuted, and struck down.

As a *Christ Worker*, you can overcome all things because the life of Jesus is manifested in your body. And while you may feel struck down, Jesus will make sure you are not crushed. Not driven to despair. Not forsaken. Never destroyed.

He really does have a bigger purpose for you – His purpose. So listen for **that quiet click of the latch**. It's Him. He is the door, and the door is opening! And He will never leave you.

Yes! In all disappointments at work and in all defeats in your career, listen for **that quiet click of the latch**. Jesus is there with His plan. He is the door, and He is waiting for you!

Prayer

Jesus, thank You for Your everlasting love. Help me remember, because of You, I am never alone no matter what obstacle is placed in my way. You always provide Your door. Let me hear the sound of it opening. Let me walk through gladly. In Your name, I pray. Amen.

Greg Smith

Week 42, Day 5

whether the time is favorable or not

Reading

2 Timothy 4:2 [NLT] Preach the word of God. Be prepared, **whether the time is favorable or not**. Patiently correct, rebuke, and encourage your people with good teaching.

Reflection

Have you ever preached something to others that you would eventually need to do yourself?

Last Sunday, I preached in our church on "Step Up When the Enemy Tries to Shut You Up." You know who the Enemy is, right? It's so easy to let Satan shut you up in life. He throws so many obstacles, and you use them as excuses for not stepping up. The timing isn't right. I'm not prepared. I don't know what to do or say. I'm nervous. I'm afraid. You know the excuses.

Well, yesterday I was sitting in my cell – mad about a particular obstacle I have no control over. It was really stupid to be this upset, and I almost didn't hear a brother calling at the gate of my cell. Finally, I heard him. He said another brother needed my help – and wanted only me to help him. At first, I said I was too busy. But then I agreed to help that brother. I put down what I was doing, forgot about that obstacle, and went to see what the brother needed.

Looking back, the Enemy tried to shut me up with my own problems. Satan did not want me to step up for that brother. He knows that every time you or I step up, it denounces him and glorifies God.

Today, as you leave home for work, prepare your heart and mind to carry Jesus' will in stepping up for His sheep, His flock, and His kingdom. It doesn't matter **whether the time is favorable or not** – forget about the obstacles you can use as excuses. All that matters is this: He calls you when the Enemy tries to shut you up.

Prayer

Father, in the name of Jesus, I pray. Thank You for Your timing in preparing me to share Your Son with others. For preparing me to step up for Your glory – **whether the time is favorable or not**. Amen.

Jimmy Davis, Jr.

Week 43, Day 1

the hope that you have

Reading

1 Peter 3:15(a) [NIV] But in your hearts revere Christ as Lord. Always be prepared to give an answer to everyone who asks you to give the reason for **the hope that you have**.

Reflection

If a court charged you and me with the crime of being Christian, would there be enough evidence to convict us? Are you sure?

Every day we are in the world – at school, work, and the marketplace. Do we bear witness to our reverence for the Lord? Or do we just go through the day like everyone else?

As a *Christ Worker*, you should have to answer – *why so much hope*? After all, everyone should see **the hope that you have** in Christ. Right? So do you have the answer ready?

Of, if you <u>aren't</u> asked this question, then maybe you need to reexamine your walk a little more. Why <u>aren't</u> you asked? Don't others see **the hope that you have**?

Today at work, remember you don't need to be a preacher or missionary to do great things for the Kingdom of God. Just keep in mind there are people around you needing to know the love of Jesus is real. And you may be the only person who can convince them.

So at work today, be ready to answer – *why so much hope*? Show them **the hope that you have**, and they <u>will</u> start to ask!!

And I will see <u>you</u> in court!!!!

Prayer

Lord, I am happy to be Yours! Help me share that joy and hope with those around me. It is easy for the tasks of the workday to crowd out that hope, so help me see those with whom I need to share Your Good News. In Your name, I pray. Amen.

Stan Best

Week 43, Day 2

about the why

Reading

Hebrews 10:25 [NLT] And let us not neglect meeting together, as some people do, but encourage one another, especially now that the day of his return is drawing near.

1 Corinthians 8:2 [NLT] Anyone who claims to know all the answers doesn't really know very much.

Reflection

It was the first day of class, and I was a new instructor. So I asked each student to briefly say something about themselves: name, employment, and plans upon earning the doctoral degree. It took about ten minutes to go around the table, and I felt pretty good about having relevant information about each one. After all, I had done the same ritual in each new class for the past 35 years. I was confident I knew enough and could now move on with the work of this course.

But after the session, one student handed me a scribbled note: "You really think you can know someone by asking just a few questions? Here are some things you don't know about me..."

Well, that note prompted an email exchange and then a visit to the student's agency. It took less than an hour, but I left knowing a lot **about the why** of this person. And I remembered learning **about the why** is far more valuable than just knowing about the what.

Your workplace is not so different than mine. You may think you have all the relevant answers about coworkers, but I bet you don't. As this workweek begins, remember there's always a "why" to each of them – and that why tells you more than just the "what."

So today at work, don't neglect learning **about the why**. You still won't have all the answers, but you will know more about how to encourage and advance that coworker. And encouraging one another is needed – especially since His return is closer than you think.

Prayer

Father God, You give me an unknown yet finite amount of time in this world to do Your work in helping others. Let me not waste that time – at my workplace or anywhere else. Help me to find out the "why" and not just the "what" – and use that knowledge to encourage and advance those around me. In Your son's name, I pray. Amen.

James D. Slack

Week 43, Day 3

rely a little less on Google

Reading

Matthew 4:4 [NIV] It is written: "Man shall not live on bread alone, but on every word that comes from the mouth of God."

Psalm 119:105 [NIV] Your word is a lamp for my feet, a light for my path.

Reflection

A sign in front of a church: *"Try God because Google doesn't have all the answers."* I laughed when I read it. But it also made me realize how much I rely on Google and the internet in everything I do.

This is especially true at work. Whenever I run into a road block, I use Google. When I need directions on how to fix an office machine, I use Google. If I need to know how to properly format a grant request, I use Google. Google is where I turn in my workplace times-of-need.

Now, there's nothing wrong for a *Christ Worker* to use Google or other search engines – in the workplace or anywhere else. But you and I have to be careful how much faith we put into our internet information sources. We have to be careful not to allow them to become our workplace gods.

So at work, remember you may <u>want</u> the internet but you <u>need</u> God.

Today **rely a little less on Google** – and *a whole lot more on Him*!

Prayer

Heavenly Father, I want to thank You for the convenience of the internet. But I <u>need</u> to thank You for giving me the wisdom to know that You are the One-and-Only true information source. I come to You for guidance first – before all others – even before I try the internet. In Jesus' name, I pray. Amen.

Crystal Featherston

Week 43, Day 4

be covet-less and shine His love

Reading

Exodus 20:17(a)(c) [NIV] You shall not covet ... anything that belongs to your neighbor.

Matthew 22:39 [NIV] Love your neighbor as yourself.

Reflection

Got a phone call from a friend last night. She was rejected for a higher-paying promotion in her organization. She applied for it, but the first cut was made by a computer search for keywords on the resume – words that my friend did not use. And now because the person getting this "coveted" position is new, my friend is part of a team to familiarize him with the organization.

And so the conversation last night centered on the fact that *the world is not fair*.

Well, is your world fair? Does it seem like everyone, but you gets the higher-paid positions? And it's your task to train them? Get along with them? Are you angry and resentful? Are you irritated when they keep asking questions? I bet you want to shout "You got the job. You should know how to do it!"

It's understandable to harbor those feelings. As I told my friend last night, life is not always fair. But as a *Christ Worker*, you know God's plans are not always your plans. And maybe the new person is in *a dark place searching for light*.

So you know what He expects of you. Right? He expects you not to covet what does not belong to you – and that promotion never did belong to you. And He expects you to love your neighbor – and that includes the new associate who just took that position you wanted.

So at work today, don't treat that new person like a thief, for he did not steal anything belonging to you. Help him around. Don't be irritated when asked the same question in the umpteenth way. Remember God expects you to **be covet-less and shine His love**.

The world is *not* fair. But calm down. Everything else – including where He needs you – will work out. Only first, you need to **be covet-less and shine His love** today at work. Period.

Prayer

Father, give me an open mind when I get passed over for a promotion. Help me be a good neighbor and Your shining light to the new person. Let me be Your ambassador in this dark world called the workplace. In Your Son's name, I pray. Amen.

John F. Long, Jr.

Week 43, Day 5

how your steps are walked

Reading

Psalm 119:133 [NLT] Guide my steps by your word, so I will not be overcome by evil.

Reflection

So many bad things happen all around us. It's easy to get frustrated. Our emotions are easily provoked. Am I right? Does this happen to you?

Brothers and sisters, remember this: a lot of people are listening to your words and watching your actions. Most important, they look to see **how your steps are walked**.

You and I have to keep allowing Jesus' words to lead us in every step we take – in our jobs, in our communities, and even in our households. It is no different on my Life Row than it is on your Life Row.

Does your walk through this day show Jesus' words? Or does your walk just show your desires and emotions? Jesus' words say to forgive. Will you walk in forgiveness today? Jesus' words say be merciful. Will you walk in mercy today? Jesus' words say to love one another. Will you walk in love today – even when it hurts? Jesus' words say be peacemakers. Will you walk in peace alongside the unpeaceful ones?

Today at work, watch **how your steps are walked**. Others are watching and listening.

Yes, today walk in the steps of Jesus. Let His words be your guide.

Prayer

Father, in the name of Jesus, I pray. Order my steps in Your word today. Let my actions give praise to You. Let my steps change the path of this world! Amen.

Jimmy Davis, Jr.

Week 44, Day 1

do what the Lord requires

Reading

Micah 6:8 [NIV] He has shown you, O mortal, what is good. And what does the LORD require of you? To act justly and to love mercy and to walk humbly with your God.

Reflection

Almost two decades ago, my husband and I lived in Eastern Europe. Our neighbors in Serbia were fighting, and economic sanctions against Serbia affected the entire region. Lots of times, you couldn't find what you wanted in the stores.

Now, you'd think the shortages would make life difficult. You'd be right, but in some ways, it actually made life easier. Want fruit? Go to the market and buy just what's in season. Want coffee? Go and purchase just what's available. Enjoy it and be grateful for it.

We got so used to limitations that we were shocked upon returning to my home country. *So many choices!* How could anyone decide? The first day back, I stood in a grocery store too overwhelmed to buy a box of cereal. I had read that having too many choices can make you feel worse than having too few choices – and I certainly found that to be the case! People find it hard to understand their options and fear making a mistake.

That's why it's comforting to know faith exists to guide your choices. The only question you ever need to ask is this: *Will this choice glorify my God?* When you ask that question, choices become easier. The best choice is the one where you **do what the Lord requires**.

At work today, you will have options. You might think not nearly enough options, or at least easy ones, but there are usually more than enough choices in any work project. As a *Christ Worker*, just **do what the Lord requires**.

You will glorify God in that choice.

Prayer

Dear God, guide my choices at work today. Make it easy for me to make the right choice even when there are lots of options. Help me choose to glorify you – in everything I think, say, and do today. In Your name, I pray. Amen.

Mary Manjikian

Week 44, Day 2

trouble comes your way

Reading

Philippians 4:13 [NLT] For I can do all things through Christ, who gives me strength.

James 1:2(b)-4 [NLT] when **troubles come your way**, consider it an opportunity for great joy. For you know that when your faith is tested, your endurance has a chance to grow. So let it grow, for when your endurance is fully developed, you will be perfect and complete, needing nothing.

Reflection

You can't really know the depth of your own character until **trouble comes your way**. And you know, one way or another, trouble is bound to show up in your workplace.

When it does, don't get caught up in the moment. I know it would be so easy to react as the world wants you to react, but don't do that. You're running a marathon, after all, not a sprint – and you're running that race for your Lord. So work on the endurance, and don't give up.

God is preparing you for something – something really important to Him – and He wants you to become perfect and complete for the tasks He has for you later on. Yes, your faith is being tested, but He promises you can survive the bleak because He is strengthening you.

So at work today, don't fall apart. Be joyful when **trouble comes your way**!

You can handle it!

Prayer

Dear God, continue to renew my mind, cleanse my heart, and make me a new creature in You. Go before me and set the stage so that, when I meet trouble, the Holy Spirit will be in my midst and will convict my thoughts, demeanor, attitude, and stamina. Today at work, let me walk boldly prepared to endure positively as Your child. In Jesus' name, I pray. Amen!

LaShonda Garnes

Week 44, Day 3

the memory of your doing

Readings

1 Corinthians 11:1 [NLT] And you should imitate me, just as I imitate Christ.

Hebrews 12:1(b) [NLT] since we are surrounded by such a huge crowd of witnesses to the life of faith, let us strip off every weight that slows us down, especially the sin that so easily trips us up. And let us run with endurance the race God has set before us.

Reflection

Sally Kate was practically a celebrity in my small town. Beautiful and talented, she was well rounded academically, spiritually, and socially. She gave much to many, and she did so in many ways. Her life imitated Christ, and that was obvious to everyone she touched. Truly, she stripped off every weight that slowed her down in the race God set before her.

But then she was gone. Just two months before graduating from college, Sally Kate died in an automobile accident. Now, 50 years later, the memory of all she did still echoes. There is a family services center, a children's home, and a memorial Park – all named in her honor, and all so vital to people living in that community. Through her legacy, Sally Kate continues to run with endurance the race God set before her.

What about the race God sets before you? The good you do on earth – regardless of how brief a stay – is worth doing in imitation of Him. If you claim the salvation offered by Jesus' death on the cross, then you will live forever in Heaven with Him – just like Sally Kate. But just like Sally Kate, you can leave a legacy. Strip off the weight that slows you down, and run with endurance His race, not yours. Buildings and parks may not be named in your honor, but just **the memory of your doing** will be an example and blessing when you are gone.

So today, do all the good you can to show God's love and to make your workplace and the world a better place. At work and elsewhere, **the memory of your doing** will make a difference.

Just like Sally Kate.

Prayer

Dear Father in Heaven, while I may never know who is following my example, please keep me focused on You – especially in my workplace. I want to influence others in positive ways. I want to bless coworkers by my example and influence while I live. I want the memory of my doing to count for something – now and after I leave this earth. In Jesus' name, I pray. Amen.

Martha Smith

Week 44, Day 4

a quiet leader without tights and cape

Reading

Judges 3:31 [NIV] After Ehud came Shamgar son of Anath, who struck down six hundred Philistines with an ox goad. He too saved Israel.

Reflection

If a bible verse were written about your workday, what would it say?

Scripture tells very little about Shamgar. He was a judge, so he must have been a leader. He was a farmer, handy with at least *one instrument of that trade* – a long wooden shaft with a metal strip known as an ox goad – to prod oxen in the right direction. Shamgar used that tool-of-trade to strike down 600 enemy soldiers. Imagine that – one farmer killing so many enemies to save His people! Certainly, he was known throughout the land. If alive today, some might claim he was a superhero wearing *tights and a cape*. In our day, he could parlay his amazing deed into endorsement deals, a run for political office, or anything else he wanted.

But in his day, Shamgar pursued no earthly accolades. He was just **a quiet leader without tights and cape**. He was content with one simple statement attached to the end of his short biblical record: he too saved God's people.

Now if God chose one farmer to rescue His people, certainly He will choose one *Christ Worker* today to accomplish tremendous things for His people. And God always chooses the unassuming person – **a quiet leader without tights and cape** – to accomplish superhuman achievements in His glory.

He will choose you today. Are you ready? Will your actions at work impact many people? Will your actions help that one person who is in greatest need? And if a bible verse were written about your workday, would it say you helped save at least one of His people?

At work today, find a way to help save that one person by pointing her to Christ. Have courage to use the instruments of your trade to step into a crisis and allow God to change lives. But do so as Shamgar did: lead in the right direction and pursue no worldly accolades.

Yes, today at work, be **a quiet leader without tights and cape**. Glorify only Him in what you do.

Prayer

Heavenly Father, thank You for depending on me to accomplish much for You this workday. Like Shamgar, give me strength to find a way to help save Your people. In Jesus' name, I pray. Amen.

Kevin Erwin

Week 44, Day 5

not a place to pretend

Reading

Galatians 2:20 [NLT] My old self has been crucified with Christ. It is no longer I who live, but Christ lives in me. So I live in this earthly body by trusting in the Son of God, who loved me and gave himself for me.

Reflection

When I was in the free world, I was a *pretender*. I did not know and love Christ, so I would go around pretending to be something I was not. A big shot. A know-it-all. Someone who could fit in with the group.

Now that I know and love Christ, I am no longer a pretender. I want people to know Christ through me and not just me through myself. And I now have two sets of friends: those who are saved and those who know about Christ but remain unsaved. With my unsaved friends, I do not pretend. Sometimes it is difficult to fit in with them, but how could they ever come to love Christ if I remain a pretender?

Where you work, are you a pretender around those who do not love Christ? How on earth will your unsaved coworkers make it to heaven if you keep pretending with them? You may have trouble fitting in, but don't you want them to be saved?

Your job is simply **not a place to pretend**. For the sake of those around you and for Christ's sake, please stop pretending. Today your earthly body has more work to do than what is on your earthly desk.

Your job is **not a place to pretend**.

Prayer

Father, in the name of Jesus, I pray. I know I have been a person of many faces. I don't want to pretend anymore. I want to be known as Your chosen vessel – no matter who approves or disapproves. Amen.

Jimmy Davis, Jr.

Week 45, Day 1

serve without outrageous nonsense

Reading

James 2:14(b)-17 [MSG] do you think you'll get anywhere in this if you learn all the right words but never do anything? Does merely talking about faith indicate that a person really has it? For instance, you come upon an old friend dressed in rags and half-starved and say, "Good morning, friend! Be clothed in Christ! Be filled with the Holy Spirit!" and walk off without providing so much as a coat or a cup of soup—where does that get you? Isn't it obvious that God-talk without God-acts is outrageous nonsense?

Reflection

When public servants campaign for office, they try to convince the voting public how they will govern. If elected through the faith of the public, the citizens will actually get the chance to see that faith in action...or not.

Too often, promises made are not promises kept. Talk of future action is never realized. After the election, too many forget to walk the walk. And that means not just knowing what's right, not just saying what's right, but doing what's right.

As *Christ Workers* – elected, appointed, or employed – we have a daily obligation to practice our faith. To translate God-talk into God-acts. To keep promises for the good of those we serve. To proclaim what is right, and then to do what is right. To do as Jesus would do.

Today at work, *put your faith into action*. For His sake, **serve without outrageous nonsense**.

Prayer

Lord, in Your name, I step up and accept the responsibility of putting You into my action. Today I **serve without outrageous nonsense**. In Your name, I pray. Amen.

Matt Whitman

Week 45, Day 2

pray for and pray with

Reading

Psalm 34:18 [HCBS] The Lord is near the broken hearted; He saves those crushed in spirit.

Reflection

What can you do to help the broken hearted in the workplace? Some bring their pain from home to work, and others receive the suffering at work and take it home. Many pretend everything is fine, but they still hurt deeply from an unjust world.

You know them. You see them. Still, you're inclined to say and do nothing. It's easier to remain blind to their troubles. Besides, what can you really do to help them?

In Jesus' name, pray for them. Then seek out and pray with them. That's what you can do – **pray for and pray with**. At least, that's a good start.

Today at work, pray for grace to feel the heartbreak of just one coworker. Pray for wisdom to help that coworker. In Jesus' name, pray with that coworker to remember the promises He keeps to all sufferers. That He is very near. That He saves those crushed in spirit.

You're not going to heal the heartache, so don't try. Healing is the Lord's work. But you can comfort that one person. So **pray for and pray with** – and know that's a good start.

Remember *prayer is the greatest component in the economy of God.*

Prayer

God, in my workplace, give me the grace required to see others who are broken hearted and crushed in spirit. There may be many, but let me help the one who works closest to me. I cannot heal, but I can comfort. I can **pray for and pray with**. I can remind – that You, and You alone are the God of kept promises. In Your Son's name, I pray. Amen.

Chris Summers

Week 45, Day 3

the hang of it

Reading

Genesis 2:7(a) [NLT] Then the Lord God formed the man from the dust of the ground.

Reflection

Right in the middle of a crowded hallway, he collided with me. Everything went flying. The embarrassed student quipped as he helped pick up my notes, "Hey, doc, nice bow tie!" A little tousled, I thanked him and wished him well. Perhaps still out of some awkwardness, he asked, "So how do you tie a bow tie? I like 'em, but I just can't get **the hang of it**."

Three decades in academia gifted me with skills to navigate around student traffic. So I would've just quickly acknowledged such instructions are "on the web" and been on my way. But this time, I didn't take that quick step. Something said "*stop!*" And so I did.

The student and I conversed in that hallway as if no one else was around. He learned I wear bow ties because of a gift from my children a long time ago, and I initially had major trouble mastering the art of tying them. His curiosity grew when I confessed that *faith* had a lot more to do with the mastery than did YouTube. I mean, there's a mechanics I don't understand. If I think too long about it, I get confused and have to start over with the knot. To this day, I haven't a clue as to how that knot works, even though I now have **the hang of it**.

The student was shocked when I said that accepting the "unknown mechanics" of bow ties calmed my doubts about *His unknown mechanics* of the Adam and Eve story. The first creation story makes sense, but Adam & Eve? Oh, come on... Dust? A rib? A talking snake? That peculiar tree? Those other cities? There were just too many unresolved issues for this "learned" mind.

But if I don't need to understand the mechanics of a simple bow tie, what made me think I have to comprehend *His mechanics* of creation? It was then, I told the student, I stopped worrying about the *how* of the Word and just accepted the *why* of faith. If God says it happened that way, that works for me! So now I have **the hang of it**!!

Like me, you probably hesitate to give testimony at work – not understanding every part of the Word. But today, just listen for His "*stop!*" And don't worry about that knot. Gravitate away from the how and toward the why. Right in the middle of anything—you'll get **the hang of it**!

Prayer

Father God, I don't understand everything about You and Your mechanics. But I don't have to. Just give me faith to follow You at work today, and I know You will help me get **the hang of it**. In Your Son's name, I pray. Amen.

James D. Slack

Week 45, Day 4

He will do it

Reading

John 14:13-14 [GNT] And I will do whatever you ask for in my name, so that the Father's glory will be shown through the Son. If you ask me for anything in my name, I will do it.

Reflection

Lately things have been difficult at work. It's close to our financial year-end, and it's a challenge to meet the community needs with the limited budget. Both colleagues and friends struggle to make ends meet regardless of their respective workplaces. In some instances, there have been ungodly layoffs – and the fear of layoffs continues. So many people struggling just to make it into tomorrow.

It seems to be a common occurrence – few resources, big needs, many fears, and always that feeling of helplessness. I struggle just to maintain a positive attitude.

I'm an early bird, and so I arrive before anyone else. I pour a cup of coffee and open my Bible. I read: *If you ask me for anything in my name, I will do it*. I look through my office window on the 19th floor and watch the dawning over the city. As I ponder this verse, the Lord confirms the truth of His Word: **He will do it**. Just as He is faithful to maintain the rising of the sun each morning, so He is faithful not to let me down.

He will guide your daily work-life. He will empower you to execute to the best of your ability all that is put forward to you. He will equip you with wisdom and skill to deliver excellent work amidst constraint and fear. Everything He does for you is to glorify our Father.

So *you must not focus on your circumstance*. Remain faithful to what you need to do at work today – ask in His name, move straight into action, and do everything so our Father may be glorified.

And when that is your purpose, know **He will do it**. Yes, whatever is wrong today concerning your job, ask in His name and glorify Him.

He will do it.

Prayer

Heavenly Father, thank You for Your everlasting faithfulness. Help me not to focus on my circumstance but to keep my eyes fixed on You. Thank You for

Your kept-promise of doing what I ask when I ask in Jesus' name. Today of all workdays, I ask for Your guidance and wisdom as I execute what is set before me – so that You may be glorified. In Jesus' name, I ask in prayer. Amen.

Thea Coetzer

Week 45, Day 5

words will surely follow

Reading

Proverbs 4:23 [HCSB] Guard your heart above all else, for it is the source of life.

Reflection

Recently a correctional officer was talking foul about a situation that just arose. This particular officer occasionally gives brothers on Life Row a hard time. He does not like me. But seeing his attitude, I chanced taking him to the side. I said he was too blessed to be so foul in his words.

There is a saying here on Life Row that may surprise you: *what comes from your mouth first comes from your heart*. If goodness comes out of your mouth, you are using your heart as the source of life for others in need. If evil comes out, your heart is no good for anyone. If that officer did not see my words as coming from my source of life, there is no telling what would have happened. But he did hear goodness, and my heart helped change his heart.

You have to guard your heart from all the bad that could come out of your mouth. If you don't guard it, your heart cannot be the source of life for others – especially those who don't like you. Hold fast to what Jesus gives your heart so it can carry out His will.

Think about this as you go to work today. Use your heart only as the source of life for others. Your **words will surely follow**.

Prayer

Father, in the name of Jesus, I pray. Thank You for healing my heart and helping me guard it so I can hold fast to what You give me in all circumstances. Use my heart as the source of life for others in need. I promise my **words will surely follow**. Amen.

Jimmy Davis, Jr.

Week 46, Day 1

eyes to see the hurt

Reading

Genesis 21:17 [NKJV] And God heard the voice of the lad. Then the angel of God called to Hagar out of heaven, and said to her, "What ails you, Hagar? Fear not, for God has heard the voice of the lad where he *is*.

Matthew 19:14(b) [KJV] Suffer little children, and forbid them not, to come unto me: for of such is the kingdom of heaven.

Reflection

I continue to walk into my classroom and see hurting children. Hurting from things they have no control over. Abandonment by a father. Nightmares from a mother cursing. Anxiety from the fighting between parents. Some children jump when I walk past because they get hit or screamed at when they are home.

By this time in my career, I suppose I should be accustomed to their hurt. But I do not grow accustomed. No, not at all. I pray I will always have **eyes to see the hurt**. How else can God use me to help ease their pain?

Well, it's taken three long months for one young man to look me in the eyes. He no longer scrunches down in his seat when I come to conference with him. What ails him? I do not know, but this I do know – God has heard the voice of this lad!

You know, God heard the voice of Ishmael, and He welcomed the children when He walked this earth. So too, I must hear the cries of the children in my presence and show them the way to our Lord Jesus.

And so must you.

Today at work, have **eyes to see the hurt**. Listen closely to hear the voices of all God's people, young and old, needing your help today. As a *Christ Worker*, remember the purpose of your service is His service. Even on the toughest days, you are here to serve God's people.

Young or old, hear their cries and have **eyes to see the hurt**.

Prayer

Dear Heavenly Father, thank You for placing me in this mission field of public service. As long as You breathe life into my body, I pray You give me Your eyes to see the pain You see and then give me strength and wisdom to lead Your children to You! In the precious name of my Lord, I pray! Amen.

Debra Neal

Week 46, Day 2

desire Him fervently

Reading

Luke 22:15 (NKJV) Then He said to them, "With <u>fervent</u> desire I have desired to eat this Passover with you before I suffer;"

Reflection

The day began quite ordinary but ended up being most significant. His last day on earth, He wanted to eat dinner with His disciples. Yes, He wanted to share a meal with His buddies.

Wow! We can so easily get lost in the divine nature of our Lord, the God that could raise Himself from the dead, that we forget that He made himself human as well. He had all the desires and needs that we have. Jesus, most of all, *desired fellowship – fervently* – with his disciples on that last day. And what better way to do that than to eat a meal together. We call it the Last Supper, but it really was the beginning of a new relationship – not just for the disciples but also for all who call Jesus "Savior."

Many public servants put their lives on the line – firefighters, police, military, and more. We are thankful. But has someone ever actually saved your life? If so, I bet you are <u>very</u> grateful. I bet you stay in touch with that person and want to be a friend for life!

Jesus saved our eternal lives, and what does He ask in return? He desires fellowship. To be invited to our dinner table – to that pick-up basketball game – to the mall – to our workplace.

Jesus loves <u>you</u> – so much He suffered and died on the cross – for <u>you</u>. And all He asks is that you **desire Him fervently** in your daily life.

So today at work, seek fellowship with Him in every way possible. Enthusiastically invite Jesus to spend the day. Beseech Him to be a part of your decisions, your meetings and emails, your frustrations and accomplishments, your lunch hour, and your commute. Passionately show Him the love He has always shown <u>you</u> by giving His life for <u>you</u>.

Yes! At work today, **desire Him fervently**. He fervently desires fellowship with you right now!

Prayer

Jesus, please come into my workday and life – into my struggles and joys. Let me show my gratefulness for saving my life. You are my best friend and my God. Thank You for my new beginning. In Your name, I pray. Amen.

Kevin J. Cooney

Week 46, Day 3

tones wantonly treacherous

Reading

Psalm 25:1, 3 [NRSV] To you, O LORD, I lift up my soul... Do not let those who wait for you be put to shame; let them be ashamed who are wantonly treacherous.

Reflection

A musician once explained that the beauty of this particular Psalm is that there are at least four different musical settings– two are quite sedate and solemn, one is "middle of the road," and one is positively bouncy. Without changing the basic message of "To you, O Lord, I lift up my soul," musicians can reflect the appropriate tone and mood for any spiritual occasion.

Just like music, words can set the tone. But in the fray of each workday, words can often escape our lips in **tones wantonly treacherous** to His glory and His purpose. Embarrassing tones for a *Christ Worker*. Shameful tones to those who wait for Him.

Yet the same words, uttered in a godly voice, can produce something completely different. They can glorify Him and His purpose in your workplace.

Yes, **tones wantonly treacherous** to Him change the mood of the message. So perhaps the lesson my mother verbalized long ago is a deep and critical truth that still rings true in public service. *"It's not just what you say, it's how you say it."*

Today at work, glorify God in what you do by the what and how of your words. Be like a musician playing the Psalm. You have an opportunity to bring to Him coworkers and constituents – anyone who comes through your office door – regardless of the occasion. True, words are important, but so is the voice and mood accompanying those words.

Even in the midst of today's stress, choose the right words. Then avoid **tones wantonly treacherous** to His purpose in your workplace.

That is how you lift up your soul to Him!

Prayer

Father, as I begin a new day of serving the public, help me remember I have chosen this career path knowing full well there would be rough days. Strengthen me so my tone reflects the Christ in me and points people toward You. In Jesus' name, I pray. Amen.

Patricia A. Maley

Week 46, Day 4

with the seed you plant

Reading

1 Corinthians 3:7 [KJV] So then neither is he that planteth anything, neither he that watereth; but God that giveth the increase.

Reflection

My job often requires me to travel, and when I do, I find time to visit churches to witness how God works in so many different ministries. On one Wednesday night, I attended the bible study of a small church. As I listened to the extremely wise 78-year-old saint teaching the class, I was touched by his humbleness and extensive knowledge of the word and ministry. Chatting with him and his wife afterwards, I asked this old man what kept him active in ministry. He answered, "You never know what God will do **with the seed you plant**."

Now I didn't fully appreciate his response until his wife told me he once led a particular person to the Lord. That person became the pastor of one of my nation's largest worldwide ministries – a preacher everyone knows! The faithfulness of this old bible teacher indirectly led millions to be saved. While most will never know his name, this 78-year-old saint was the instrument of eternal change – because he was faithful to *plant a seed* that someone else watered and God increased it in great measure.

You and I often get discouraged by our circumstance. We grow frustrated in our limited contributions to *anything*, including work. We question our influence on others – especially coworkers and the citizens we serve. The older you get, the more you wonder about it.

Yet know God understands your circumstance. Your job is more than a money-maker to Him. Your career is more than an earthly path to Him. What you do has value to Him. Your work *is* a ministry – a blessing God has entrusted to you. And you may never know the outcome, but still be faithful and *plant a seed*. God will be faithful to His word and give the increase.

Yes, today at work, you have the value of a 78-year-old saint! And who knows what God will do **with the seed you plant** today? In His tomorrows, God will give the increase!

Prayer

God, give me the stamina to be faithful in planting seeds. May I seize the opportunities You provide and be thankful for the blessing of being used to further

Your kingdom. Increase that which I have planted so You may receive the glory. In Jesus' name, I pray. Amen.

Bill Dudley

Week 46, Day 5

share in that joy

Reading

Philippians 2:17 [NLT] But I will rejoice even if I lose my life, pouring it out like a liquid offering to God, just like your faithful service is an offering to God. And I want all of you to share that joy.

Reflection

I am always blessed with joy in helping my church build the Body of Christ here on Life Row. But one of the best joys came when I helped a very young brother. Once a Christian, he allowed his circumstance to pull him away from God. He felt the wickedness of his sin was too much for the church. Satan re-owned him, and Satan did not want to give that life back.

But God did not let me give up on this young brother. I dug deep in the Word and in prayer.

I rejoice in telling you this young brother finally lost his life – again – to Christ. He poured out his old life like a liquid offering to God. And just three weeks ago, he preached a powerful sermon in my church! Oh, I did **share in that joy!**

Faithful service can happen anywhere, and it must happen <u>everywhere</u>. Someone cannot get over his circumstance. Someone's wickedness of sin blocks her from the church door. This person may sit next to you on the bus going to work. You may carpool with her. You may work right next to him each day.

Today at work, your faithful service is needed in rebuilding someone's faith. Be His instrument in bringing that person back to Christ. Make Satan give up a life that does not belong to him. It will be the hardest work you do, and it will be work not done in a day.

But in the end, when that person loses his life – again – to Christ, you <u>will</u> **share in that joy!**

Prayer

Father, in the name of Jesus, I pray. Thank You for showing me the joy of helping others see Your love and grace. Give me courage to help someone today – that lost person who needs You most. I yearn so much to **share in that joy!** Amen.

Jimmy Davis, Jr.

Week 47, Day 1

enough evidence to convict

Reading

Philippians 3:17 [ESV] Brothers, join in imitating me, and keep your eyes on those who walk according to the example you have in us.

Reflection

I once had a coworker who never preached and never talked about church, but everyone knew he was the most sincere and honest Christian because of the way he lived. He represented Christ to everyone at work. Even non-Christians came to him in times of trouble. Certainly, there was **enough evidence to convict** him of being Christ-like!

How about you?

How do you handle yourself at work? How do you react to stress? Do you curse and swear? What do you say about others? Do you gossip? If you were put on trial by your coworkers, accused of being Christ-like, would there be **enough evidence to convict**?

Just a reminder: others are *watching your example*. And this is especially true at work. It doesn't matter if you wear a cross. Makes no difference if your Bible is up front on your desk. Do others see Christ in your words and deeds?

Today at work, draw others closer to Him by your example. And if you're accused of being Christ-like, just make sure there is **enough evidence to convict**!

Prayer

Dear Lord, live Your life in me – an example of how You lived while on earth. At work today, help me be so much like You and so less like me. In Your name, I pray. Amen.

Chris Summers

Week 47, Day 2

exercise by walking in faith

Reading

Colossians 3:7-10 [NIV] You used to walk in these ways, in the life you lived. But now you must also rid yourselves of all such things as these: anger, rage, malice, slander, and filthy language from your lips. Do not lie to each other, since you have taken off your old self with its practices and have put on the new self, which is being renewed in knowledge in the image of its Creator.

Lamentations 3: 23-24 [NIV] Because of the LORD's great love we are not consumed, for his compassions never fail. They are new every morning.

Reflection

Do you exercise daily? I walk early each morning, and I take my dog with me. (And to be honest, I don't know which end of the leash enjoys it most!) For me, sunrises bring new hope for each day. And looking at God's sunrise allows me to reflect on the daily renewal of His mercies.

You know, scripture uses the word "walk" to describe how we are to live our lives. As *Christ Workers,* you and I must rid ourselves of the ways we used to walk – in anger, malice, slander, filthy language, lies. We must **exercise by walking in faith** to put on the new self. That's the only way we can remove the old self that does not conform to God's ways.

So I can't just walk the dog each morning without pondering the previous day. I try to think whether I showed gratitude to Christ for what He has done for me. I realize I must not only exercise by walking in body, I must also **exercise by walking in faith**.

Are you walking through the daily work grind in a manner worthy of Christ? Or is there a reflection of your old life casting a shadow? Do you truly **exercise by walking in faith** – interacting with everyone as Christ would – or are you simply exercising, walking, alone?

You may not physically exercise before work, and if you do, you may not include your dog! But just don't forget to **exercise by walking in faith** this morning. Like the sunrise, the beauty and glory of God must be reflected in your workday – in your office, meetings, and conversations.

So as you prepare for work, enjoy the sunrise and put on your new self. For His mercies are new every morning!

Prayer

As the sun rises, God give me grace to be rooted and grounded in Christ so that I may exercise my faith walk this day and every day – showing the love, mercy, and grace of Jesus to others. I ask this in Your Son's name. Amen.

Jan Bedogne

Week 47, Day 3

every bit as relevant

Reading

2 Timothy 3:16-17 [ESV] All Scripture is breathed out by God and profitable for teaching, for reproof, for correction, and for training in righteousness, that the man of God may be competent, equipped for every good work.

Malachi 3:6(a) [ESV] I the Lord do not change.

Reflection

"Irrelevant." "Meaningless." "Pointless." "Those laws were for so long ago." "God wouldn't have said that today." "This doesn't apply to me."

When I was earning my bachelor's degree, I heard *those words and phrases* all the time. Even when the topic centered on jobs and careers – and how to get and keep one. So many in undergraduate school did not understand *God does not change*.

While this world continues to fall away from Christ, He still preaches that the "new" way of life must be the "old" way of life – and the "new" ways of climbing the career ladder must be consistent with the "old" way God still wants. And so I can't believe God would say things way back then that are irrelevant or meaningless or pointless today – especially when it comes to how you and I view our lives and career paths.

The world has less tolerance for what you believe as a *Christ Worker*. And I know at work you constantly have people wanting you to embrace the idea that God does not care how you live and what you do. But *God does not change*!

At work today, fight against those words and phrases. Stick with His words and phrases. Know God's words and phrases are **every bit as relevant** today as they were in the time of Jesus. So at work, continue to follow God's commands, and do so with the assurance that He cares.

Yes, wherever your career takes you, God is there for you and He never changes. His words and phrases are **every bit as relevant** in your workplace – today as yesterday. And tomorrow.

Prayer

Heavenly Father, thank You for Your word and Your truth. I praise You that

Your word is constant and just like You; it never changes. In Your Son's name, I pray. Amen.

Brock Wolitarsky

Week 47, Day 4

ahead of the game

Reading

Galatians 6:9 [ESV] And let us not grow weary of doing good, for in due season we will reap, if we do not give up.

Philippians 2:3 [ESV] Do nothing from selfish ambition or conceit, but in humility count others more significant than yourselves.

Reflection

Meetings. Deadlines. Newly assigned deadlines. And always the extemporaneous. It's Monday, and I already have a robust to-do list. And so I renew a daily commitment to complete tasks way in advance. Yes, I'm very proud of staying **ahead of the game**!

But walking towards my office, with coffee in hand, I see my former intern waiting at the door. He is a recent full-time hire, so we are now coworkers, and frankly, his problems are no longer mine as I have my own robust to-do list.

Yet his frantic face tells me he's nervous about his first major project. And he's behind the curve. A deadline is approaching, and a presentation is even closer at hand. He desperately needs help to calm down, stay focused, and gain confidence.

At this moment, I have a choice; send him on his way dooming his confidence to failure and his project to incompletion. Or forget about staying **ahead of the game** on this day, right now, and help this coworker.

How you react to situations can define your faith. Do you respond with compassion or selfishness? As a *Christ Worker*, you are required by Christ to sacrifice your time to further the Kingdom and put others first.

So at work today, help that young coworker who is overloaded. You may experience stress for doing so, but you can take it. After all, you are **ahead of the game**.

Today at work, your willingness to sacrifice time for a coworker can be the ultimate way to show Christ's love.

And doing that, my friend, will keep you truly **ahead of the game**.

Prayer

Lord, I sacrifice my time and life for You. Bless my interactions with coworkers today, and help me overcome selfishness. This day belongs to You, and the real game is You. Help me stay in pace with Your game, not mine! In Your name, I pray. Amen.

Joseph N. Harrell, III

Week 47, Day 5

that same one Jesus had

Reading

Philippians 2:3(a),4-5 [NLT] Don't be selfish... Don't look out only for your own interests, but take an interest in others, too. You must have the same attitude that Christ Jesus had.

Reflection

One day last week, I was jogging outside, and my eye came across something on the basketball court. It was the kind of thing that could have ended up bad for everyone in the yard.

So I stopped jogging and walked over to the brother on the basketball court. I said let's talk – but he hesitated. But soon we started walking and talking for the rest of the hour we had outside. While I might have gotten into trouble just walking with this brother, it wasn't me I was looking out for. I was just trying to *have that attitude* – you know, **that same one Jesus had.**

Later that day, a note from that brother was passed to me from down the row. He thanked me for allowing God to use me in such a way to keep him out of trouble. He thanked me for taking an attitude that was more concerned about him than me.

Who are you willing to take an interest in at work today? Is there someone messing up? Taking an easy way to get the job done – but a way that does not glorify God? Cutting corners out of selfishness? Doing something out of arrogance? Spreading rumors? Not working well with others?

Is there someone who does not have that attitude – **that same one Jesus had**? And what about your attitude at work? Is it the same one you take to church?

As you start the workday, take an interest in others. Share that special attitude – you know, **that same one Jesus had**. If you do, you will truly be helping His kingdom.

Prayer

Father, in the name of Jesus, I pray. Sometimes I get caught up in my own interest. My own selfishness. Only You can enlighten my eyes and heart so I can show others the same attitude of Your Son. Enlighten me this day. Amen.

Jimmy Davis, Jr.

Week 48, Day 1

no matter what is said and done

Reading

Psalm 55:12-14 [NLT] It is not an enemy who taunts me—I could bear that. It is not my foes who so arrogantly insult me—I could have hidden from them. Instead, it is you—my equal, my companion and close friend. What good fellowship we once enjoyed as we walked together to the house of God.

Luke 6:27 [NLT] But to you who are willing to listen, I say, love your enemies! Do good to those who hate you.

Reflection

A few years back, a coworker and I were very close. But something happened – we lost our way and decided to go our separate ways. I was hurt for a long time, and a part of me wanted to apologize. But I didn't apologize. I couldn't because I felt I did nothing wrong. And besides, this former friend started to spread rumors about my family. It was dreadful.

I wanted to lash out and defend myself. I wanted to tell everyone she was lying and trying to make me feel bad since we were no longer friends. But then Jesus took my hand and asked if I were listening. He then reminded me of His love and instructed me to pass His love to that former friend. So **no matter what is said and done**, I must <u>love</u> that person.

At work today, is there a coworker hurting you? A supervisor? Are rumors flying about? If you listen to Him, you will hear this: **no matter what is said and done**, you must love that person.

So today at work, it's not going to be easy. You and I both must find a way to walk in fellowship **no matter what is said and done**. You and I must be willing to listen to Him.

Prayer

Thank You, God, for allowing me to listen to You. Give me courage to love those who do not love me. In Your Son's name, I pray. Amen!

Maureen Bereznak

Week 48, Day 2

with justice and mercy

Reading

Matthew 23:23(b) [NIV] you hypocrites! You give a tenth of your spices – mint, dill and cumin. But you have neglected the more important matters of the law – justice, mercy and faithfulness. You should have practiced the latter, without neglecting the former.

Reflection

Public servants are often implementers of the law. In fact, my country's constitution requires administrators to execute the laws of the land. And we certainly try to do that, as I'm sure you do in your country. But is that enough?

We tend to think of upholding the law as just following its legal intent. But scripture says it's more than that – it must be entwined **with justice and mercy**. Sure, faithful to the intent of the law, but mercy and justice must also be served. Now that is a big challenge in any country – implementing the law faithfully but **with justice and mercy**.

As you rush from one task to another, from one crisis to another, it's easy to forget doing so **with justice and mercy**. But you are a *Christ Worker*.

So today at work, don't just give a tenth to your tasks. Remember what Christ expects. Don't just implement mechanically. Implement **with justice and mercy**.

In your office or in your community – in the committee room or on the street – don't be a hypocrite in the eyes of Christ. Go do your job **with justice and mercy**.

You are, after all, His servant and worker.

Prayer

Lord, Creator of the Universe and the foundation of the Law, thank You for giving me knowledge that the law and regulations must be administered with more than just mechanics. Help me remember this in my busy day as I go forth to perform my vocation. May Your Spirit fill my heart and my tasks today. In Your name, I pray. Amen.

Allen Stout

Week 48, Day 3

all alone in your workplace

Reading

Matthew 27:46(b) [KJV] and about the ninth hour Jesus cried with a loud voice, saying, Eli, Eli, lama sabachthanl? That is to say, My God, my God, why hast thou forsaken me?

Hebrews 13:5(b) [KJV] for He hath said, I will never leave thee, nor forsake thee

Reflection

It's so easy to feel like you are **all alone in your workplace**. Given the economy, you see many people feeling that way. Wondering about the future. Worried about layoffs. It's hardest on Christians because troubled times can erroneously bring on some anger toward God. In your workplace, you may feel like you are all alone in standing up for our Lord.

When you feel this way, do not forget Jesus was all alone on that cruel cross. Oh, history records other people watching, but our Lord was by himself as He felt the worst possible suffering! Even our supreme God had to forsake Him for our benefit.

Praise God you will never have to go through that kind of loneliness. True, things might happen to make you believe you are the only light in a dark world. Or that you are the only darkness in a bright world. But just remember His promise: *I will never leave thee*!

Today at work, thank God for your Christian brothers and sisters, and thank God for Jesus. As bad as things might get, know you are not **all alone in your workplace**.

Eli, Eli, lama sabachthanl? No way! Be certain He has not!

Prayer

Dear God, thank You for sending Your son to die on the cross for my sins – for removing a debt I could never pay. Thank You, Lord, for willingly taking that punishment all alone so I can go free and never be all alone! Let me spread this Good News today in my workplace. In the name of Jesus, I pray! Amen.

Debra Neal

Week 48, Day 4

the singularity of serving

Reading

1 Corinthians 3:6 (NIV) I planted the seed, Apollos watered it, but God has been making it grow.

Reflection

How often do we fall short of His glory? As public servants, perhaps it's because you and I fail to see **the singularity of serving** both the King of the Universe and the citizens of our community.

In growing the community, make sure you're actually farming the land of the Owner and not just the sharecrop you claim. Both seeds and water need to be blessed by God. Work the soil with faith, and irrigate hope with nothing but pure and unconditional love for God. Only then will the blossoming of His fruit and vegetation become a healthy harvest for those we serve. Only then will you see **the singularity of serving** God and community.

Today at work, God wants to use you in mighty ways. He wants to do so until you retire or until He calls you home. Your job is to grow in His knowledge and wisdom in order to meet the challenges you face and to bless those you serve.

So today, go work in His garden! See **the singularity of serving** both King and citizens. Surely, His glory will shine, and your community's harvest will be bountiful!

Prayer

Father, make me a good farmer today. Bless Your field in which I work. Give me strength and wisdom not to deny You anything – including my loyalty and dedication to the commands of Your Word. You instruct me to be like Your Son, and this is how I want to be. It is in Your Son's name that I pray. Amen.

Ellen C. Stamm

Week 48, Day 5

things from the vending machines

Reading

John 4:34(b) [MSG] The food that keeps me going is that I do the will of the one who sent me, finishing the work he started.

Reflection

The only food you get in a lock-down is bologna sandwiches and hotdogs. And for the last several weeks, we were on lock-down. Now there's nothing wrong with bologna and hotdogs – but three times a day for several weeks? You get a little tired of it.

Well, last Friday the lock-down was lifted – just in time for my scheduled visitation. I get two each month, and a good brother travels many miles to visit me – he is my only visitor for over 10 years. And when he comes, he follows the custom here of bringing in a large bag of quarters so I can eat **things from the vending machines**: hamburgers, chicken sandwiches, hoagies. I probably eat five or six sandwiches during our four-hour visits, and the food is really good.

But the True Food accompanying our conversation – the food that keeps both of us going – is the food the Holy Spirit brings to our table! Oh sure, we talk about a lot of things – sports, family, friends, news, his challenges and mine – but all is anchored in Jesus' heart. Everything we talk about – the fun and the serious stuff – always leads to Him. And this True Food helps keep me and my friend on the path of *working on the work* Jesus started in both of us.

And so the True Food is great! Last week there was no room on my plate for an order of anger at those who caused the lock-down or even a side of bitterness about being stuck in my cell for those many days – eating only bologna and hotdogs. No, I was nourished with much more than **things from the vending machines**!

Today at work, no matter how frustrated you get – no matter what kind of lock-down you find yourself in – the only thing that will keep you going is the True Food from doing the will of the One who sent you. Your nourishment will not come from bologna or hotdogs. It will not be **things from the vending machines** in your breakroom. It will come from His table, not yours.

And you will have need on your plate for nothing more!

Prayer

Father, in the name of Jesus, I pray. Continue to feed me Your nourishment, not mine, so I can keep *working on the work* you started in me. I thank You for Your banquet! Amen.

Jimmy Davis, Jr.

Week 49, Day 1

do your Father's business, quietly

Readings

Matthew 6:1-4 (NIV) Be careful not to practice your righteousness in front of others to be seen by them. If you do, you will have no reward from your Father in heaven. "So when you give to the needy, do not announce it with trumpets, as the hypocrites do in the synagogues and on the streets, to be honored by others. Truly I tell you, they have received their reward in full. But when you give to the needy, do not let your left hand know what your right hand is doing, so that your giving may be in secret. Then your Father, who sees what is done in secret, will reward you.

Reflection

There are reasons for "employee recognition" programs. You know, sometimes you see a sign in the parking lot "reserved for employee of the month." Such rewards are meant to lift morale, encourage workers to do their best, and acknowledge top performance.

But Christians also know there can be danger in such programs. There is always a fine line between boasting and accurately reporting one's performance. Reporting makes you and me good stewards. But if we applaud ourselves, then that is the only reward we get!

Now, how empty is that?

As a *Christ Worker*, don't be a hypocrite. Don't boast to others and, if you win an award, don't applaud yourself. If you are truly serving others for the sake of Christ, God knows it. Your reward will be forthcoming, and it will be eternal.

Winning an award can be an appropriate response to your good performance. But just **do your Father's business, quietly**. And don't worry about who fills that reserved spot in the parking lot. You already have a special place reserved in heaven!

Today at work, **do your Father's business, quietly**.

Prayer

Dear Lord, show me Your ways and Your heart. Help me do for others in Your name – for You and not for me. Thank You for my eternal reward. I am eternally grateful. In Your name, I pray. Amen.

Kathleen Patterson

Week 49, Day 2

not just His worker

Reading

2 Corinthians 5:21 [NIV] God made him who had no sin to be sin for us, so that in him we might become the righteousness of God.

Reflection

You ever stepped in to do something for someone who did not expect your help? Did something that cost you a lot? Time? Money? Physical pain? Suffering?

Have you?

Well, that's what Jesus did for you at Calvary.

So at work today, remember what Christ did for you and what He has called you to do. Be His representative, no matter how hard it may be, to everyone you meet. Why? Because of what He did for you. Don't forget He chose you to be – **not just His worker** in this world – but to be with Him throughout eternity.

Keep this wonderful fact close throughout the workday: you are **not just His worker**; you are more – much, much more.

Prayer

Lord, thank You for choosing me! Give me courage and opportunity to express my thanks to You during this workday by the way I live my life for You. Let me help others know that You have chosen them, too. In Jesus' name, I pray. Amen.

Gilbert O. Craven

Week 49, Day 3

lift you up in due time

Reading

Job 6:2(b) [NIV] If only my anguish could be weighed and all my misery be placed on the scales!

Hebrews 10:23 [NIV] Let us hold unswervingly to the hope we profess, for he who promised is faithful.

1 Peter 5:6 [NIV)\] Humble yourselves, therefore, under God's mighty hand, that he may **lift you up in due time**.

Reflection

For more than a decade, my life has been stripped of nearly everyone and everything. My parents died. My sister and brother moved far away. I've been ill and suffering greatly, like a burn victim with skin stripping away again and again just as it starts to heal. A semi-truck ran over my car. My house was broken into. And I was laid off from work.

So I've cried out to God. I cried long and hard. Why is all this happening to me? I blamed Him. Each day I shouted, "Why are You breaking me again and again and again!"

A couple of months ago, He actually answered. I heard His Voice: "If I take everything ... if you have nothing ... if I am all you have left ... *will you still love Me?*"

I didn't know how to answer, but I knew He was talking to me. I finally whispered back to that Voice, "In spite of circumstances, in spite of how life looks from the outside, in spite of a thousand different things, the answer is YES! *I love You, Lord.*"

His question was a great gift. It allowed me to put life in perspective. How blessed I really am! The God of all creation loves me so much He would take the time to strip my life so I might know the joy of truly loving Him. I have regained the blessing of trusting Him. I know *He who promises so much is so faithful.* I know He will lift me up in His due time.

God is preparing you for the times ahead. In life and in work, you will struggle. But you were chosen for this time. And as a *Christ Worker*, you're called into all the tomorrows you have to stand against darkness and to offer His light to the world. Despite your suffering, people count on you.

Today, you'll want to weigh your anguish – put all your miseries on the scale. You'll want to blame God. But don't! No, just seek Him, cling to Him, and sing His praises. It is He who promises. It is He who is faithful. It is He who will **lift you up in due time**.

Yes, at work and elsewhere, He <u>will</u> **lift you up in due time**. Until then, know He is blessing you richly!

<u>Prayer</u>

Father, You are the Hope I profess. I come to You humbly knowing You will lift me up in Your time – not mine. Thank You for blessing me so richly. In Jesus' name, I pray. Amen.

Lori Jordan

Week 49, Day 4

in the reminding business

Reading

Psalm 40:3 [HCSB] He put a new song in my mouth, a hymn of praise to our God. Many will see and fear and put their trust in the LORD.

Song of Solomon 2:15 [HCSB] Catch the foxes for us – the little foxes that ruin the vineyards – for our vineyards are in bloom.

Reflection

Workday morning! Getting my thoughts back onto work after a wonderful evening with loved-ones is not easy – especially when it's so beautiful outside.

My computer is very slow to start-up in the mornings, and consequently, I don't shut it down at night. But this morning I'm encountering problems with it... I reboot (again) as the icons disappear (once again) and still nothing happens... Go away little fox!

I decide to get a cup of tea while awaiting the second-coming of my computer. I notice a quote hanging off the string of the tea bag: "Sing from your heart." Ah... even in the workday morning, God is **in the reminding business**. And then He puts a new song in my mouth, Jessi Colter's *His Eyes are on the Sparrow*. And so I sing in praise of him: "I sing because I'm happy, I sing because I'm free. His eye is on the sparrow, and I know He watches me."

God is so amazing! I may be sitting in a small cubicle and not flying outside like a sparrow, but the Lord has just set me free, and that's something to sing about!

Even in the workday morning, He blesses me beyond belief. He knows what my heart needs at this very moment – at every moment.

Today at work, be aware of the little foxes (thoughts, people, technology) that visit early in the morning to ruin your vineyard (your peace, relationships with coworkers, your witness). God has planted you at this specific workplace for such a time as this. And He is **in the reminding business**.

So even on this workday morning, trust in Him and *bloom*... let others pick up the aroma of God's peace in your worklife.

And when the little foxes show up, look for signs of His glory throughout the day. After all, He's **in the reminding business** – even on workday mornings!

Prayer

Thank You, Lord, for Your immeasurable love, patience, grace, and mercy. Help me recognize the little foxes that come to ruin my vineyards. Let them not distract me from doing Your work and being a blessing to others. Lord, I don't always see my cup overflowing, but I know You will remind me that it always does. In Your name, I pray. Amen.

Suzanne Bourque

Week 49, Day 5

the man-made bars

Reading

Judges 6:14-15 [MSG] But GOD faced him directly: "Go in this strength that is yours. Save Israel from Midian. Haven't I just sent you?" Gideon said to him, "*Me*, my master? How and with what could I ever save Israel? Look at me. My clan's the weakest in Manasseh and I'm the runt of the litter."

Reflection

I heard a brother crying out that he could not help his family in any way because he sat here on Life Row. I remember the times when I felt that way – of being helpless to others because of **the man-made bars** surrounding me. They make you feel like you're the helpless runt of the litter.

I reminded that brother that I've been behind **the man-made bars** decades longer than him. I told him he has to get over it and just go do Jesus' will. If the Lord has need of him helping his family, the Lord will provide the way. And the Lord does not view him as the helpless runt of the litter. So he needed to *just go do His will*!

Have you ever felt like the helpless runt of the litter? Have you cried out about **the man-made bars** you live and work behind? You know they're of your own making, don't you? Our Lord puts no bars around you. No, He sets you free! So don't look at who you are or where you are. Look at who Jesus wants you to be and where he is sending you. *Then just go do His will*.

Today at work, maybe there is more to do than you think you can handle. More paperwork. More deadlines. More stress and anxiety. Then there are the family concerns you bring with you to work. You look around and see so many people suffering – so many you don't think you can help.

But you can! You are not the helpless runt of the litter. You are a *Christ Worker*. He is shaping you to do His will. So just go do His will.

At work today, break out of **the man-made bars**. If I can, so can you!

Prayer

Father, in the name of Jesus, I pray. Continue to give me confidence – not in me, but in You. For without You, I remain the helpless runt of the litter not being able to do anything or help anyone. No, Lord. Give me confidence in You. With the help of the Holy Spirit, give me strength to just go and do Your will. Amen.

Jimmy Davis, Jr.

Week 50, Day 1

bring many to the Well

Reading

John 4:15(a), 39-42 [NIRV] The woman said to him, "Sir, give me this water. Then I will never be thirsty…"… Many of the Samaritans from the town of Sychar believed in Jesus. They believed because of the woman's witness. She said, "He told me everything I've ever done." Then the Samaritans came to him and tried to get him to stay with them. So he stayed two days. Because of his words, many more people became believers. They said to the woman, "We no longer believe just because of what you said. We have now heard for ourselves. We know that this man really is the Savior of the world."

Reflection

Ever gone to see something out of curiosity, but then was convicted because of your own encounter? Perhaps it was someone with a different background. Or maybe it was a person speaking a different language. Well, scripture tells of the Samaritan whose nationality, race, and gender allowed her to bring a whole city to the feet of Jesus.

In our day – with so many fixed opinions about race, nationality, culture, marital status, and economic plight – it's easy to forget God created you and me (EVERYONE) *perfectly* – just as we are for this exact time and place. He doesn't want sin, but He doesn't want you to be ashamed of who you are or what you've done. No. He wants you to share your story as a *witness to His Glory and Grace* so that you might speak a language that will **bring many to the Well**.

It's hard to be open about your personal story. Some may laugh. Others may judge and take retribution in one way or another. This is especially true in the workplace.

But today at work, be like that Samaritan woman. Have courage to witness about your encounter with Christ. In the elevator, tell a coworker or citizen about what He said to you at the Well. At lunch, be proud to show how much God loves even <u>you</u> – despite what you've done in the past. Throughout the day, let Him use your story to **bring many to the Well**.

True, you may seem like a curiosity. Don't worry. Just plant the seeds and let Jesus do the convicting.

Yes, at work today, share your witness. Soon others won't need your story to believe. And they, too, will **bring many to the Well**.

Prayer

Thank You, Father, for my story about how You gave me water at the well. At work today, give me courage to witness out loud! I pray this in Jesus' name. Amen.

Kathryn Saunders

Week 50, Day 2

destroyed by pride

Reading

Proverbs 16:18-19 [NKJV] Pride goes before destruction, and a haughty spirit before a fall. Better to be of a humble spirit with the lowly, than to divide the spoil with the proud.

Reflection

Recently, my division executed an event for which we worked hard over many months. The event lasted for most of the day, and it was a tremendous success. Since I had been in the planning stage, as well as implementation stage, I was feeling pretty good about myself and the accomplishment to which I contributed.

When I returned to my office after the event, I had an unexpected visitor. Someone came to complain about my demeanor toward one of his assistants. In a couple of minutes, I went from the proverbial "penthouse" of pride (for the success of the program) to the "basement" of shame (for the way my pride must have come across to that assistant). When this person left my office, I was certainly deflated. But then I realized this was the Lord's way of reminding me about being prideful.

I thank God for keeping me grounded in humility so that I am not **destroyed by pride**.

Everyone in the public service works harder than most people imagine. And you and I can be justifiably proud of the job well done. Yet pride is a dangerous thing, for if it causes us to puff up. Worse, it destroys our ability to glorify God.

As a *Christ Worker*, do not lose touch with the humble spirit. Do not be **destroyed by pride**. Today at work, glorify only God.

Prayer

Lord, at work today let me not be **destroyed by pride**. I seek to glorify You and only You in my workplace and in the work that I do. I seek to remain humble in Your service. In Your name, I pray. Amen.

David Boisselle

Week 50, Day 3

lead and follow by His example

Reading

Colossians 3:23 [MSG] Servants, do what you're told by your earthly masters. And don't just do the minimum that will get you by. Do your best. Work from the heart for your real Master, for God, confident that you'll get paid in full when you come into your inheritance. Keep in mind always that the ultimate Master you're serving is Christ. The sullen servant who does shoddy work will be held responsible. Being a follower of Jesus doesn't cover up bad work.

Reflection

We've heard it before: "Government workers are lazy, incompetent, and only interested in making life difficult for the citizens who pay their wages!" It isn't true, of course, yet many work in that hostile culture. And we all have to endure each day the damaging consequences of that mantra: "Do more with less." The constant indictment of public service is enough for anyone to give up and just go through the motions.

But God is very clear in His instructions: Don't just get by. Don't cover up bad work. Don't allow the complainers to dismiss your integrity and disqualify the quality of your work. No, we are to *repay each complaint with excellent service and exceptional kindness*. We do this, not because we're better than secularists and non-Christians, but because we serve the best Master of all. Yes, we are to **lead and follow by His example** – the example of Christ.

Today at work, you and I may not be immune to troubles imposed by a hostile culture. But those troubles will not negatively affect the quality of our work. And, if we **lead and follow by His example**, won't others begin to ask "What makes the *Christ Worker* so different?" Won't they be drawn to Christ through our best work?

As this workday begins, **lead and follow by His example**. It is what your Lord commands. It is what this hostile world needs most.

Prayer

Father, I am so grateful for Your ever-present guidance in my work and in my life. May my work never be less than my very best. May my obedience to Your instructions demonstrate to others that You are the Way, the Truth, and the Life. In Your Son's name, I pray. Amen.

Anne-Marie Amiel

Week 50, Day 4

even in this wilderness

Reading

Jeremiah 2:2(b) [NLT] I remember how eager you were to please me as a young bride long ago, how you loved me and followed me even through the barren wilderness.

Galatians 6:9 [NLT] So let's not get tired of doing what is good. At just the right time we will reap a harvest of blessing if we don't give up.

Reflection

The stakes are high, demand is increasing, and politics supersedes everything. You and I were once excited about work and career. Was it just yesterday? But today – perhaps this very minute – you've become cynical and I'm so tired. To both of us, nothing seems right. You begin to wonder, is this the right job for me? I wonder, am I on the right career path? How did the newness of the day, the excitement of the doing, wear off so fast?

All public servants feel this way at times. We are strapped with shrinking resources and dwindling support, and our back is always burdened with unlimited demands.

But we are *Christian* public servants – *Christ Workers*. We are unique. When that drain begins to happen, we run to God. After all, we serve a sovereign God of the *Final Say*.

So He calls you and me to do good and be eager – **even in this wilderness**. And today – right now – He is planning to give both of us a *harvest of blessing*.

On this workday, forget about all the stuff going on. Don't get tired of doing what is good. Be eager to serve Him – **even in this wilderness**. Count on it – that harvest is surely coming!

Prayer

Father God, thank You for every opportunity to serve You and Your people. Grant me wisdom, anointing, humbleness, and enthusiasm to serve – **even in this wilderness**. I know You are planning to bless me in so many ways! In Your Son's precious name, I pray. Amen.

LaShonda Garnes

Week 50, Day 5

let God work out the negative

Reading

Genesis 50:19-20(a) [MSG] Joseph replied, "Don't be afraid. Do I act for God? Don't you see, you planned evil against me but God used those same plans for my good, as you see all around you right now—life for many people."

Reflection

When I was sentenced to death, I was taken away from all my loved-ones. But today, God uses that sentence for my good. People not only judged me but said I was worthless. But today, people from all walks of life say that who I have become shows them Jesus' grace and mercy. And even though I am in an 8'x 5'cell 23 hours each day, today I get to share His Gospel with people around the world.

Now, I did not act as God. No, I trusted God to act for me. You see, I **let God work out the negative** in my life.

So **let God work out the negative** in your life, in your work, and in your career. Let Him do so for your good. Then you will not only be able to forgive others, you will also be a blessing to others.

Yes, **let God work out the negative** – in your life, in your work – in you!

Prayer

Father, in the name of Jesus, I pray. Thank You for Your awesome love for me. Father, it is You who worked everything out for my good – even when I felt hopeless. Amen.

Jimmy Davis, Jr.

Week 51, Day 1

something going on

Reading

Hebrews 3:13(a) [GW] Encourage each other every day while you have the opportunity.

Romans 15:7 [Aramaic Bible in Plain English] Because of this, you shall accept and bear with one another, just as also The Messiah has accepted you for the glory of God.

Reflection

There's **something going on**. A coworker my friend hardly knows approached him in the elevator. She receives a daily workplace devotional via e-mail and wanted to share. They laughed when my friend said he receives it, too. Before the door opened, they quickly prayed together. Then at Wednesday night church, someone said she mentioned our Sunday school project during a break at work. Other coworkers began to chime in about their own church projects. In that break room, coworkers started to talk about Christ shaping their lives!

Look around at your workplace! Is there **something going on**? Are Christian coworkers actually getting to know each other – I mean, *as Christians*??

You know, each of us must walk our own path with Christ, but we are not alone on that journey. Just as Jesus encouraged those around Him, should we not do the same? To know that other Christian coworkers have your back is a marvelous feeling! It means someone is praying for you. It means others can help you do things and speak words in His name – things and words that may make you hesitant without the encouragement of other Christians.

What a purpose He has for us as we work together and grow in our spiritual walks! We become more like Him as we sharpen each other.

So, today at work, see if there's **something going on**. Find a way to let others know you are a Christian. Take each opportunity to encourage and bear with a brother- or sister-in-Christ.

And, who knows, you may be the one sharing this devotional in your elevator!

Prayer

Father, I come before Your throne of grace and mercy. As I walk alongside You, help me encourage others on their journey with You. In Your glory, help me make my workplace feel not so lonely and distant from You. Everything I need is in You. And it is in Your Son's name, I pray. Amen.

Ellen C. Stamm

Week 51, Day 2

His beauty in your chaos

Reading

Psalm 111:2 [NIV] Great are the works of the LORD; they are pondered by all who delight in them.

Reflection

Well, it's over – an event at work that took months to plan and prepare for. The event went well, serving about one hundred military wives. Yet things got kind of crazy that afternoon as I helped this person over here, pointed that volunteer to over there, and cleaned up the messes everywhere made by little children. It was very easy to be consumed by the busy-ness of the day and to fail to see the beauty all around me. But in the midst of the chaos, I took a deep breath and noticed the real work of the day. Military wives, whose husbands are so far away, were smiling. Women who serve and sacrifice so much were making new friends. They were relaxing, laughing, and just having a good time.

If you're like me, you can get glued to the particulars of the task or notice only the seeming chaos surrounding the job. You can forget to see the beauty of God's own work.

So as this workweek begins, don't lose sight of *the work God is doing in your work*. When tasks become consuming or crazy, take a deep breath and look for **His beauty in your chaos**. The opportunity to serve a citizen, help a coworker, complete the task, work hard – the chance to change the heart and life of someone else – are all part of His work in your work.

So yes, don't forget His work really is found within the busy-ness of your work. As a *Christ Worker*, take a deep breath and look for **His beauty in your chaos**.

Prayer

Thank You, Father, for every little blessing – even the smallest of things like a smile or a laugh. I pray that my mind will be set on You this workweek so that even when things get crazy I can see how You are working in my life and the lives around me. In Your Son's name, I pray. Amen.

Brooke A. H. Neale

Week 51, Day 3

become the Rock in your workplace

Reading

Matthew 16:18(a) [NIV] And I tell you that you are Peter, and on this rock I will build My church...

Romans 12:2(a) [NIV] Do not conform to the pattern of this world, but be transformed by the renewing of your mind.

Reflection

In my country, it is quite common for firefighters to acquire nicknames. Most receive a nickname based on something done in emergencies or because of personality.

You know, Jesus gave Simon son of Jonah a nickname – "Peter the Rock." We don't know if the nickname was based on work done or personality. After all, Peter's work was just about to begin, and Simon's personality was reportedly, well, a bit impetuous, brash, impulsive, loud, outspoken, and self-confident. Let's face it; Simon son of Jonah was even arrogant. Yet Jesus must have had faith that Peter the Rock could transform Simon's personality traits for God's will in the emergency of building His church. And you know what? One of Peter's best qualities became his willingness to transform the things in his life that weren't pleasing to our Lord.

There's a chance that you might also have a workplace nickname – one perhaps spoken only behind your back. Do you exhibit some of the personality traits of Simon son of Jonah? I know I do. Frankly, I sometimes act much more like Simon than like Peter the Rock.

Yet our Lord chooses you and me to be *Christ Workers* – His servants – to build His church in our workplaces and in our interactions with those we encounter in our jobs. We can be *Christ Workers* only when we let God transform us by renewing our dedication to doing His will in our lives – including in our worklives.

As a *Christ Worker*, what are you willing to do for God? Are you willing to transform your character? Are you willing to serve in a manner that shows Jesus' love towards everyone? It doesn't matter what your current nickname may be. What matters is that you and I are willing to hear, obey, and change when God calls us.

Today, **become the Rock in your workplace**, and see what eternal nickname He gives you!

<u>Prayer</u>

Lord Jesus, thank You for choosing me to do Your work. Today, transform me into Your "Rock" – a living example of Your love of those I serve. In Your name, I pray. Amen.

Stephen Pincus

Week 51, Day 4

to live in real peace

Reading

John 14:27(a) [NIV] Peace I leave with you; my peace I give you.

Reflection

The winter season is hitting where I live. Colder weather, less daylight, and rising heating bills that correspond to the weight I'm gaining from physical inactivity. Melancholy can set in for a variety of reasons.

At these times, you can feel pretty alone. So can your coworkers. So can the citizens you serve. If you are alert to what's going on, you might treat the symptoms. Use and share sound advice ranging from exercise tips to deep-breathing relaxation techniques. All of this is good, but **to live in real peace**, despite an uncertain world and a potentially dismal season, needed is more.

As a Christian, you know **to live in real peace** requires the peace that only comes from Jesus. As a *Christ Worker*, you know that **to live in real peace**, your community needs that same kind of peace. So do your coworkers and individual citizens you serve. Yes, Jesus is needed **to live in real peace**. After all, He knows you better than you know yourself.

So on this workday, reach out for Him. Then find a way to reach Him out to others. A simple reflection on His peace. A humble demonstration of His peace found in your heart. Go ahead and thank Him openly for that peace. Find a way to show the Hope for getting through the melancholy – for getting through this world – to coworkers and citizens.

Before this workday fades, find a way to show all that Jesus is needed **to live in real peace**.

Prayer

Heavenly Father, I humbly ask for Your peace that goes beyond what I can understand – the peace that You promise. I ask for unexplainable joy that comes from that peace – joy even in my workplace – in the midst of weather that makes me melancholy. I ask for Your strength to bring glory to You in accomplishing only what can be done by Your hand. In Jesus' name, I pray. Amen.

Rose Heyward

Week 51, Day 5

my Lord's presence changes everything

Reading

Genesis 28:16(b) [NLT] Surely the LORD is in this place, and I wasn't even aware of it!

Reading

Last week during church, as we were praising and worshiping our Lord, some free-world brothers heard us and came over to worship with us. Afterwards one said to me, "I wish I could worship with you guys all the time because my church doesn't have the Holy Spirit like here." Those free-world brothers were *aware of the Lord* in my place.

Surely, **my Lord's presence changes everything**! It doesn't matter that my place is what you call "death row." It doesn't matter how dark my place is or how hopeless my situation looks. Does it matter about your place? How about your situation? It shouldn't because **my Lord's presence changes everything**!

As you go to work today, be aware of the Lord's power to change the atmosphere. You are a *Christ Worker*, so know that His power can flow through you and around you.

Today, remember that your own death row can easily be changed into His Life Row. He is in your place, just as He is in mine.

Surely, **my Lord's presence changes everything**!

Prayer

Father, in the name of Jesus, I pray. Continue to keep me aware of Your presence so that I can see all Your power – so I can show others that Your presence is everywhere – even in what seems the worst place or the worst situation. You can change the atmosphere. You can change people and conditions. You can change anything and everything. You have changed me. Amen.

Jimmy Davis, Jr.

Week 52, Day 1

keep a carol in your mind

Reading

Isaiah 26:3 (TLB) He will keep in perfect peace all those who trust in him, whose thoughts turn often to the Lord!

Reflection

Today's my first workday since Christmas, and frankly, I'm a little depressed that Christmas is over. Now I have to face the grim reality of the workday world: commuting in rush-hour traffic, the uncertainty of weather, finding a parking place, shuffling into the office, starting anew with the daily stress of schedules, commitments, deadlines, challenging clients, and difficult managers. It's as if my colorful, happy balloon has suddenly burst. Stark reality descends.

But getting into that cold car and turning on my favorite radio station, I find joy. No way! Are they still playing Christmas carols? What a wonderful surprise! Somehow, Christmas remains!!

I begin to remember the *emotional Christmases* of my past. Family and friends, the proverbial visit to Grandma's house, and all the music, color, and lights. But having become a practicing Christian just weeks ago – I now recall the *spiritual essence* of Christmases past and why all the joy is here today because of it.

I pull into the parking lot, walk into work, and remain afloat on my thoughts of it all. It's not just the Christmas music that has me up – no, it's so much more. It's the birth of the Most Special One – and it's His rebirth in my heart each day since I truly met Him.

So today at work, **keep a carol in your mind**. You know it's not just the Christmas music – it's the reminder of His birth that will keep you afloat. Yes, **keep a carol in your mind** and remember in your heart why this workday must surely fill you with joy.

Yes, **keep a carol in your mind** every workday, and just see what the New Year brings!

Prayer

Dear God, may both the child in my heart and the adult in my head always remember why I am joyful of Christmas. Give me strength and courage to share this Good News throughout each workday of the year. In Your Son's name, I pray. Amen.
Patricia Baum

Week 52, Day 2

the opportunity to understand and grow in Him

Reading

2 Peter 3:18 [NKJV] but grow in the grace and knowledge of our Lord and Savior Jesus Christ. To Him *be* the glory both now and forever. Amen.

Reflection

I'm so excited! A Harvard professor wants me to go to a conference on his campus. But his message was kind of cryptic. Why me? Was I supposed to present my research? Did he want me to speak? I started to think about all the possibilities – an opportunity to travel to the States and an invitation to Harvard University!

So I went to see my senior mentor to talk about it and ask what my role would be at this important conference. Well, he sat me down and brought a bit of reality. He said, "just email the Harvard professor. Ask your questions, and wait for his response. And be honored – regardless of whether he wants you to present, speak, or just sit in the audience."

Simple. Real. Why didn't I think of that?

The reality brought by my mentor, as usual, taught me a lesson. To be present doesn't mean you always have to be noticed. To make a difference, even at a professional conference, you don't always have to give but just receive and absorb.

And there's another lesson. As a *Christ Worker*, all I need do in my work is to grow in grace and knowledge – and give Him the glory! Don't focus on me. Don't focus on the world. Don't focus on the what-ifs. Just use **the opportunity to understand and grow in Him**.

So that's what I'm doing – using **the opportunity to understand and grow in Him**.

At work today, you do the same. Opportunities are like seeds. You may not know what to expect. You may not see the detail. Your hopes may not match reality. But just remember Who gives you this seed of opportunity in the first place. And then act accordingly.

Yes, today use **the opportunity to understand and grow in Him**. And give Him the glory!

Prayer

Lord, I thank You for the many opportunities You will provide me today. Seemingly small or apparently large, all are great. Help me make the most of each as I work to grow in You. And I give You the glory through each opportunity – now and forever. In Your name, I pray. Amen.

Stephanie Van Straten

Week 52, Day 3

your Father

Reading

Matthew 6:9; 33 [NKJV] In this manner, therefore, pray: Our Father in heaven, Hallowed be Your name… But seek first the kingdom of God and His righteousness, and all these things shall be added to you.

Reflection

When my daughter was little, we were out walking in the rural countryside. She was busy demonstrating her independence from her daddy by running ahead in spite of my warnings to stay close. Suddenly an angry dog came around the corner. This dog must have been huge in my daughter's eyes. She turned back to me and ran with all her might, literally leaping into my arms. I instantly *swung her onto my shoulders* so I had both hands free to deal with the dog.

That day changed my daughter's relationship with me. While she developed her independence, she now listens to me and stays close when I tell her to. She knows her daddy is not only her protector but also someone who has her best interests at heart.

You know God warns you and me to stay close to Him, but do we listen? The honest answer is not as much as we should.

God wants you to see Him as **your Father** who protects, provides, advises, and loves. Too many fathers here on earth fail at this, but **your Father** in Heaven is the best Father – He does not fail to live up to the standard of fatherhood because He is the standard. God wants you to run into His arms when trouble arises – to depend on Him for everything. He wants you to seek His advice and wisdom. He wants you to listen to Him. He is a truly great Father who desires a relationship with you – yes, even you – His creation, His child.

At work today, will you seek His advice and wisdom? In the middle of an angry situation, will you run into His arms for protection and peace? Or will you choose to go it alone?

At work today, no matter how big or small the issue, breathe a prayer to **your Father** for help and wisdom. Know **your Father** is listening and watching.

Know **your father** is always ready to *swing you onto His shoulders*.

<u>Prayer</u>

Lord, You are my Father who loves <u>me</u> – even when I am at work. I will seek You throughout the day – because I am always in need. In Your name, I pray. Amen.

Kevin J. Cooney

Week 52, Day 4

someone in your workplace searching

Reading

Romans 5:8 [HCSB] But God proves His own love for us in that while we were still sinners, Christ died for us!

Reflection

There is **someone in your workplace searching**. That person is searching today – right before your eyes. I bet you know who it is. But you may not know how to reach that coworker. I mean, it's difficult to do the simple thing: walk right up to a coworker and just ask, "Do you know Jesus?" You fear you might get into trouble, or worse, you fear your effort might turn that person's search away from Christ.

But you've read something this morning that could help. That God's grace, motivated by His love, reached out and pursued you while you were yet hostile toward Him. That you were lost, and He pursued you. That you were once searching, but you found the answer.

Today at work, you have the opportunity to extend God's grace to someone who does not know Jesus. It may not be easy, but don't give up. Pray for the power of God's love to motivate you. Pray for a perspective of grace to see and compassionately understand the fears of that lost coworker.

Yes, at work today, who has Jesus placed on your heart to befriend or tenaciously pray for? There is **someone in your workplace searching**.

Let the end of that search begin today.

Prayer

Father, thank You for sending Your Son to die for my sins. Please use me today as Your instrument in showing Your love to others. Let the search begin to end today. In Jesus' name, I pray. Amen.

Chris Summers

Week 52, Day 5

God is in your workplace

Reading

Genesis 20:11(b) [KJV] Surely the fear of God is not in this place;

Reflection

Ever feel like God is not in your workplace? Perhaps you feel like you are the only Christian where you work – so how could He possibly be there?

Well, Abraham felt the same way about the place he was in. And look what happened. He trusted himself, not God, and lied and deceived others.

When you feel like God is not in the place where you're at – including your workplace – then you might feel as if you don't have to show the God who lives in you and through you. You become like everyone else in that place. You lose the *fear of God*.

As this work-year comes to a close and as the new work-year is about to begin, do not doubt **God is in your workplace**. Don't lose the fear of God. He is there to help you – if you trust Him. He is inside you and around you.

So at work throughout each year, trust God to help you reveal Him to others by allowing Him to flow through you.

And never doubt **God is in your workplace**!

Prayer

Father, in the name of Jesus, I pray. Thank You for trusting me where You have me – so I can trust You and not me. I know You are in my workplace – I know You live in me – this year, this coming year, and all years. Amen.

Jimmy Davis, Jr.

About the Editors

Kevin J. Cooney, Ph.D., worships our Lord at the Church on the Ridge in Snoqualmie, Washington. He is a Visiting Professor at Ritsumeikan Asia Pacific University in Beppu, Japan. He previously served as the Director of the Pacific Rim Center at Northwest University where he held a dual appointment as Professor of Business and Political Science. He was also on the faculty at Union University and Arizona State University. Kevin earned the Ph.D. in political science from Arizona State University, which was followed by a post-doctorate certification in marketing and management from the University of Florida. He is the author of several books and numerous academic papers on East Asian security and economics. After over twenty years of teaching, Kevin left full-time academic work in 2014 to pursue writing and consulting. When not traveling for work, he lives in Snoqualmie with his beautiful wife Atsuko; their incredibly gifted children, Aiyana and Kian; and their dog, Knight.

William (Bill) Dudley, MPA, worships our Lord at Beacon Baptist Church in Virginia Beach, Virginia, where he is a singer/songwriter and Worship Pastor. He earned the Master of Public Administration (MPA) Degree from the Robertson School of Government at Regent University in Virginia Beach. Bill is a retired 32-year Naval Officer and ordained minister. He works for the U.S. Department of Defense. Bill resides in Virginia Beach with his beautiful wife, Annette. They have four incredibly gifted children – Stephen, David, Tiffany, and Faith.

Jonathan Lantz, MPA, worships our Lord at Trinity Church in Virginia Beach, Virginia. He earned the Master of Public Administration (MPA) Degree from the Robertson School of Government at Regent University in Virginia Beach. He is currently pursuing a career in local administrative government and is passionate about effecting change in local communities. Jonathan is currently an intern with the Chesapeake City Manager in Chesapeake, Virginia. God has blessed him with an appreciation for the outdoors, and he loves spending time exploring the Virginia Beach area.

Christopher Sean Meconnahey, MPA, worships our Lord at St. Andrew's United Methodist Church in Virginia Beach, Virginia. He earned the Master of Public Administration (MPA) Degree from the Robertson School of Government at Regent University in Virginia Beach. He currently works for the Department of Defense in Norfolk, Virginia. He lives in Virginia Beach with his beautiful wife, Samantha, and their incredibly gifted daughter, Madelyn.

Tammy L. Peavy worships our Lord at Crossgates Baptist Church in Brandon, Mississippi. She is a Fire Safety Education Officer for the Mississippi State Fire Marshal's Office in Jackson, Mississippi, and she has taught fire prevention in Katete, Zambia, Africa. She also assisted in the delivery of a fire truck to the citizens of Katete. Tammy resides in Pearl, Mississippi with her dogs, Jake and Rascal.

Stephen Pincus, M.A., worships our Lord at St. Joseph Catholic Church in Hampton, Virginia. He earned the Master of Arts (MA in public administration) Degree from the Robertson School of Government at Regent University in Virginia Beach, Virginia. Stephen began his career as a firefighter for the City of Newport News, Virginia, in 1984. Now retired, he rose through the ranks to Public Affairs Chief. Stephen resides in Yorktown, Virginia, with the blessings of his life – his beautiful wife, Amy, and their two incredibly gifted sons, Stephen, Jr. and Mark.

James (Jim) D. Slack, Ph.D., Ph.D. worships our Lord at Bluff Park United Methodist Church in Hoover, Alabama. He earned the Ph.D. in political science from Miami University and the Ph.D. in Christian (crisis) counseling from Cornerstone University. He is a professor in the Department of Public Policy & Administration at Jackson State University in Jackson, Mississippi, where he writes in the area of "death policy." He is also a Faculty Fellow in the International Center for Ethics, Justice and Public Life at Brandeis University in Waltham, Massachusetts. Jim follows our Lord to minister in prison, and he routinely visits Jesus on death row. He is a member of the Emmaus Community. His beautiful wife, Janis, has put up with him for nearly 35 years. They are blessed to have three incredibly gifted children – Sammy, Sarah, and (Sarah's husband) Brandon.

About the Contributors

Alexander, Deanna, M.P.A. – Week 31, Day 1
    County Supervisor
    Milwaukee County
    Milwaukee, Wisconsin USA

Allen, Gary R. – Week 33, Day 2
    City Councilor
    District 6
    Columbus, Georgia USA

Amiel, Anne-Marie – Week 23, Day 2; Week 34, Day 4; Week 50, Day 3
    Risk Manager
    Columbus Consolidated Government
    Columbus, Georgia USA

Arbitter, Angela, M.P.A. – Week 25, Day 3; Week 30, Day 4; Week 37, Day 2
    International Justice Mission
    Gulu, Uganda

Barnes, Michael – Week 4, Day 3
    Student
    Robertson School of Government
    Regent University
    Virginia Beach, Virginia USA

Baum, Patricia, RN, BSN – Week 1, Day 1; Week 8, Day 4; Week 36, Day 1; Week 52, Day 1
    Clinical Trial Specialist
    Neurosurgery Department
    Beth Israel Deaconess Medical Center
    Boston, Massachusetts USA

Bayer, Paul, M.A. – Week 7, Day 4
    Robertson School of Government
    Regent University
    Virginia Beach, Virginia USA

Bedogne, Jan – Week 15, Day 1; Week 47, Day 2
    Vice President of Finance and Human Resources
    Parroco Production Group
    Chesapeake, Virginia USA

Beller, Tracie M. – Week 26, Day 4
    M.A. Candidate
    Robertson School of Government
    Regent University
    Virginia Beach, Virginia USA

Bereznak, Maureen – Week 3, Day 2; Week 8, Day 1; Week 15, Day 2; Week 36, Day 3; Week 48, Day 1
    Council Woman
    Lewisberry Borough, Pennsylvania USA
    and Research Analyst
    State House of Representatives
    State of Pennsylvania
    Harrisburg, Pennsylvania USA

Best, Morgan – Week 5, Day 4; Week 13, Day 2
    Elementary School Teacher
    Wake County Public Schools
    Raleigh, North Carolina USA

Best, Stan – Week 16, Day 1; Week 17, Day 2; Week 19, Day 1; Week 20, Day 2; Week 31, Day 4; Week 34, Day 3; Week 36, Day 2; Week 38, Day 4; Week 43, Day 1
    Training Manager
    Apprentice School
    Newport News Shipbuilding Company
    Newport News, Virginia USA
    and Masters of Theology Candidate
    St. Leo University
    Chesapeake, Virginia USA

Biggs, Joycelyn – Week 30, Day 3
    Public Affairs Specialist
    Marine Corps Logistics Base Albany
    Albany, Georgia USA

Boisselle, David, D.S.L. – Week 1, Day 3; Week 8, Day 3; Week 23, Day 4; Week 28, Day 4; Week 50, Day 2
    President & CEO
    Agape Leadership Consulting, LLC
    Chesapeake, Virginia USA

About the Contributors 383

Bourque, Suzanne – Week 49, Day 4
    Classification Grievances Coordinator | Coordonnatrice de griefs de classification
    Agriculture and Agri-Food Canada | Agriculture et Agroalimentaire Canada
    Government of Canada | Gouvernement du Canada
    Ottawa, Canada

Brown, Christie, M.P.A. – Week 34, Day 1; Week 39, Day 2
    Director of Communications
    School of Optometry
    University of Alabama at Birmingham
    Birmingham, Alabama USA

Butler, Steve, Ph.D. – Week 1, Day 2
    U.S. Department of Justice
    Washington, D.C. USA

Carr, Krystiana, M.P.A. – Week 19, Day 4
    Human Resources Assistant
    U.S. Army ROTC Program
    Hampton University
    Hampton, Virginia USA

Coetzer, Thea – Week 45, Day 4
    Director (Compliance)
    Office of the Service Delivery & Transformation Manager
    City of Tshwane
    Pretoria, South Africa

Conroy, Richard T., M.S.C.J. – Week 4, Day 4
    U.S. Federal Bureau of Investigation National Academy
    and Assistant Professor
    Dallas Baptist University
    Dallas, Texas USA

Cooney, Kevin J., Ph.D. – Week 9, Day 2; Week 11, Day 2; Week 19, Day 3; Week 24, Day 4; Week 29, Day 1; Week 32, Day 2; Week 46, Day 2; Week 52, Day 3
    Visiting Professor
    Ritsumeikan Asia Pacific University
    Beppu, Japan

Couturier, Anne-Marie – Week 4, Day 2
    Senior Learning Advisor | Conseillère principale en apprentissage (retired) Corporate Programs | Programmes ministériels
    Human Resources Directorate | Direction des ressources humaines
    Treasury Board of Canada Secretariat | Secrétariat du Conseil du Trésor du Canada
    Ottawa, Canada

Cox, Alan – Week 20, Day 1
    Housing Commissioner
    Department of Neighborhoods
    City of Toledo
    Toledo, Ohio USA

Craven, Gilbert O. – Week 33, Day 1; Week 49, Day 2
    M.A. Candidate
    Robertson School of Government
    Regent University
    Virginia Beach, Virginia USA

Crone, Loren M. M.P.A. – Week 37, Day 3
    Chaplain and Lieutenant
    Marine Corps Embassy Security Group
    U.S. Navy
    Washington, D.C. USA and throughout the world

Davis, Jimmy, Jr. – Day 5 on each week, Week 1 - Week 52
    Z-557 Unit N-10
    Death Row
    W.C. Holman Correctional Facility
    Atmore, Alabama USA

Denis, Suzanne – Week 5, Day 1; Week 21, Day 1; Week 40, Day 2
    Director of Quality Development of Expertise | Directrice de la qualité et du développement de l'expertise
    Regional Center for Rehabilitation | Centre régional de réadaptation La RessourSe
    Gatineau (Québec) Canada

Dickens, Logan, M.P.A. – Week 28, day 3
  Special Projects Analyst
  Virginia Department of Medical Assistance Services
  Richmond, Virginia USA

Dudley, Bill, M.P.A. – Week 12, Day 3; Week 22, Day 4; Week 24, Day 1; Week 28, Day 1; Week 29, Day 2; Week 32, Day 4; Week 38, Day 2; Week 42, Day 1; Week 46, Day 4
  Pastor and Logistician
  U.S. Department of Defense
  Naval Base Norfolk
  Norfolk, Virginia USA

Erwin, Kevin – Week 44, Day 4
  Assistant Principal
  Simmons Middle School
  Hoover School District
  Hoover, Alabama USA

Everette, Erica – Week 16, Day 2; Week 35, Day 2; Week 41, Day 2
  MPA Candidate
  Robertson School of Government
  Regent University
  Virginia Beach, Virginia USA
  and Eligibility Review Analyst
  Department of Medical Assistance Services
  State of Virginia
  Richmond, Virginia USA

Featherston, Crystal, M.P.A. – Week 10, Day 2; Week 43, Day 3
  Budget Office
  City of Virginia Beach
  Virginia Beach, Virginia USA

Flannagan, Jenny Sue, Ed.D. – Week 16, Day 4
  Professor
  School of Education
  Regent University
  Virginia Beach, Virginia USA

Flint, Alan S. – Week 5, Day 2
  Retired (elected) Parish & District Councillor
  Crich, Derbyshire, United Kingdom
  and Elder & Secretary

Crich Baptist Church
Crich, Derbyshire, United Kingdom

Garnes, LaShonda, M.P.A. – Week 2, Day 2; Week 35, Day 1; Week 37, Day 4; Week 44, Day 2; Week 50, Day 4
    Business Operations Manager
    Public Works & Utilities Department
    City of Wichita
    Wichita, Kansas USA

Garth, Sara, M.A. – Week 10, Day 1
    Robertson School of Government
    Regent University
    Virginia Beach, Virginia USA

Griffing, Noah M. – Week 20, Day 4
    M.A. Candidate
    Robertson School of Government
    Regent University
    Virginia Beach, Virginia USA

Pineiro Graham, Samantha – Week 17, Day 3
    J.D. Candidate
    Law School
    Regent University
    Virginia Beach, Virginia USA

Granger-Malone, Shelia – Week 6, Day 2
    Q/C Development Lab Supervisor
    Axiall Corporation
    Madison, Mississippi USA
    and M.P.P.A. Candidate
    Department of Public Policy and Administration
    Jackson State University
    Jackson, Mississippi USA

Hanson, Larry – Week 21, Day 4
    City Manager
    City of Valdosta
    Valdosta, Georgia USA

Harrell, Joseph N. III, M.A. – Week 10, Day 4; Week 35, Day 4; Week 47, Day 4
    J.D. Candidate
    Robertson School of Law
    Regent University
    Virginia Beach, Virginia USA

About the Contributors   387

Henry, Samuel, M.A. – Week 17, Day 1
    Deputy
    Training, Readiness and Exercises
    U.S. Transportation Command
    Norfolk, Virginia USA

Heyward, Rose, SPHR, CPC – Week 51, Day 4
    Director of Human Resources
    County of Spotsylvania
    Spotsylvania, Virginia USA

Hill, Phoenecia – Week 26, Day 1
    MPA Candidate
    Robertson School of Government
    Regent University
    Virginia Beach, Virginia USA

Hinton, Reagan – Week 12, Day 4
    J.D. Candidate
    School of Law
    Regent University
    Virginia Beach, Virginia USA

Hunt, Gregory – Week 25, Day 2
    Z-521 Unit N-6
    Death Row
    W.C. Holman Correctional Facility
    Atmore, Alabama USA

Jordan, Lori – Week 49, Day 3
    Administrative Assistant, Business Development
    Arkansas Economic Development Commission
    State of Arkansas
    Little Rock, Arkansas USA

Kay, Jessica – Week 33, Day 3
    ECCS 911 Operations Supervisor
    City of Virginia Beach
    Virginia Beach, Virginia USA

Ketcham, Larry – Week 2, Day 3
    City Engineer
    City of Laramie
    Laramie, Wyoming USA

Knight, Joanna, M.P.A. – Week 15, Day 3
    Mother
    Virginia Beach, Virginia USA

Lacourse, Lyse-Ann – Week 21, Day 3; Week 29, Day 4
    Administrative Coordinator | Coordonnatrice administrative
    Office of the Chief Actuary | Bureau de l'actuaire en chef
    Office of the Superintendent of Financial Institutions | Bureau du surintendant des institutions financières
    Government of Canada | Gouvernement du Canada
    Ottawa, Canada

Lantz, Jonathan, M.P.A. – Week 3, Day 3; Week 28, Day 2; Week 38, Day 1
    Intern
    City of Chesapeake
    Chesapeake, Virginia USA

Lassiter, Lou, C.P.A. – Week 33, Day 5
    Assistant County Administrator
    Chesterfield County
    Chesterfield, Virginia USA

Long, John F. Jr., -- Week 9, Day 3; Week 41, Day 4; Week 43, Day 4
    Reverend
    and Equipment Specialist
    Surface Forces Logistics Center
    U.S. Coast Guard
    Baltimore, Maryland USA

Mahoney, Wendy – Week 6, Day 1
    Executive Director
    Mississippi Coalition Against Domestic Violence
    Jackson, Mississippi USA
    and Ph.D. Candidate
    Department of Public Policy and Administration
    Jackson State University
    Jackson, Mississippi USA

Maletoungou, Sosthene, M.A, M.Div – Week 2, Day 1
    Education Consultant for West Africa
    Christian Reformed World Missions
    parts unknown (for security reasons), West Africa

Maley, Patricia A. AICP – Week 40, Day 1; Week 46, Day 3
    Senior Planner Design and Review/DRPC Coordinator
    Department of Planning and Development
    City of Wilmington
    Wilmington, Delaware USA

Manjikian, Mary, Ph.D. – Week 18, Day 3; Week 31, Day 3; Week 44, Day 1
    Professor and Associate Dean
    Robertson School of Government
    Regent University
    Virginia Beach, Virginia USA

Meconnahey, Christopher Sean, M.P.A. – Week 27, Day 3
    Military Sealift Command
    U.S. Department of the Navy
    Norfolk, Virginia USA

Missildine, Laura Ashley – Week 5, Day 3
    7th Grade Language Arts Teacher
    Simmons Middle School
    Hoover School District
    Hoover, Alabama USA

Monaheng, Amelia – Week 1, Day 4
    Personal Assistant to the Minister of Police
    South African Police Service
    Pretoria, South Africa

Monnin, Rachael, M.P.A., J.D. – Week 18, Day 4
    Chesapeake, Virginia USA

Neal, Debra – Week 14, Day 2; Week 18, Day 2; Week 29, Day 3; Week 34, Day 2; Week 46, Day 1; Week 48, Day 3
    6th Grade Teacher
    South Amherst Middle School
    Firelands School District
    South Amherst, Ohio USA

Neale, Brooke A. H., M.P.A. – Week 51, Day 2
    Donor Relations Officer
    Childbirth PATHS International, Inc.
    North Point, Florida USA

Patterson, Eric, Ph.D. – Week 25, Day 4
    Professor and Dean
    Robertson School of Government
    Regent University
    Virginia Beach, Virginia USA

Patterson, Kathleen, Ph.D. – Week 49, Day 1
    Professor
    School of Business & Leadership
    Regent University
    Virginia Beach, Virginia USA

Peavy, Tammy L. – Week 28, Day 1
    Fire Safety Educator
    State Fire Marshal's Office
    Mississippi Insurance Department
    Jackson, Mississippi USA

Pincus, Stephen, M.A. – Week 10, Day 3; Week 13, Day 4; Week 22, Day 1; Week 24, Day 3; Week 51, Day 3
    Public Affairs Chief
    Newport News Fire Department
    Newport News, Virginia USA

Pulsford, Meredith, M.P.A. – Week 20, Day 3
    Department Manager – Human Resources
    McDonalds Corporation
    Virginia Beach, Virginia USA

Roberts, Gary E., Ph.D. – Week 6, Day 4; Week 13, Day 1; Week 24, Day 2; Week 38, Day 3; Week 39, Day 4; Week 42, Day 2
    Professor and Director
    Master of Public Administration Program
    Robertson School of Government
    Regent University
    Virginia Beach, Virginia USA

Robinson, Tammy, M.B.A. – Week 32, Day 1
    Medical Management Specialist I
    Medicare Medical Management
    Anthem, Inc.
    Youngstown, Ohio USA

About the Contributors 391

Rogers, Maureen, CPA, CPFO – Week 15, Day 4
    Finance Director
    City of Shawnee
    Shawnee, Kansas USA

Saunders, Kathryn – Week 11, Day 3; Week 17, Day 4; Week 23, Day 3; Week 50, Day 1
    Head Soccer Coach
    Texas Southern University
    Houston, Texas USA

Scaife, Wilisha G. – Week 12, Day 1
    Program Director
    Department of Elementary Education
    Ball State University
    Muncie, Indiana USA

Scharein, Andy – Week 26, Day 3
    Acquisition Manager
    U.S. Department of Defense
    Tel Aviv, Israel

Schenkel, Adam – Week 35, Day 3
    Robertson School of Government
    Regent University
    Virginia Beach, Virginia USA

Shoop, Hannah – Week 30, Day 1
    7th Grade Language Arts Teacher
    Simmons Middle School
    Hoover School District
    Hoover, Alabama USA

Slack, James D., Ph.D., Ph.D. – Week 4, Day 1; Week 9, Day 4; Week 14, Day 4; Week 22, Day 2; Week 31, Day 2; Week 37, Day 1; Week 41, Day 1; Week 43, Day 2; Week 45, Day 3
    Professor
    Department of Public Policy and Administration
    Jackson State University
    Jackson, Mississippi
    and Faculty Fellow
    Educational Network for Active Civic Transformation (ENACT)

International Center for Ethics, Justice and Public Life
Brandeis University
Waltham, Massachusetts USA

Smith, Greg – Week 3, Day 1; Week 42, Day 4
Kansas State Senator
District 21
Overland Park, Kansas USA

Smith, Martha, M.A., J.D., SPHR – Week 40, Day 4; Week 44, Day 3
Vice President for Human Resources & Administration
Regent University
Virginia Beach, Virginia USA

Stamm, Ellen C. – Week 9, Day 1; Week 11, Day 4; Week 19, Day 2; Week 48, Day 4; Week 51, Day 1
Department of Toledo-Lucas County Planning Commission
City of Toledo/Lucas County
Toledo, Ohio USA

Standorf, Wendy, PHR; IPMA-CP – Week 8, Day 2; Week 14, Day 3; Week 27, Day 4
Human Resources Director
City of West University Place
West University Place, Texas USA

Steele-Clearman, Valerie – Week 39, Day 1
MPPA Candidate
Department of Public Policy & Administration
Jackson State University
Jackson, Mississippi USA

Stout, Allen – Week 7, Day 1; Week 48, Day 2
Professor and Director
Inland Empire Campus
University of La Verne
Ontario, California USA

Summers, Chris – Week 2, Day 4; Week 7, Day 3; Week 11, Day 1; Week 13, Day 3; Week 18, Day 1; Week 21, Day 2; Week 22, Day 4; Week 27, Day 1; Week 30, Day 2; Week 42, Day 3; Week 45, Day 2; Week 47, Day 1; Week 52, Day 4
        Chaplain
        W.C. Holman Correctional Facility
        Alabama Department of Corrections
        Atmore, Alabama USA

Theroux, Paul, M.P.A. – Week 39, Day 3; Week 41, Day 3
        Maintenance Program Manager
        U.S. Department of Defense
        Naval Base Norfolk
        Norfolk, Virginia USA

Van Straten, Stephanie – Week 3, Day 4; Week 14, Day 1; Week 23, Day 1; Week 27, Day 2; Week 32, Day 3; Week 52, Day 2
        M.D. Candidate
        School of Clinical Medicine
        University of Witwatersrand
        Johannesburg, South Africa

Walker, Adrieme, FLMI, ACS, AIRC – Week 6, Day 3
        Policy Service Consultant
        Southern Farm Bureau Life Insurance
        Jackson, Mississippi USA
        and Ph.D. Candidate
        Department of Public Policy and Administration
        Jackson State University
        Jackson, Mississippi USA

Whitman, Matt – Week 12, Day 2; Week 16, Day 3; Week 40, Day 3; Week 45, Day 1
        Deputy Mayor
        City of Halifax
        Halifax, Nova Scotia Canada

Wilson, Ronald – Week 7, Day 2
        Development Review Coordinator
        Franklin County
        Town of Rocky Mount, Virginia USA

Wolitarsky, Brock, M.A. – Week 25, Day 1; Week 26, Day 2; Week 47, Day 3
        Research Assistant
        Discovery Institute

Seattle, Washington USA

Zasadny, Katherine, M.P.A – Week 36, Day 4
    Hiawatha Care Center
    Cedar Rapids, Iowa USA

Subject Index

a better formula – Week 13, Day 1
about the why – Week 43, Day 2
a burnt bridge – Week 24, Day 1
a fool by comparison – Week 29, Day 1
a good Christian marriage – Week 38, Day 4
a hotdog, a spare rib, or even buttered popcorn – Week 27, Day 1
a different way of life – Week 4, Day 5
a mountain can surely move – Week 25, Day 2
a quiet leader without tights and cape – Week 44, Day 4
a simple display of faith – Week 38, Day 2
a teachful way – Week 31, Day 4
ahead of the game – Week 47, Day 4
all alone in your workplace – Week 48, Day 3
always a gut check time – Week 24, Day 1
always better than yours – Week 14, Day 1
an even greater responsibility – Week 39, Day 2
and don't be afraid – Week 27, Day 4
approved in His sight – Week 28, Day 4
as you water others – Week 22, Day 5
at the bottom of the box – Week 16, Day 4
audacious faith – Week 30, Day 4
awake from a selfish sleep – Week 14, Day 5
be bold and testify – Week 16, Day 3
be covet-less and shine His love – Week 43, Day 4
be gentle to all – Week 42, Day 1
be the servant and you will be the leader – Week 16, Day 1
because that person is Jesus – Week 36, Day 5
become the Rock in your workplace – Week 51, Day 3
being His team player – Week 42, Day 2
believe and don't be afraid – Week 14, Day 1
believe, trust, and turn – Week 31, Day 1
born into different cloth – Week 33, Day 1
bring many to the Well – Week 50, Day 1
cannot run well without Him – Week 41, Day 3
carry His word in your toolbox – Week 19, Day 2
carry the hurting to Him – Week 34, Day 3
catch your breath – Week 23, Day 2
cease striving and just be – Week 11, Day 4
cling onto His promise – Week 11, Day 3
commit your work to Him – Week 20, Day 3
connect with the Father – Week 30, Day 1
correct with love – Week 38, Day 1

cross that road – Week 10, Day 3
define success as He does – Week 39, Day 4
delivery is everything – Week 30, Day 3
desire Him fervently – Week 46, Day 2
destroyed by pride – Week 50, Day 2
do His chores – Week 25, Day 1
do not be troubled – Week 22, Day 4
do that one small thing – Week 36, Day 3
do the hope of Christ – Week 18, Day 4
do what the Lord requires – Week 44, Day 1
do your Father's business, quietly – Week 49, Day 1
don't abuse God's freedom – Week 27, Day 5
don't become weary – Week 12, Day 4
don't let work get in the way – Week 33, Day 3
doors to His need – Week 37, Day 1
dressed for success in any season – Week 6, Day 3
enough evidence to convict – Week 47, Day 1
enter His gates with thanksgiving – Week 4, Day 4
even in a land of all fiction – Week 9, Day 5
even in this wilderness – Week 50, Day 4
even Mr. Night – Week 14, Day 4
every bit as relevant – Week 47, Day 3
exceptional for His sake – Week 11, Day 5
exercise by walking in faith – Week 47, Day 2
eyes to see Jesus – Week 3, Day 5
eyes to see the hurt – Week 46, Day 1
face it with God – Week 32, Day 3
faithful in all He does – Week 28, Day 3
fight through the waves – Week 12, Day 3
firewall against spiritual hackers – Week 15, Day 4
far scarier than a heart attack – Week 41, Day 1
forget self-help – Week 28, Day 2
forgive those who trespass – Week 40, Day 1
get up and get back to work – Week 17, Day 2
gentle words and patient persuasion – Week 9, Day 3
give and receive unwarranted forgiveness – Week 5, Day 1
giving your best is not optional – Week 38, Day 3
grace to others – Week 40, Day 4
God is in your workplace – Week 52, Day 5
God notices misery – Week 24, Day 5
God's handiwork of change – Week 3, Day 4
Good but not God – Week 39, Day 1
great things without number – Week 21, Day 1
grow in size when you share – Week 17, Day 5
Happy Birthday – Week 33, Day 5

have to believe – Week 3, Day 1
He always responds with faith – Week 35, Day 4
He will do it – Week 45, Day 4
He's gardening you – Week 23, Day 3
hear His whisper – Week 41, Day 3
help from a God-given gift – Week 41, Day 4
high time to awake – Week 1, Day 3
highlight the beauty – Week 27, Day 2
His beauty in your chaos – Week 51, Day 2
His gift of diversity – Week 8, Day 4
His living plan – Week 21, Day 5
His power rests on you – Week 9, Day 1
His way and choose life – Week 14, Day 3
His word, nothing more – Week 20, Day 5
His work where we work – Week 37, Day 4
hold up the hands – Week 40, Day 5
how your steps are walked – Week 43, Day 5
impossible to deny Christ – Week 24, Day 4
in a manner worthy – Week 6, Day 5
in the reminder business – Week 49, Day 4
it's faith that gets you places – Week 10, Day 2
Jesus heals best – Week 36, Day 1
Jesus is found – Week 21, Day 4
Jesus is waiting for you – Week 18, Day 1
Just do what you can – Week 38, Day 5
just pushing through the day – Week 13, Day 2
keep a carol in your mind – Week 52, Day 1
keep pushing through – Week 35, Day 1
kneel before others – Week 12, Day 1
know the people you work with – Week 32, Day 4
lead and follow by His example – Week 50, Day 3
lead by the heart, not by the world – Week 8, Day 1
leave the rest up to Him – Week 33, Day 4
let all things die – Week 28, Day 5
let God work out the negative – Week 50, Day 5
let your attitude match your message – Week 23, Day 5
let's do this day together – Week 39, Day 2
letting the evil one get to you – Week 8, Day 2
lift you up in due time – Week 49, Day 3
like a passing shadow – Week 7, Day 1
like sandpaper on your heart – Week 15, Day 1
love all others – period – Week 2, Day 3
love less like others expect – Week 23, Day 1
loving the unlovable – Week 40, Day 2
make sure your heart is engaged – Week 1, Day 1

matches to light that candle – Week 17, Day 1
miss the right results – Week 15, Day 5
more like God – Week 9, Day 2
more powerful than any earthly temptation – Week 1, Day 2
motivation, delivery, and timing matter – Week 25, Day 4
my Lord's presence changes everything – Week 51, Day 5
never be a double standard – Week 32, Day 2
no bad days at the office – Week 6, Day 2
no longer fishing for catfish – Week 2, Day 5
no matter how many NO's you endure – Week 32, Day 1
no matter how people respond – Week 40, Day 1
no matter what is said and done – Week 48, Day 1
not a place to pretend – Week 44, Day 5
not Maslow, but Christ's – Week 13, Day 3
not just fixing the immediate – Week 20, Day 4
not just for rest but for praise – Week 7, Day 4
not just His worker – Week 49, Day 2
not my responsibility – Week 6, Day 4
not to hit back – Week 37, Day 5
not to sell out – Week 30, Day 5
not to your cave – Week 8, Day 5
nothing but the truth – Week 26, Day 1
ointment of healing – Week 29, Day 2
on knees and not in flesh – Week 6, Day 1
one of the least – Week 4, Day 3
only a coworker – Week 19, Day 4
only test you need to pass – Week 15, Day 2
our Lord detests lying lips – Week 33, Day 2
pause and look – Week 34, Day 1
pray and seek His face – Week 12, Day 2
pray as your first resort – Week 17, Day 4
pray for and pray with – Week 45, Day 2
prayer, praise, and proclamation – Week 18, Day 2
prayers will be my weapons – Week 20, Day 1
put all the chaos aside – Week 5, Day 4
put on Jesus – Week 12, Day 5
really hurting Jesus, Week 41, Day 5
really not that far from paradise – Week 15, Day 3
rely a little less on Google – Week 43, Day 3
remember to be patient – Week 35, Day 3
remove the X – Week 40, Day 3
rest in the words – Week 19, Day 5
see another side of them – Week 16, Day 5
seems more impossible than not – Week 27, Day 3
serve without outrageous nonsense – Week 45, Day 1

Subject Index 399

share in that joy – Week 46, Day 5
show love instead – Week 26, Day 1
some kind of peace in the middle of the storm – Week 18, Day 5
someone in your workplace searching – Week 52, Day 4
something going on – Week 51, Day 1
sow from the heart condition – Week 22, Day 3
steps are ordered by the Lord – Week 24, Day 3
still enough – Week 26, Day 4
stolen goods hidden there – Week 32, Day 5
such a despicable boss – Week 31, Day 2
tears from the soul – Week 35, Day 5
tempted by powerful sin – Week 1, Day 5
tendency for memory lapse – Week 37, Day 3
take a chance and lead with love – Week 23, Day 4
that business of making all things new – Week 2, Day 4
that Hand will move – Week 5, Day 2
that quiet click of the latch – Week 42, Day 4
that same one Jesus had – week 47, Day 5
that second look – Week 35, Day 2
that simple rule – Week 17, Day 3
the arrogance of the day – Week 36, Day 2
the best training ground – Week 7, Day 5
the biggest word ever – Week 5, Day 5
the brother serving trays – Week 34, Day 5
the condition of the heart – Week 11, Day 1
the desires of your heart – Week 8, Day 3
the first step in healing – Week 9, Day 4
the heavenly outcome of work – Week 25, Day 3
the hang of it – Week 45, Day 3
the Hope of all nations – Week 2, Day 1
the hope that you have – Week 43, Day 1
the man-made bars – Week 49, Day 5
the meal of sharing something greater – Week 25, day 5
the memory of your doing – Week 44, Day 3
the only thing you need to remember – Week 29, Day 3
the opportunity to understand and grow in Him, Week 52, Day 2
the process of discipline – Week 37, Day 2
the right formula – Week 11, Day 1
the seed or the nourishment to the seed – Week 2, Day 2
the simple thing – Week 13, Day 5
the singularity of serving – Week 48, Day 4
the Ultimate Fixer – Week 5, Day 3
the virtue of spiritual poverty – Week 7, Day 1
things from the vending machines – Week 48, Day 5
think in a godly manner – Week 30, Day 3

this kind of hope – Week 21, Day 3
to die with loose ends – Week 3, Day 2
to live in real peace – Week 51, Day 4
tones wantonly treacherous – Week 46, Day 3
troubles come your way – Week 44, Day 2
unlovely in the eyes of some – Week 36, Day 4
use your inner lens – Week 10, Day 4
wait and watch with one another – Week 34, Day 2
wake up and shake off the dust – Week 4, Day 1
wear the proper attitude – Week 19, Day 1
well done good and faithful – Week 22, Day 1
watches you and watches over you – Week 31, Day 3
what can mere people do to me – Week 1, Day 4
what lies ahead – Week 4, Day 2
what seems the impossible – Week 22, Day 2
what we know – Week 19, Day 3
when a bully comes your way – Week 7, Day 2
when anger wells up – Week 16, Day 2
when the work is burned – Week 11, Day 2
where's your sweet spot – Week 21, Day 2
whispered in your ear – Week 34, Day 4
who's my daddy – Week 42, Day 4
with justice and mercy – Week 48, Day 2
with spiritual eyes – Week 26, Day 3
with the seed you plant – Week 46, Day 4
without selfishness or envy – Week 18, Day 3
words will surely follow – Week 45, Day 5
yelling and shouting – Week 28, Day 1
you lack nothing – Week 29, Day 4
you step up – Week 31, Day 5
you will be strong – Week 29, Day 5
your Father – Week 52, Day 3
your turn to be bold – Week 20, Day 2

www.ingramcontent.com/pod-product-compliance
Lightning Source LLC
Chambersburg PA
CBHW031959220426
43664CB00005B/72